Argonauts of West Africa

Argonauts of West Africa

Unauthorized Migration and Kinship Dynamics in a Changing Europe

APOSTOLOS ANDRIKOPOULOS

The University of Chicago Press
Chicago and London

The University of Chicago Press, Chicago 60637
The University of Chicago Press, Ltd., London
© 2023 by The University of Chicago
Published 2023
Printed in the United States of America

32 31 30 29 28 27 26 25 24 23   1 2 3 4 5

ISBN-13: 978-0-226-82260-0 (cloth)
ISBN-13: 978-0-226-82262-4 (paper)
ISBN-13: 978-0-226-82261-7 (e-book)
DOI: https://doi.org/10.7208/chicago/9780226822617.001.0001

Library of Congress Cataloging-in-Publication Data

Names: Andrikopoulos, Apostolos, author.
Title: Argonauts of West Africa : unauthorized migration and kinship
    dynamics in a changing Europe / Apostolos Andrikopoulos.
Description: Chicago : The University of Chicago Press, 2023. |
    Includes bibliographical references and index.
Identifiers: LCCN 2022032906 | ISBN 9780226822600 (cloth) |
    ISBN 9780226822624 (paperback) | ISBN 9780226822617 (ebook)
Subjects: LCSH: Africans—Kinship—Netherlands—Amsterdam. | Africans—
    Netherlands—Amsterdam—Social conditions. | Africans—Legal status,
    laws, etc.—Netherlands—Amsterdam. | Noncitizens—Netherlands—
    Amsterdam—Social conditions. | Illegal immigration—Netherlands.
Classification: LCC DJ92.A47 A64 2023 | DDC 362.84/960492352—
    dc23/eng/20220926
LC record available at https://lccn.loc.gov/2022032906

♾ This paper meets the requirements of ANSI/NISO Z39.48-1992 (Permanence of Paper).

To Anna

Contents

Navigating Kinship

"Where is Joshua?" I asked my Greek friend Eleni about her Nigerian husband almost one hour after I arrived at their place in Amsterdam. Eleni had met Joshua in Greece in 2003. A few years later, they got married and moved to Amsterdam. "He's talking on the phone with his friend Chidi," she replied, explaining that these days he talked with him on the phone for hours. Chidi and Joshua had met in Thessaloniki, Greece's second-largest city, where they worked together as street vendors. From there, Chidi went to Italy and later the United States, where he got married to an African American woman. The main topic of the long phone conversations between Chidi and Joshua were the attempts by Chidi's brother, Victor, to enter Europe. Victor, with his own passport, had managed to travel only from Nigeria to the Republic of Georgia, where he was stranded. Victor's original plan was to travel from Georgia to Turkey and from there to clandestinely cross the border and enter Greece. However, Joshua strongly advised him to reconsider this plan because, as he had learned from his brothers in Thessaloniki, it would be extremely difficult for him to find employment in crisis-hit Greece. Instead, Joshua suggested Victor join him in the Netherlands, where there were relatively more job opportunities—though certainly considerably fewer than in previous years. Joshua tried to find documents for Victor, or, more precisely, he looked for someone willing to lend his passport to Victor to allow him entry into the Netherlands. It has not been uncommon for West African and other migrants to use someone else's identity documents to travel or find work in the Netherlands and elsewhere. Nigerian migrants call this practice *ori olori*, which can translate as using someone else's head (Akanle 2009, 188; Adebanwi and Obadare 2022, 83).[1] Eleni was aware of this plan and not at all surprised by it. It was not the first time she had heard about the circulation of identity documents among West African migrants. About ten years ago, while cleaning the apartment of her boyfriend "Walter," she found a passport in the closet bearing the name Joshua. Upon this discovery she left him to temporarily return to her family home. Joshua begged her to hear him out. Eleni recalled, "He said that the only way he could get a visa, and he paid for this and did other things, was to do it with the papers of someone else because he couldn't do it under his own name." She forgave him and helped him to get legalized status by marrying him.

Faced with exclusion by the increasingly hostile immigration policies in Europe, migrants have responded by drawing on kinship and generating new kinds of sociality. Innovative forms of kinship emerge in contexts of accelerated change and uncertainty. This book investigates how West African migrants with precarious legal status mobilize and produce kinship, especially siblinghood and marriage, to obtain identity documents, such as visas, work permits, residence permits, and passports, which enable them to travel, work in formal jobs, and stay legally in Europe. More specifically, it examines the role of kinship for West African migrants as they circumvent restrictive immigration policies and border controls, secure waged employment in the strictly state-regulated Dutch labor market, and acquire legal residence in the Netherlands. In this regard, this book focuses on the interplay of citizenship and kinship. It examines the process of kinship in a setting of unequal access to citizenship and its means of proof: identity documents. Thus, the aim of this study is to examine the role of civic inequality in the ways migrants work with kinship.

In the social sciences and political philosophy, there has been a general tendency to assume that the emergence and growing influence of the state will restrict the societal role of kinship and its entanglement with politics and other domains of social life. But in the contexts I study, it is precisely the ever more intensive interventions by the state—notably new measures to control mobility across borders, access to the labor market and citizenship—that trigger new efforts by migrants to mobilize and develop kinship to use it for gaining a foothold in new surroundings. Changes in the wider contexts, such as the 2009 European economic crisis and shifts in EU membership (Eastern enlargement), prompted further innovations by West African migrants in the creation of kinship networks. A focus on kinship, a classical anthropological topic, turns out to be surprisingly relevant for understanding migrant struggles to retain agency in the face of mounting external pressures. Yet in this new context, this focus also requires a critical appraisal of the basic tenets of existing approaches to kinship. Close attention to kinship's dynamics and flexibility is imperative, as the new generation of kinship scholars advocates.

But even more important is the attention to inequality as a complement to the common pattern of studies of migration and recent approaches to kinship to pair kinship with reciprocity.

The protagonists of this book are migrants from Ghana and Nigeria—the Argonauts of West Africa—as well as other migrants, from other African countries, the Caribbean, and Eastern and Southern Europe, with whom West Africans collaborate and develop relations of kinship. Obviously, the title of this book is a playful alteration of Malinowski's 1922 *Argonauts of the Western Pacific*, a classic text that established ethnographic fieldwork as an anthropological method and contributed to theoretical debates on exchange and reciprocity. But the book's title is also a reference to the story of Argonauts in ancient Greek mythology. Like the Greek Argonauts who embarked on a risky voyage, passing through the Clashing Rocks, in quest of the Golden Fleece in the kingdom of Colchis, the Argonauts of West Africa navigate difficult and constantly changing situations to migrate to Europe and build a future. West African migrants' shifting practices within a changing environment are well captured by the notion of navigation, as theorized by Henry Vigh (2009). Social navigation designates "motion within motion," as it refers to the dynamic relation "between the environment people move in and how the environment itself moves them, before, after and during the act" (Vigh 2009, 425). The lives of migrants are profoundly affected by new technologies of border control and shifting conditions in Europe, such as economic crises, labor market transformations, and new demographic realities. But West African migrants do not remain passive to these changes (Adesina and Adebayo 2009, 9). They constantly develop strategies, malleable and responsive to wider changes, to survive and fulfil their aspirations. For both Greek and West African Argonauts, the role of kinship is central to navigating new obstacles and attaining their goals. Jason, the leader of Argonauts, managed to obtain the Golden Fleece with the help of the king of Colchis's daughter Medea, who became his wife. West African migrants similarly use creatively old and new forms of kinship in their endeavor to travel to and find work and remain in Europe.

Nevertheless, in the stories of both Greek and West African Argonauts, kinship takes on a dynamic of its own, which makes it more difficult to control than the Argonauts initially believed, and shows its dark, ugly side. Jason succeeded because of Medea's help, but when he abandoned her for another woman, Medea took revenge by killing their two children. For West Africans, kinship may offer solutions to their problems, but it also creates new and sometimes more difficult ones. Migrants do not always pleasantly experience what kinship does and enables others to do to them. Against the usual tendency to associate kinship with reciprocity, trust, and care, this book is attentive to the ambiguities of kinship and advocates an approach to kinship that considers these unpleasant practices not as anomalies of kinship but as its dark side.[2]

Joshua finished his long phone call and joined us in the living room. "How is your wife?" Eleni asked, teasing him about the close relationship he had recently developed with Chidi. Joshua apologized for being away and briefly explained that Chidi had asked him to help his brother Victor travel from Georgia to the Netherlands, which he intended to do. I interrupted, asking Joshua directly, "With someone else's documents?" He looked down at the floor, smiled, and said, "Ooh, Apostolos! You know too much!" Questions about the borrowing and loaning of identity documents from an outsider, such as me, often left my migrant interlocutors feeling uncomfortable, afraid, or embarrassed, although they frequently talked and laughed about it among themselves. Similar to what Herzfeld (2016) described as "cultural intimacy" in reference to the more disreputable aspects of national identity that contribute to the reproduction of shared national sentiments among citizens but are excluded from official national narratives, the feelings of embarrassment and fear associated with the exchange of identity documents reinforced an awareness of commonality among those involved in the practice. Eleni urged Joshua to update us on the latest developments. Joshua told us he had met Ugo, "a brother from the Bijlmer" who was a Nigerian with a Dutch residence permit and "very much a lookalike" of Victor. The Bijlmer, officially Amsterdam Zuidoost, is the district in Amsterdam where most African migrants live. In exchange for €2,500, Ugo agreed to travel with his wife to Tbilisi and give his passport to Victor, who would then use it to travel to Amsterdam together with Ugo's wife. After Ugo's wife and Victor arrived in Amsterdam, Ugo would declare to the Dutch embassy that his passport and the Dutch residence permit had been lost and would request the issuance of new travel documents. "Why do you need Ugo's wife in this story?" I asked. Joshua said Ugo's wife would be necessary for showing Victor what to do and how to behave at Amsterdam's Schiphol Airport, as a holder of a Dutch permit, especially in case someone addressed him in Dutch. Her role would become more important if the immigration officers began to doubt whether the passport belonged to him. She could provide them with a marriage certificate and claim that Victor was indeed her husband "Ugo." Everything was set, with only the approval of Chidi's African American wife still pending. Once she allowed Chidi to pay the €2,500, Joshua could initiate the process. In the meantime, Victor would have to wait in Georgia.

Victor's journey to the Netherlands depended on being financed by his brother in the United States, who had succeeded in his migratory goals and obtained a green card after marrying an American citizen. Because Victor did not meet the qualifications for legal entry into the Schengen Area, he had to follow other strategies to achieve his aspiration of migrating to Europe. Victor's project not only required a significant amount of money but also involved the time and effort of many other individuals to coordinate and realize the plan. With some of these individuals, he already shared kinship ties, such as with his brother Chidi, but others he had never met. Nevertheless, the relations among all these people were expressed in the language of kinship (*brother*, *wife*) and unity (*us*, *we*). Although each of them had a different reason to participate, they all worked together for the project's success. For Victor, the departure from Nigeria and passage across international borders marked his entry into a new web of relationships and the beginning of a life in which he could access various resources only by relying on others and impersonating someone else. This brought Victor closer to other migrants with similar experiences and to persons who could help him gain access to those resources. For example, one of the reasons Joshua was motivated to help Victor was that he had experienced similar difficulties in the past, including using someone else's identity. Victor and Ugo also bonded because of their unequal civic status. In the process of his migration to Europe, Victor became closer to people such as Joshua, with whom he shared similar experiences, and others, such as Ugo, who held a relatively more privileged position. In the second case, Victor had to not only cooperate with Ugo but also learn about and impersonate him, at least during the time he was crossing the border.

For Victor and many other migrants, identity documents are at the center of their struggle to enter and stay in Europe because, as material expressions of citizenship and legal status (Anderson 2020, 55) and "tangible evidence of bureaucratic inscription" (Horton 2020, 4), they can open doors to mobility, employment, and residence rights. I consciously avoid describing migrants' practices of appropriating identity documents as "identity fraud," which inevitably leads to a state-centered epistemology that reinforces the symbolic power of the state and its ability to impose its own categories and frames of understanding (Bourdieu 2000).[3] "Truth," as Foucault (1990, 133) suggested, "is linked in a circular relation with systems of power." In this regard, classifications of "fake" and "genuine" are political categories (Le Courant 2019, 477) and not objective qualities of either documents or the persons who use them.[4] The use of "identity fraud" as an analytic notion also directs attention to certain issues that the state considers important, such as the site of document production and whether the one using these documents is a "legitimate" holder of them. From migrants' perspective, these are also important issues, but they are subsumed by migrants' primary concerns about whether documents are effective and how they can be door openers for them.

Furthermore, the state's definition of "identity fraud" presumes a conception of the person as a bounded and well-defined entity. This conception of personhood is not a reality upon which the state operates but rather a product of states' technologies of governance (Turner 1986; Caplan 2001; Groebner 2007). For the state to attribute rights and obligations to those subjected to its power, it has to first ensure that these are legible subjects, or in the words of the philosopher J. G. Fichte ([1796] 1889, 378), a pioneer of German nationalism, that "each citizen shall be at all times and places . . . recognized as this or that particular person." As I elaborate further in the next chapter, personhood is always an incomplete process in the making (Nyamnjoh 2017). For these reasons, I prefer to treat "identity fraud" and other state categories as objects of analysis and examine how categorizations of "genuine" and "legitimate" are constructed by the state to be perceived as self-evident and how this process affects migrants' effort to appropriate identity documents. To do so, I introduce *unauthorized identity craft*.

Unauthorized identity craft refers to the complex processes of crafting multiple and intersecting relations—with persons, objects, states, and their institutions—that allow migrants to access identity documents and establish a relation with them that is assessed as "legitimate" by immigration control agents. Migrants carefully create, remake, and dissolve relations that allow them to access and appropriate identity documents. Victor had to craft, directly or indirectly, multiple relations with persons (Chidi, Joshua, Ugo, Ugo's wife, immigration officers), objects (passport, marriage certificate), and institutions (immigration authorities). All these relations were established and sustained through various means, such as money transfers, performance, empathy, and appeals to kinship and its norms. Victor's crafting of this set of relations was to eventually help him establish a relation with Ugo's passport that would be assessed as legitimate by Dutch immigration officers. Although all these relations were important for Victor to obtain the passport and successfully appropriate it, he would have to strategically perform some of these relations to immigration officers and hide others from them. This process of crafting relations is not essentially different from other processes of identity making. However, I call this process "unauthorized" because if some of these relations were to come under the state's gaze, they would be classified as "illegal" and possibly be penalized.

Possibilities of Kinship

Migration research has prioritized ethnicity over other forms of social clo-sure and identification to explain the process of migration and migrant in-corporation. Inspired by reflexive critiques of migration research (Wimmer and Glick Schiller 2002; Wimmer 2009; Dahinden 2016) and more gener-ally by constructivist and processualist approaches to ethnicity (Barth 1969; Brubaker 2004; Eriksen 1994), I have been reluctant to take ethnicity as a unit of analysis in my previous research projects and in the research on which this book is based. In my first study in Thessaloniki (2004–2005), following the example of other scholars (Baumann 1996; Wimmer 2004), I took a neighbor-hood as a unit of analysis and approached my respondents as residents of that area and not specifically as members of a particular ethnic group (Andriko-poulos 2017). This allowed me to find out whether and to what extent ethnic-ity was important in their lives, instead of taking its significance for granted. In that neighborhood, I came across a small but noticeable number of Afri-can residents who, very willingly, talked to me about their relations with their neighbors and shared their life stories with me. When I moved to Amsterdam in 2007, I happened to meet some of the Nigerian migrants I had previously interviewed in Thessaloniki. I became fascinated by their intricate migration trajectories and started new research on the migration process from Nigeria to the Netherlands and the survival strategies of Nigerian migrants in Am-sterdam. A merely spatial unit of analysis, such as a neighborhood, was not adequate to explore these questions, so I considered alternative methodologi-cal options that would help me avoid the essentialization of ethnicity.

The study of social networks and the analysis of how resources circulate among network actors appeared to be a good choice. However, I feared that such a methodological approach would direct me to kinship, a topic I was quite reluctant to address. At the time, I saw kinship as an old-fashioned con-cern of earlier generations of anthropologists who studied societies with no or weak state organization and more or less implicitly seemed to assume that kinship loses its significance in modern state-organized societies. Moreover, in African studies, the introduction of the concept of ethnicity signaled an in-crease of interest in urban processes, demographic transformations and (de) colonization; it replaced the concept of tribe that had referred to clan-based societies, seen as static.[5] How could kinship be a better choice than ethnic-ity for a study on African migrants in Europe? How could a focus on kin-ship avoid the pitfalls of an ethnic lens, such as the essentialization of identi-ties, when ethnicity in African studies had been introduced to analyze the processes of social transformation and the dynamics of group formation in new contexts where tribe and kinship seemed to be losing their relevance? I was worried that a focus on kinship would exoticize African migrants and reproduce stereotypes about them as "traditional" and "family-oriented" people.

Nevertheless, the lives of legally precarious African migrants, such as that of Victor, convinced me of the urgency of studying kinship in migratory contexts. It would be impossible to understand the motivations, aspirations, choices, and survival strategies of West African migrants without considering kinship. Relationships they describe in terms of kinship are typically those that are crucial to their realization of their aspirations and that ensure that the requisite resources are available at the right time for their daily survival. They may thus have borrowed from "family" to be able to migrate, traveled with the passport of a look-alike "brother" or "sister," found jobs in Amsterdam using the identity documents of those "brothers" and "sisters," and obtained a family reunification visa or legalized their status in the Netherlands through "marriage." Furthermore, the newly formed kinship relations in Europe, especially siblinghood and marriage, crossed boundaries of ethnicity and connected legally precarious West African migrants with citizens and legal residents of African, Afro-Caribbean, and European descent. Various forms of exchange took place across ethnic boundaries and resulted in collaborations between people of different ethnic backgrounds, countries of origin, socioeconomic positions, and—most important—legal status. The study of these kinship assemblages offers a fascinating entry point to go beyond ethnicity. However, it also requires going beyond the way kinship has been theorized as an institution of "traditional," stateless societies.

The social relations that organized and regulated the lending of Ugo's passport to Victor as well as the marriage of Joshua to a Greek woman in the Netherlands and of Chidi to an African American woman in the United States (both Joshua and Chidi then qualified for a residence permit) indicate how migrants generate different kinds of kinship in response to state policies and regulations. The dominant presence of the state in the lives of legally precarious migrants did not lead to the disappearance of kinship; it continuously regenerated it. This book delineates how these migrants acquire, through kinship, resources that are difficult to access. It examines the forms of exchange and collaboration between West African migrants, mostly Nigerians and Ghanaians, with other African migrants, Dutch Afro-Caribbeans, and citizens of peripheral European countries.[6] The exclusion of many West African migrants from civic membership in the Netherlands designates citizenship as a scarce and desirable status. Civic membership and the proofs of it—identity documents—become valuable resources in a setting of civic inequality. Therefore, the questions I seek to answer are how unequal access to citizenship (civic inequality) triggers new dynamics of kinship for West African migrants in Amsterdam and how new practices of kinship are linked to identity documents.

More generally, exploring the relationship between kinship and inequality—notably, unequal access to citizenship and other state institutions—is analytically and theoretically important. Showing how state-generated inequality affects new assemblages of social collaboration and re-creates kinship relations contributes to the long-standing effort to overcome the dyadic opposition between traditional and modern societies. It also contributes to debunking the presupposition that kinship organizes social, political, and economic life only in traditional societies while in modern societies kinship plays only a marginal role in political and economic activities.

Moreover, this book contributes to discussions about the role of kinship in migration processes. In the interdisciplinary field of migration research, kinship has been a central topic in early accounts of chain migration (Litwak 1960; MacDonald and MacDonald 1964; Choldin 1973; Tilly and Brown 1967) and subsequently migrant networks (Massey et al. 1987; Akanle 2013; Akanle et al. 2021). In this field, kinship has been conceptualized as a conduit to resources and a form of social capital that helps people migrate. The ethnographic cases in this book demonstrate that kinship is indeed important for migrants to obtain resources that are difficult to access. But they also show that this support comes at a cost and that in highly precarious situations kinship often proves to be unreliable (see Menjívar 2000; Del Real 2019).

A recent contribution to the debate over kinship and migration is the edited volume *Affective Circuits* (Cole and Groes 2016b). The book introduced the notion of affective circuits, which refers to the social formations that emerge from the exchange of material resources, emotions, money, and ideas and connect migrants with their families in their countries of origin and elsewhere. Through mobility, migrants access resources that they can channel to their affective circuits. Migrants' engagement in different forms of exchange with their relatives ultimately allows them to reposition themselves from the periphery to a more central position within their affective circuits, where they have greater control over circulating resources. There, migrants claim new forms of authority, respectability, and valuable personhood. This conceptual approach added a new perspective to the debate on migrant networks, as it shifts the focus from how networks facilitate migration to how mobility helps migrants to move through their networks. Combining this insight with the notion of social navigation, I suggest that kinship is not only the boat migrants board to navigate turbulent waters. It is also the sea, sometimes rough, that migrants must swim through facing the danger of drowning, especially if they underestimate the risks and believe kinship to be a safe haven.

In addition to this edited volume, a couple of recent ethnographic studies have also dealt with the role of kinship in different facets of migration from Africa: Charles Piot's (2019) book on the emergence of innovative forms of kinship in the context of applying for a US visa in Togo under the guidance of an ingenious migration broker; Julie Kleinman's (2019) urban ethnography on young and adventurous West African men whose short-term exchanges outside a Paris train station enabled them to participate in long-term transnational exchanges with their families in Africa; Cati Coe's (2014) monograph on Ghanaian migrant parents in the United States whose repertoires of family life had to adjust to their separation from their children; Pamela Feldman-Savelsberg's (2016) book on how Cameroonian migrant mothers forged belonging and new networks in Germany through their children; Joris Schapendonk's (2020) study on how the circulation of people, money, ideas, and imaginations within African migrants' networks across Europe connect different places and give raise to a postnational Eurospace. Outside the African context, there are also important contributions exploring the articulation of migrants' kinship practices with immigration policies (Boehm 2012; Charsley 2013; Freeman 2011; Constable 2003). All these books, with attentiveness to ethnographic detail, examined how kinship adjusts to changing conditions of migration and is responsive to restrictive immigration regimes and global inequalities. In that regard, *Argonauts of West Africa* shares similarities with these studies. But there are also differences. In contrast to most studies that considered kinship in migratory contexts, this book places within the frame of analysis both marriage and siblinghood and examines new forms of kinship that cross ethnic boundaries.

From West Africa to Western Europe: Navigating Inequalities with Kinship

This book is primarily based on ethnographic fieldwork that I carried out in Amsterdam with legally precarious migrants from West Africa. By the term *legally precarious migrants*, I refer not only to those who do not have the right to reside legally in the Netherlands but also to migrants who have a temporary legal status but fear that they will soon lose the right to reside legally. For migrants who do not have a residence permit, I use the term *(legally) unauthorized* instead of the commonly used term *undocumented*. The story of

Victor and the detailed case studies in the following chapters show that these migrants are anything but undocumented.

Legal precarity is not an autonomous, external condition that exists in a vacuum. It is an aspect of the unequal relationship between the state and migrants. This relationship renders some migrants more insecure than others (Chauvin 2017, 2010). While it is often assumed that migration policies in the Global North have become more restrictive, the reality is that they have become more selective, privileging certain types of migration, such as of highly skilled workers, and deterring the mobility of so-called lower-skilled workers (Olaniyi 2009; De Haas et al. 2018). By making illegal certain types of labor migration, migration policies contribute to escalating the precariousness of a significant part of the workforce (De Genova 2002; Castles and Kosack 1972; Olaniyi 2009).[7]

Legally unauthorized migrants are certainly "legally precarious," but they are not always in the most extreme situation of legal precarity. It is important for states to first "embrace" their subjects, using techniques such as identification, registration, and census, to control them and differentiate between members and nonmembers (Torpey 2000). As a result, "individuals who remain beyond the embrace of the state necessarily represent a limit on its penetration" (Torpey 2000, 11). Ivie, a Nigerian woman who was granted a temporary residence permit as a victim of human trafficking, told me that she felt more insecure about her stay in the Netherlands than she earlier had as an unauthorized migrant. Her residence permit could be renewed every six months only as long as police investigations were going on, a nerve-racking process. From the moment she appeared in the records of the Dutch state, her fear of deportation intensified. "Now, they have my name, they have my address, they have everything," she told me. "And they keep saying that it is better if I go to a rehabilitation center in Africa." As Sarah Horton (2020, 6) aptly noted, "in rendering migrants not only known to the state but *legible*—that is, locatable through the information tied to migrants' identities—documents also make migrants more vulnerable." Eventually, Ivie obtained a family-type residence permit after she married a Dutch citizen. Although the extension of both types of permits, either as a human trafficking victim or as a spouse, were uncertain, and she had no full control over it, getting her papers through marriage gave her more freedom and agency—at least she believed that to be so.

Beyond the vulnerabilities that precarious legal status entails, this study is interested in the modes of action that uncertainty elicits (Cooper and Pratten 2015). As Ivie's story shows, migrants might deal with the uncertainties of their legal status by turning to kinship. But can kinship help them overcome these uncertainties? If so, how? Does kinship not introduce new uncertainties? Can kinship eventually bring order, stability, and predictability to their lives? To answer these questions, it is important to go beyond normative discourses, which usually portray kinship relations in a positive light. If we want to understand what kinship does to the lives of migrants—and not only migrants—we need to observe people's practices, how they behave with one another, and how norms of kinship affect their interaction.[8] The ethnographic study of social life in its all messiness and contradictions is necessary. Before I develop these arguments more fully, in conversation with recent advances in kinship theory, I examine the new barriers African migrants face to enter and stay in Europe, particularly the Netherlands, and how they turn to kinship in search of solutions.

CHECKING OUT

"I lived in the Netherlands for ten years, for *tien jaar*," Joe said to me when I met him in the office of his trading company in Ghana. During our conversation, Joe inserted any Dutch word he knew in his sentences, mostly numbers and greetings, even though these Dutch words did not really ease our communication. I guessed it was an attempt to impress his clients and employees who observed his interaction with me, a white European.[9] Joe's brothers were among the first Ghanaians who migrated to Amsterdam in the mid-1980s. His brothers had originally migrated to Nigeria, where the booming oil economy had created many employment opportunities (Akyeampong 2000, 205). However, the drop in oil prices in the early 1980s resulted in a sudden deterioration of the Nigerian economy. In 1983, the Nigerian government deported all unauthorized migrant workers, about a million of whom were Ghanaian (Van Hear 1998, 77). Like other Ghanaian deportees, Joe's brothers used their savings from Nigeria and migrated to Europe. Once they settled in the Netherlands, they paid a quite expensive broker's fee to bring Joe with them. The broker placed Joe in a group of seven Ghanaian musicians who were invited to participate in a folklore festival in France. In fact, none of the seven men who traveled were musicians. All had been instructed by the broker to assume the identity of a different member of the band. Joe and the other six men traveled from Accra to Paris without any problem. Joe immediately took the train to the Netherlands. In Amsterdam's train station, a police officer asked to inspect his passport. Joe became stressed. He was not so afraid that the officer would doubt his identity, because his passport and visa had his own picture. Instead, he worried that he did not know with certainty whether he was allowed to travel to the Netherlands with a French Schengen visa.

He did not need to have worried about this: holders of a Schengen visa can travel to any country in the Schengen Area. After a quick check of the visa's expiration date, the officer returned the passport to Joe. Then as planned, Joe overstayed the visa and remained in the Netherlands.

In media reports about African migration to Europe, unauthorized migrants are portrayed as persons who escaped pervasive poverty and took a dangerous journey, crossing the Mediterranean clandestinely to enter Europe. This representation is to a certain extent inaccurate and misleading (Nshimbi 2020). In West African contexts, migration to Europe is not simply seen as a way out of poverty. Local terms for migration and migrants emphasize the adventurous aspect of migration and the possibilities it entails for migrants' social becoming and respectability.[10] Migratory aspirations are formed not only by the lack of perspectives in the country of origin but also by the desire to become like other migrants who have returned with wealth and converted it into local forms of respectability (Awedoba and Hahn 2014; Effevottu 2021; Okunade 2021; Ikuteyijo 2020). In Ghana, migration is described as going "beyond the horizon" (*aburokyire*), and migrants are called *been-to* or *burgers*, terms associated with prestige, economic success, and cosmopolitanism (Nieswand 2014; Bakuri 2018). Moreover, although global inequalities and developmental disparities shape all kinds of mobilities between Africa and Europe, African migrants in Europe are rarely among the poorest in their countries or origin. Migration is costly and the very poor cannot afford it. Migration to Europe by sea, across the Mediterranean passage, is certainly a reality for thousands of Africans (Adepoju and van der Wiel 2010; Andersson 2014; Lucht 2011). And sadly it is a deadly reality for many. But what is often not realized is that most unauthorized African migrants enter Europe through formal border passages, either with visas that they later overstay or with someone else's documents or counterfeit ones (De Haas 2008, 1308; Flahaux and De Haas 2016).[11]

Ghanaians and Nigerians with low or modest finances are usually ineligible for visas to any European country. For them, it is difficult even to get a short-term Schengen tourist visa, for which they must prove that they have the financial means to support their trip. A stable income and a few thousand euros in bank savings are considered the bare minimum. "Well, we want to make sure that people can pay their stay in Holland. And also if they have income here [in Ghana], there is more [of a] guarantee that they are not going to the Netherlands for economic reasons to work there in an illegal way," an immigration officer at the Dutch embassy in Accra explained to me. A bank statement showing sufficient funds is one of the most important documents in the assessment of a visa application. Indicative of the difficulty in meeting

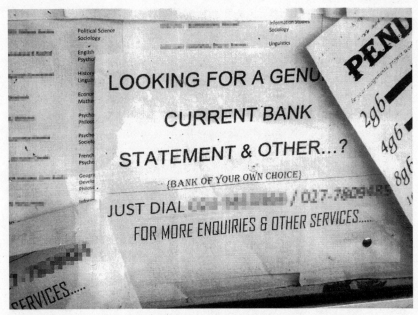

FIGURE 1.1. Advertisement for "genuine" bank statements, Accra, 2012. Photo by the author.

this requirement is that in 2014 only 35 percent of Ghanaians and 44 percent of Nigerians have actually a bank account, let alone one with significant savings.[12] Given the importance of a bank statement to this process, many aspiring migrants without "sufficient funds" do not even apply for a visa, or if they do, they submit counterfeit bank statements bought from intermediaries in the black market (fig. 1.1).[13]

As migration policies become more selective and restrictive, cross-border marriage remains one of the few available migration channels for West Africans from lower socioeconomic backgrounds. In principle, EU countries cannot deprive foreign spouses of their right to move to Europe and live together with their EU partners, as this would violate the EU citizen spouse's right to family life. However, over the past two decades, the Netherlands and many other EU countries have introduced a number of measures, such as income thresholds, civic integration requirements, and age limits, which essentially restrict marriage-based migration (Beck and Beck-Gernsheim 2010; Kofman 2018; D'Aoust 2022).

While the state sets the formal criteria for visa categories, including family visas, and determines who has the right to migrate, it is not the only authority that regulates human mobility across borders. Kinship networks can also exert control over cross-border mobility either by assisting aspiring migrants in meeting formal requirements or by providing them support to migrate through legitimate and illegitimate means. In either case, kinship has its own eligibility requirements that usually differ from the state's categories of deservingness (Gaibazzi 2014; Drotbohm 2020). Families assess the risks involved in determining who to help migrate and how. Among other considerations, an important concern is how to ensure that recipients of support will not be ungrateful and forget their families once they establish themselves abroad. This type of risk assessment differs from that of the state, which is mostly concerned with issues of national security, welfare-state protection, and cultural reproduction of the nation and national community. Aspiring migrants who are excluded from state's privileged categories of migration may fulfill their migratory goals with support from their kin—of course, as long as their kinship networks are able to mobilize resources and convert them into migration-facilitating capital (Kim 2018).

Migrants pay for the costly services of migration brokers, usually with money from multiple family members and friends (Olaniyi 2009, 157). The role of brokers has become particularly important in the projects of many migrants today, affecting migration destinations and costs (fig. 1.2). Migration brokers

FIGURE 1.2. Advertisement for visa agent, outside the Accra Mall shopping center, Accra, 2012. Photo by the author.

are frequently involved in the choice of destinations, which may not be the ones aspiring migrants initially desire (Alpes 2017a; Van Liempt 2007, 139–41). For aspiring migrants in Ghana and Nigeria, the most desirable destinations are the United States, the United Kingdom, Canada, and the Schengen Area countries. These are also the most difficult destinations to reach and the ones for which migration brokers charge the highest fees. West Africans, like many migrants, might have preferences, but they are bound by immigration restrictions and what they can afford.

West Africans increasingly migrate to new destinations in Africa, Asia, and the Middle East (Flahaux and De Haas 2016). To a large extent, migration to these destinations is related to growing barriers for low-skilled workers to migrate *legally* and *directly* to the Global North. Migration to other countries of the Global South is usually seen by migrants as the first segment in a serial migration (Ossman 2013; see also Zuluaga 2015; Paul 2011). They hope it will allow them to make some money and invest it in the next segment of their trip, which typically is to Europe or North America (Konadu-Agyemang 1999, 411–12).

FINDING WORK

Upon his arrival in Amsterdam, Joe learned from his brothers that a common strategy for unauthorized migrants to find work is by borrowing the papers of other migrants. The relationship between those who borrowed and those who loaned their documents was usually described by both parties as brotherhood or sisterhood. However, Joe's brothers alerted him that this was a risky practice, not so much for the risk of being discovered but for the dangers of becoming so reliant on the person whose document you borrow. To protect him from the possible perils of this practice, Joe's brothers put together money and, with the assistance of an intermediary, bought him a French passport. The intermediary sent Joe's passport photo to a poor French citizen of Afro-Caribbean origin in Guadeloupe, a French overseas department, and instructed him to apply for a passport using Joe's photo. The few thousand euros that Joe's brothers paid were shared by the intermediary, the Guadeloupean man, and the officer who received a bribe to process the passport. When Joe received the passport, he used it to obtain a driver's license and later work as a taxi driver.

The next challenge unauthorized West African migrants face in Europe is how to find employment and earn their living. The organization of each country's labor market determines the ways unauthorized migrants find a place in it. In Greece, for example, unauthorized African migrants have worked as street vendors in the somewhat tolerated informal sector, where identity documents are not needed (Andrikopoulos 2018). In the Netherlands, the labor market is strictly regulated, and thus, unregistered jobs are limited for those without documents. Up until relatively recently, a common practice for unauthorized African migrants was to work in registered jobs with the documents and under the name of another (legal) black migrant (Sociale Inlichtingen en Opsporingsdienst 2005; Garcés-Mascareñas and Doomernik 2007). This practice of "identity loan" (Horton 2015) required collaboration between authorized and unauthorized migrants that often created innovative forms of kinship. It is worth outlining here how identity loan became a prominent practice for unauthorized migrant workers and why it eventually declined and today has mostly disappeared.

Unauthorized West African migrants who arrived in the 1980s did not have to engage in identity loan to find work. In those days, the employment of unauthorized migrants was largely tolerated by Dutch authorities.[14] Migrants could obtain a "social-fiscal" number (Sofi number) by presenting Dutch authorities their own passports, or the counterfeit documents they used to enter the Netherlands, and then apply for tax-paying jobs. Only in 1991 did legal residence in the Netherlands become a requirement for issuance of a Sofi number (Meeteren 2014, 71; Doomernik 2008, 137).

After 1991, unauthorized migrants could not obtain a Sofi number in their name, so faced a major obstacle in accessing the labor market. The difficulty of obtaining a job increased in 1994 with the introduction of the Law of Employment of Foreigners, which required employers to hire only those foreign workers who possessed a work permit, and the Compulsory Identification Act, which required employees to be able to prove their identity in the workplace. At the same time, Dutch authorities intensified their controls of unregistered labor as "black work" (*zwartwerken*). In this context, working under the name of a legal resident became one of the few possibilities for unauthorized migrants to earn their living.

The attempts by Dutch authorities to combat unauthorized migration resulted in the valorization of identity documents as scarce assets. This was a condition that enabled the circulation of identity documents among migrants, but the driving forces were labor market needs and employment opportunities for unauthorized migrants. Transformations of the Dutch economy had an important impact on the conditions of migrant participation in the labor market. The two most relevant changes were the remarkable economic growth—the "Dutch miracle" that created new jobs[15]—and the implementation of policies that greatly flexibilized the labor market.[16] In this setting, job agencies (*uitzendbureaus*) came to occupy an important position in the Dutch labor market, formally functioning as employers of flexible workers who were sent to companies to perform job assignments. From the mid-1980s until the late 2000s, the Dutch economy had been growing and demand for labor increasing. The booming Dutch economy not only tolerated the labor of unauthorized migrants but also greatly needed it. My research participants emphasized that in that period, it was much easier for unauthorized migrants to find employment through a job agency, sometimes without even going through an interview. Most found jobs in cleaning companies, restaurants, hotels, and other service jobs. The fact that the work site was in a different location from the employer (job agency) made it easier for them to get the position using someone else's papers.

Since the late 2000s, the practice of identity loan has been declining. All my interviewees agreed that the practice is no longer as common as it was in the preceding two decades. In 2005, the Foreign Nationals Employment Act introduced a new administrative fine for companies and private individuals who employed unauthorized migrants (De Lange 2011). For every unauthorized employee, companies would be fined €8,000. In 2013, the fine increased to €12,000. Dutch officials, lawyers, and migrants told me that the gradual disappearance of the practice of identity loan was the result of the newly introduced severe fines for employers. The restrictive legislation, and its implementation, has no doubt affected identity loan practices. But the reality is more complex. Two important developments equally affected the employment of unauthorized migrants and the practice of identity loan.

First, the 2008 financial crisis halted the Dutch economy's growth. The unemployment rate more than doubled from 3.6 percent in 2008 to 7.8 percent in 2014 (Eurostat). The job market shrank, and the first jobs lost were in the "flexible sector." Unauthorized migrants then had to compete with other migrants and Dutch citizens for fewer jobs. Since then, the situation has only worsened. Especially during the COVID-19 pandemic, when "flexible" jobs in the service sector decreased drastically, unauthorized migrant workers found themselves in an extremely difficult situation.

Second, in May 2007, the Netherlands lifted the transitional restrictions for citizens of the eight member states (Poland, Hungary, Lithuania, Latvia, Estonia, Czech Republic, Slovakia, and Slovenia) that joined the European Union in 2004.[17] This entailed widespread legalization of migrant workers, predominantly Polish, who were already residing in the Netherlands but had not possessed employment rights and thus were in the same position as unauthorized African migrant workers. Now, however, unauthorized African migrants had to compete with Eastern European migrants who had full employment rights and had started arriving in the Netherlands in larger numbers (fig. 1.3). In addition to migrants from the new EU member states, migrants from Southern

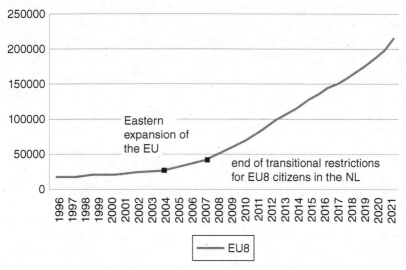

FIGURE 1.3. First-generation migrants from the EU8 in the Netherlands. *Source*: Centraal Bureau voor de Statistiek Data.

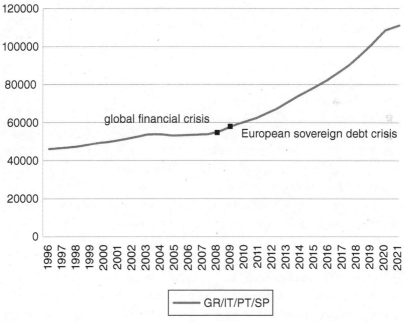

FIGURE 1.4. Total number of first-generation migrants from Greece, Italy, Portugal, and Spain in the Netherlands. *Source*: Centraal Bureau voor de Statistiek Data.

Europe, especially Greece, also significantly increased (fig. 1.4). This increase was an outcome of the intensification of inequalities that the European debt crisis caused in the aftermath of the 2008 financial crisis. In Greece, for example, severe measures imposed by the European Commission, European Central Bank, and International Monetary Fund as conditions for bailout loans led to a spectacular increase in the unemployment rate (almost 30 percent for the general population and 60 percent for those younger than twenty-five) and consequently emigration. In the Netherlands, employers preferred to hire migrant workers from Europe's eastern or southern periphery because their legal status would not put their businesses at risk of high administrative fines. Peripheral European migrants, especially from Poland, eventually displaced unauthorized African migrants in the formal job market.

Interestingly, while the growing presence of peripheral European migrants in the Netherlands has contributed to the displacement of unauthorized West African workers from the formal labor market, it has also presented new possibilities for their legalization. Many unauthorized migrants regularized their status through marriage with these newly arrived EU citizen migrants, who had the right to petition for the legalization of their spouses in the Netherlands (chapter 5). Marriage to an EU citizen became a new way for West African migrants to obtain a residence permit. As one of the few remaining routes to migrant legality, these marriages gained significance as the Dutch state gradually imposed restrictions on marriage-based legalization with Dutch citizens.

GETTING PAPERS

During his years in the Netherlands, Joe explored different options for getting a residence permit in his name. Many of his male peers managed to legalize their status through marriage, either with Dutch women of Afro-Caribbean origin or, later, with women from Europe's periphery. Joe did not want to do the same because he was already married to a Ghanaian woman. Moreover, marriage-based legalization was becoming increasingly difficult. Having no other realistic option, he continued living with precarious legal status. One day, a police officer stopped him for a routine inspection. He checked his French passport and, to Joe's bad luck, addressed him in French. Joe failed to reply in French, which raised the officer's suspicion. Joe was arrested and later deported to Ghana. When I found him in Ghana, he had not given up his plans to return to Europe. In the meantime, he had become a successful businessman in Ghana and funded the migration of his wife, who was a nurse and qualified for a health-care worker visa, to the United Kingdom. Joe stayed in Ghana until his wife was able to meet all the British requirements (income and minimum length of employment) to sponsor a family visa for him. About a year later, Joe joined her in the United Kingdom.

Since the early 1990s, the Netherlands, like many European countries, started to gradually impose restrictions on family migration, and thus on marriage-based legalization, making the process more selective, difficult, and costly. In 1993, the Dutch government introduced an income requirement according to which the partner who wanted to bring a spouse to the Netherlands would have to be employed and earn at least 70 percent of the minimum wage. In 2001, the income requirement was raised to 100 percent of the minimum wage. A few years later, in 2004, the income requirement changed again to 120 percent, and more restrictions were introduced, such as a minimum age, twenty-one, for both partners.[18] In addition to these strict conditions, since 2006, family migrants have been required to pass, before and after entering the Netherlands, a civic integration and Dutch-language test (Bonjour and Duyvendak 2018). Unauthorized migrants can become legalized through marriage to a Dutch citizen or legal resident only by returning to their country of origin to take the civic integration exam; if they pass, only then can they return to the Netherlands with a family visa and residence permit. These strict measures constrained the right to family life for many Dutch citizens and legal residents and for many migrants, and especially men, effectively blocked the marriage channel to legalized status.

The introduction of an income requirement for family reunification implied that the right to family life became available only to working citizens and permanent residents. Thus, it deprived a large part of the population from it, notably those who were unemployed, underemployed, or relied on welfare benefits. The income requirement made the family-based residence permit less easily accessible even to those whose citizen spouses were employed but did not work full-time or did not have stable employment or earned very little. The minimum wage was calculated on the basis of full-time employment (forty hours per week), which was not easily achievable for employees in "flexible" sectors of the labor market.[19] In the large fast-food restaurant where I worked and also conducted my fieldwork, all employees worked an unstable number of hours that depended on the volume of work. As a result, my colleagues and I rarely worked for forty hours a week, and so no one was able to earn the minimum wage, let alone 120 percent of it. The increase in the income requirement from 100 percent to 120 percent of the minimum wage automatically deprived almost 30 percent of the working population in the Netherlands of the possibility of family reunification.[20] This 30 percent of the population also finds women, young people, and ethnic minorities to be overrepresented. In the end, the increased income requirement resulted in a 37 percent decrease in the number of family-related residence permits (Leerkes and Kulu-Glasgow 2011, 111).

Many of the first West African migrants in the Netherlands, particularly men, regularized their status through marriages with Dutch citizens. Usually these Dutch citizens were of Afro-Caribbean origin, from the former Dutch colonies (Suriname, Dutch Caribbean). West Africans and Dutch Afro-Caribbeans shared a common racial background but had different access to rights. The two groups, though, came close together and established relations of kinship through marriage. The ever-increasing restrictions implemented by the Dutch government regarding marriage migration and marriage-based legalization devalued the civic resources of Dutch Afro-Caribbeans. The possibility of West African men obtaining residence permits through marriage to Dutch Afro-Caribbean women was severely constrained because these women's disadvantaged position in the labor market did not usually allow them to meet the new income requirements.[21] Eventually, this also affected types of collaboration between Africans and Dutch Afro-Caribbeans, at least in the realm of marriage (chapter 3).

At the same time, European regulations to ensure the free movement of EU nationals within the European Union—a cornerstone of EU citizenship—required member states to protect the family life of mobile EU citizens. Therefore, EU member states, such as the Netherlands, could not impose strict requirements and conditions on European migrants who wanted to live together with their spouses and children.[22] In practice, this meant that West African migrants' marriages to non-Dutch EU citizens (e.g., Polish, Greek) were not subjected to the same restrictions as marriages with Dutch citizens. The disparity of national and EU legislation created what legal scholars (Tryfonidou 2008; Bierbach 2017a) have described as "reverse discrimination": national citizens and their foreign spouses are treated less favorably than EU citizens and their foreign spouses.[23] As EU regulations became more liberal and national measures for family reunification more conservative, the number of marriages of West African men to women from Europe's periphery increased (chapter 5). This shift in marital practices fueled Dutch authorities' suspicions of instrumentality. Unable to impose any serious restriction on these marriages, Dutch authorities could only investigate the motives of unauthorized migrant men who wanted to marry EU citizens.

Kinship, Politics, and the Market

Migrants' creativity in using kinship in response to legal changes and the Dutch government's and European Union's regulating the family in order to implement political and economic agendas both reveal the intricate entanglements of kinship with state politics. This kind of articulation invites a reconsideration of kinship as an institution of tradition and a separate domain from politics and the market economy. In classic anthropological and sociological accounts, kinship has been conceptualized as the organizing structure of "primitive" or "traditional" societies, inseparable from other domains of society, such as economy, political organization, and religion (for a critical review of this perspective, see McKinnon and Cannell 2013; McKinnon 2013; Thelen and Alber 2018b). In this view, kinship supposedly became irrelevant to and disentangled from other social domains in so-called modern societies. This marginalization was due in part to the presence of a centralized state authority, which supposedly granted equal rights and obligations to its citizens, and in part to the capitalist market, which had transformed socially embedded economic relations into impersonal transactions. According to this narrative, the presence of the state and the capitalist market caused a transformation in the conceptions of personhood: from persons-relatives, whose social existence was firmly embedded in the web of kinship in traditional societies, to autonomous, rights-bearing, and rational persons-citizens in modern societies.

The deeply problematic and flawed modernity-tradition dichotomy and all associated binaries have their origin in the colonial legacy of anthropology. Euro-American anthropologists constructed the "myth" of a kinship-based primitive society to contrast and portray their own societies as democratic and economically rational. The illusion of "primitive society" functioned as a mirror image of anthropologists' own imagined view of their societies (Kuper 1988). From an empirical perspective, the conceptualization of modern society as composed of equal and autonomous individuals, in contrast to kinship-based traditional societies with interdependence as the core of coexistence, is mainly based on philosophical, legal, and religious sources rather than the study of everyday practices (Carsten 2004). Indeed, the anthropology of kinship, especially before Schneider ([1968] 1980) and Strathern (1992), studied small, stateless societies at the global periphery and hardly ever societies in Europe and North America.[24]

In recent decades, however, anthropologists have begun studying kinship in Euro-American contexts and have persuasively demonstrated that the boundary between modern and Western, and traditional and non-Western, cannot be sustained through kinship as the marker of difference (McKinnon and Cannell 2013; Thelen and Alber 2018a). Heading in the same direction, this study calls for a closer examination of the role of the state and citizenship in the process of constructing kinship in contemporary settings. Moving

beyond the normative consideration of citizenship as an institution of equality, this ethnography explores the implications of citizenship on the daily lives
and practices of people who are excluded from it. Given that civic inequality
is also an aspect of state-organized societies (Brubaker 1992; Bosniak 2008;
Wallerstein 2003; Duyvendak, Geschiere, and Tonkens 2016), this book examines how exclusion from citizenship and other forms of state membership
(e.g., residence permits, visas) affects human sociality and the dynamics of
kinship. Such emphasis on the consequences of the intrinsically exclusionary
character of citizenship is more necessary than ever in an era of increased
transnational mobility and globalization. But more generally, especially in
these contexts of mobility and change, a new theorization of kinship is needed
that pays close attention to kinship's interrelation with politics, its flexible
and dynamic character, and its ambiguities (Andrikopoulos and Duyvendak
2020). Recent developments in kinship theory move in this direction.

Ambiguities of Kinship

Contrary to the structural-functionalist model of kinship that was once dominant in Africanist anthropology, emphasizing fixity and ascription, newer approaches to kinship, intellectually influenced by feminism, studied and conceived of it in terms of practices and processes of becoming (Carsten 2020;
McKinnon 2016). This more recent approach to kinship, often called "new
kinship studies," emerged after a period of reflexive critique within the anthropology of kinship, expressed predominantly by David Schneider (1984;
[1968] 1980). The critique exposed the ethnocentric underpinnings of how
kinship was theorized and studied to the extent that Schneider questioned
the appropriateness of using kinship as an analytic category for cross-cultural
comparisons.[25]

Addressing these critiques, new theorists introduced concepts for the study
of kinship that do not prioritize procreation as the means of establishing kinship. Carsten (2000, 4) suggested the term *relatedness* as an inclusive concept for use in cross-culturally studying "indigenous idioms of being related."
Sahlins (2013, 21) suggested conceptualizing kinship as a "mutuality of being" in which "relatives" refer to those "who belong to one another, who are
parts of one another, who are co-present in each other, whose lives are joined
and interdependent." For Sahlins, "all means of constituting kinship are in
essence the same" (29) and may range from commensality, mutual aid, and
shared experiences to adoption, marriage, and procreation. "Relatedness"
and "mutuality of being" prioritize local understandings of how people see
themselves as related and include all the ways of constituting intersubjective

participation in the study of kinship. These are useful conceptualizations for the study of kinship in migratory and transnational contexts where boundaries of culture are contested and transgressed and innovative forms of kinship emerge.

Nonetheless, the theorization of "mutuality of being" and the way "relatedness" has been applied in ethnographic studies tend to ascribe a prominent role to sharing and reciprocity as a basic mechanism of kinship.[26] Several studies (Carsten 1997; Pauli 2013; Thelen, Coe, and Alber 2013) have shown most convincingly the key role of sharing in the process of kinship. Yet the importance attached to sharing in the theorization of kinship as a mutuality of being or relatedness risks obscuring the complexities, tensions, and inequalities that exist within kinship relations. There is a similar risk in studies of migration, where kinship is also associated with sharing, reciprocity, and altruism (Adler Lomnitz 1977; Massey et al. 1987; Faist 2000; Akanle 2013).[27]

Sharing and reciprocity imply closeness, mutuality, and often equality. This conceptualization of kinship bears the risk of locating practices such as violence, treachery, jealousy, fights, and secrecy outside the realm of kinship. As other anthropologists (Geschiere 2013; Lambek 2011; Delaney 2001; Piot 1996; Fennell 2016), and especially sociologists and psychologists (Dobash and Dobash 1979; Gelles 1972, 2017; Smart 2007), have warned, these unpleasant practices and emotions are part and parcel of kinship relations. Feminist and Marxist scholars have already pointed out the extent to which ideologies of kinship naturalize patriarchy and power dynamics within the family and mask hierarchical relations of production (Yanagisako and Delaney 1995; Collier 1988; Siskind 1978; Goody 1990; White 2004). These caveats are important for this ethnographic study. Although feminists have been primarily concerned with gender inequality, their insights are useful for the study of other forms of inequality, such as civic inequality. Taking inequality as an entry point for studying kinship makes us more careful about idealizing kinship relations and enables us to see beyond the positive discourse on kinship our informants often engage in.

Research Population and Fieldwork

The vast majority of West African migrants in Amsterdam originate from Ghana and Nigeria. According to data from the Statistics Department of the City of Amsterdam, 11,463 Ghanaians (7,498 first generation) and 1,712 Nigerians (1,096 first generation) are registered in Amsterdam.[28] These figures do not include unauthorized migrants, so do not represent the total number of migrants from these two countries. Ghanaians are by far the largest group of West African migrants in Amsterdam, and even the largest among sub-Saharan migrants, followed by Nigerians. Migrants from Ghana and Nigeria, as well as other English-speaking migrants from sub-Saharan Africa, socialize together, collaborate in various domains, live in the same neighborhoods, attend the same churches, and work in similar sectors. Furthermore, they also face the same legal barriers to coming to and staying legally in the Netherlands. Although the lives of legally precarious West African migrants in Amsterdam are the focus of this research, ethnographic fieldwork was not limited to them. The research population of this ethnographic research includes wider circles of their quite heterogeneous social networks, which included other African migrants, migrants of African descent from former Dutch colonies in the Caribbean (Suriname and the Dutch Caribbean, which comprises Curaçao, Aruba, and Sint Maarten, constituent countries of the Dutch Kingdom, and Bonaire, Saba, and Sint Eustatius, special municipalities of the Netherlands), migrants from Southern and Eastern Europe, and white Dutch people.[29]

It is difficult to draw a clear timeline as to when the fieldwork actually started and finished because I have been living in Amsterdam since 2007 and my communication with many of the research participants had already started before I formally began my fieldwork, which lasts today.[30] Nevertheless, systematic fieldwork in Amsterdam, in the sense of full-time dedication to research, including keeping regular field notes, lasted for fourteen months, from October 2011 until November 2012.[31] During this period, I relocated to and lived in Amsterdam Zuidoost, or "the Bijlmer," as it is usually called. In 2012, 72 percent of Ghanaians and 51 percent of Nigerians registered in the municipality of Amsterdam resided in this district of Amsterdam.[32] The Zuidoost is ethnically highly diverse, and due to the high concentration of black migrants, either from Africa or the Caribbean, it is known among Amsterdam's residents as the city's "black neighborhood."[33]

Book Overview

The journey of the *Argonauts of West Africa* has set off. The first empirical chapter of this book, chapter 2, follows Jason, a Ghanaian migrant, in his repeated and complex efforts to travel "to an advanced country." It examines how he managed to achieve his migratory and life goals by engaging in "unauthorized identity craft." The chapter develops this notion, which I presented in the introduction, engaging with the debate over the role of the state in the constitution of persons as autonomous individuals and bounded entities. Going beyond the inclusive capacities of citizenship, the chapter investigates the impact of the inherently exclusive side of citizenship on the formation of personhood. After repeated attempts and failures, Jason learns how to craft the right identity that would enable him to enter Europe. Embodying different persons, Jason manages to overcome barriers imposed by increasingly hostile global migration regimes. Following Jason in his journey across the world, we see how many people, places, and relations stand behind a man's mobility.

Chapter 3, the next stop in *Argonauts'* journey, examines the practices of unauthorized migrants in finding employment and earning their living in the Netherlands. Unauthorized migrants borrow the identity documents of other "look-alike" migrants and find employment in their name. This practice entails substantial risks and often has unexpected consequences for document lenders and borrowers. Kinship seems to provide some stability and safety for those involved in the practice to deal with possible dangers. Thus document lenders and borrowers forge relations that they name as siblinghood in hopes that these relations would comply with the kinship norms of solidarity and reciprocity. Not surprisingly, the appeal to kinship does not always have the anticipated outcomes and exposes migrants to new problems and risks.

In the last two empirical chapters of this book, the focus shifts to the marriages of West African migrants. These two chapters explore, on the one hand, how marriage becomes a means for West African migrants to navigate legal precarity and, on the other hand, how those marriages are affected by legal changes at national and European levels.

Chapter 4 examines how legally precarious African migrants gain long-term residency rights and citizenship in the Netherlands through marriages to Dutch citizens of Afro-Caribbean descent. These two racialized groups, West Africans and Afro-Caribbeans, have differentiated access to rights in the Netherlands. The chapter explores how transatlantic kinship, expressed in a language of siblinghood ("black brotherhood"), between African migrants and Afro-Caribbean Dutch citizens facilitates marriages between them. It also examines the effects of Dutch policies designed to restrict access to migrant legality through marriage, which effectively resulted in the devaluation of Afro-Caribbean Dutch citizens' civic resources. Does the attempt of the Dutch state to regulate marriage migration and marriage-based legalization affect the forms of collaboration between Africans and Afro-Caribbeans? If so, how?

The last empirical chapter examines the shift in marital practices of West African migrants, especially Nigerians, from choosing Dutch citizens of various ethnic backgrounds as spouses to European citizen spouses from countries of Europe's periphery. The chapter looks closely at the forms of exchange that take place in the marriages of West African men with women from

Europe's periphery and the circulation of emotions, money, civic resources and sexual pleasure. It shows that West African migrants navigate the highly asymmetrical dynamic of mixed-status marriage by choosing as partners peripheral Europeans, who are EU citizens but most of whom are working-class migrants and in a similar structural position in Dutch society. Under these conditions, the exchange of resources, money, emotions, and sexual pleasure between spouses results in a more reciprocal dependency.

By exploring how West African migrants rely on kinship in attempting to overcome the uncertainties of their legal status, I want to overcome the dilemma of seeing migrants as either victims of structural inequalities or active agents navigating repeatedly updated constraints. It seems that kinship offers a means to deal with institutional structures of civic inequality. However, kinship's unpredictable dynamics, especially in a context of extreme inequality, may prove more difficult to control than many expected.

Unauthorized Identity Craft

A plane from Lagos lands at London Heathrow. All passengers pass successfully through immigration control—all passengers, that is, but one. A young man, who looks at least in his late twenties, is held up by a female immigration officer, who has apparently noticed something amiss with his travel document.

"What's your real name?" the officer asks him.

"My name is Okpegwa Benson."

"OK. Whose passport is this?"

"The passport is somebody's that gave it to me. I would normally call him Uncle London. I have problem at home."

A male immigration officer intervenes. "Where did you get this passport from?"

"A good Samaritan gave it to me."

"A good Samaritan?" the male officer scoffs. "Good Samaritans forge passports nowadays?"

Benson says, "In Lagos. I stressed everything to him and told him everything that happened."

The female officer says: "This document contains an indefinite leave stamp. Whose stamp is this?"

"The person I bought this thing from."

"What is the name of that person?"

"We normally call him Uncle London."

"How do you know Uncle London?"

"When I came to Lagos to see my friend, my friend took me there. Since I have problem I should go and meet him so that I can just . . . [he] give me a helping hand."

Benson claims he was born in 1993, that he is fifteen, a student who fled Nigeria when his parents were murdered. The male officer asks him when he first went to high school. Benson first says 1990, but then 2006: "I said 1990. If I went to school in 1990 by now I'm supposed to be a graduate. I want to say 2006 because I'm in year three." He gave the first answer, he says, because he feels intimidated by the officers, who do not seem convinced by Benson's story.

"I believe that you're not fifteen," the female officer says. "To me, you look older."

"I am fifteen," Benson insists. He repeats it over and over.

"How will I believe that you're fifteen?" the officer says.

"Take it from me," Benson says.

The officers do not believe him. He carries no other identification. In accordance with the law, they order an age test. Pending the test, Benson is placed in a house for minors in London. Soon after, Benson vanishes from the house without a trace.[1]

* * *

The video recording of this encounter, broadcast for a TV program that depicts migrant encounters with the UK Border Agency, went viral on social media, especially among African migrants. This chapter deals with what state authorities call "identity fraud for immigration purposes" (National Document Fraud Unit 2016; Grütters and Zwaan 2010). I prefer to use the term *unauthorized identity craft* to emphasize migrants' perspectives and practices. As used by states, *identity fraud* implies a differentiation between genuine and fraudulent documents and their legitimate and illegitimate use. Migrants are well aware of these distinctions, which strongly influence their practices. However, for migrants, the value of identity documents, and therefore what differentiates one document from another, does not directly result from where the documents were produced or who the state considers their legitimate holders. Instead, the value of an identity document is produced by its capacity to enable its holder, who might be illegitimate according to the state, to cross international borders (Alpes 2017b). Often, producers of identity documents, which the state categorizes as fraudulent, refer to them as "genuine" without intending to deceive their clients but to stress the documents' effectiveness.[2] As aptly described by Adebanwi and Obadare (2022, 77), the producers of these documents contest "state's right, power and capacity to produce, authenticate, and validate documents, thereby establishing what is *true* and *valid* about papers."

Identity documents have been used by the state as a means to establish its relationship to subjects and ultimately exert control over them (Hull 2012; Torpey 2000; Caplan and Torpey 2001; About, Brown, and Lonergan 2013). At the same time, state-issued identity documents "turned the certified individual into a legal person—a positive distinction that ensured the individual as citizen privileged access to certain resources" (Groebner 2007, 237). During immigration controls, when personhood and state membership are controlled and contested, unauthorized identity craft raises important questions of wider theoretical relevance. How do migrants claim to be the legitimate owners of the documents they hold, and how do immigration authorities ascertain the relationship between a document and its holder? How is the relationship between an identity document and a person established? If identity documents are only formal proofs of state membership, what makes a person a genuine citizen?

The circulation of identity documents among migrants is a common practice and, as with Benson and Uncle London's passport as well as Victor's and Joe's stories in the previous chapter, access to documents often involves an appeal to, or a language of, kinship. Existing and newly formed kinship relations are important in unauthorized identity craft because they enable aspiring migrants to find documents and afford their cost (Gaibazzi 2014; Le Courant 2019; Chu 2010; Mays 2020; Ordóñez 2020) and/or because they help them establish their relationship to the document in the eyes of state authorities (Piot 2019; Kim 2011; Freeman 2011; Alpes 2017a). The key role of kinship in unauthorized identity craft is not just an example of kinship's significance in modern settings but also indicates that kinship relations might be strengthened and revitalized when people face forms of inequality generated by the state. Through the presumably "traditional" channel of kinship, migrants can access identity documents, the "artifacts of modern knowledge" (Riles 2006) and emblematic symbols of modern bureaucracies that enable them to cross international borders.

A major challenge for migrants is how to connect their bodies to the person that an identity document represents. And more specifically, how to do so in a way that will suspend the doubts of immigration bureaucrats and, ideally, make the relation appear indisputable. The practice of "kinning" is central to unauthorized identity craft. Originating from studies of transnational adoption (Howell 2006), kinning describes the forging of a set of relations that connect a fetus or a newborn child with the adoptive family and its social networks. It is through the process of kinning that the adoptee transforms from an unrelated person into a relative, from stranger into family member.

In the process of kinning, Mariner (2019, 537–38) emphasizes, paperwork is also important in producing and redoing kinship. "Papers literally enliven and extinguish persons," as Yngvesson and Coutin noted (2006, 179).

In a similar process, migrants who want to appropriate identity documents as their own engage in practices of kinning that connect their bodies with the person that the identity documents represent. The bureaucratic person that an identity document represents becomes, through the process of kinning, a social person—a person with social life—that is embodied by the migrant. By establishing a web of relations with other persons, things, and institutions, migrants craft identities that correspond to the documents they use. The process of unauthorized identity craft is similar whether migrants try to appropriate other persons' identity documents or documents that represent completely new identities or documents that partially correspond to their identities. In all these cases, migrants craft relations in their effort to embody new subjectivities.

Crafting is a difficult and complicated process that requires skills and often resources. Migrants have learned how to craft alternative identities from previous unsuccessful attempts, from experiences of other migrants and increasingly from migration brokers.[3] In a fascinating study of a visa broker in Togo, Charles Piot (2019) described how the broker had set up a business for supporting visa lottery winners who could not pay the expensive consular fee and airfare to the United States.[4] Kodjo, the visa broker, found sponsors for the expenses, which were unaffordable for average-income Togolese, and in exchange the winner would marry the sponsor and migrate together to the United States. Kodjo also prepared the new couple for their visa interview and gave them detailed instructions on how to perform their relationship at the US consulate. About a month before the visa interview, Kodjo asked the new couple to move to an apartment that he had prepared for them. At any moment before the interview, a consulate officer could make an unannounced visit to the couple's apartment to check whether they indeed lived together and whether their neighbors confirmed their relationship. For this reason, Kodjo had decorated the apartment with photos of the couple and instructed neighbors how to answer possible questions by consulate officers. Moreover, by living together, the spouses could get to know each other well and thus answer with confidence questions about their supposed relationship in the visa interview. In this case, we see how many relations Kodjo had to establish and masterfully craft for his paying clients to get a US visa as spouses of visa lottery winners.

Many have anticipated that the digitization of border controls and the use of biometric information in immigration proceedings would have brought unauthorized identity craft to an end. The assumption is that biometric identification, through techniques such as fingerprinting, facial recognition, and iris scanning, relies on unique, indisputable evidence from the body and as such is impossible to fabricate. There is no doubt that the increasing use of biometric technologies in immigration controls—biometric passports, DNA tests for family ties, and so on—has made it substantially more difficult (and more expensive) for migrants to engage in practices of unauthorized identity craft. However, these practices have not disappeared. For example, biometric information collected in the application process for a visa allows immigration officers at borders to perform a biometric matching and confirm a visa holder's identity. The introduction of such techniques made it almost impossible for look-alikes to use someone else's documents. Nevertheless, this did not prevent them from using counterfeit documents to meet the visa requirements (e.g., bank statement, employment contract, invitation letter) or apply for a visa with a biometric passport acquired using a counterfeit birth certificate (Scheel 2019; Kim 2018).

Furthermore, biometric techniques are usually used in combination with other verification techniques, and their use remains at the discretion of the state officer. Another example from Piot's (2019, 63–65) ethnography is indicative. In one of the couples Kodjo prepared for a visa interview, the woman was pregnant from her actual husband. Her pregnancy was not an obstacle for the first visa interview. She went to the embassy with the person who appeared in the application as her "husband," and they both performed the role of the couple expecting their first child. The woman hoped that the visa would be granted shortly after the interview so she could give birth in the United States. But due to a delay in the process, the woman gave birth in Togo. The birth of the child created a new problem. If the mother wanted to take the child with her to the United States, the embassy might require a DNA test to assess the parents' genetic relation with the baby. These kind of requests have become increasingly common in family-related visa processes (Kritzman-Amir 2021). The test would reveal that the woman's "spouse" was not the (biological) father of the child. In turn, this would raise suspicion about the authenticity of the couple's marriage. Kodjo assessed the risk and advised the couple to request a visa for the baby and take the baby with them to their next appointment. Again, Kodjo prepped the couple for the interview and trained the man how to perform as a new "father." He insisted that the man should appear at the consulate holding the baby in his arms and then pass it back and forth to his "wife" during the interview. The plan "worked like a charm": the consul was friendly with the couple and even took the baby in her arms. She granted visas to all three without requesting a DNA test.

This example shows that biometric techniques are embedded in a social sphere and coexist with other modes of identification and verification. In this case, a DNA test could document only the genetic relation between the child and the two adults. But kinship is a social relation, and as such, it can be verified through other means. The performance of parenthood by the couple was sufficient to convince the consul that the child was theirs. Biometric identification and the digitization of legal identities have neither replaced nor erased the social person (Dalberto and Banégas 2021, 15; Dalberto, Banégas, and Cutolo 2021). The growing reliance of immigration authorities on "the truth from the body" certainly signals a move toward an "overindividualized corporeality" (Fassin and d'Halluin 2005). Despite this tendency, the person as a social being remains at the center of immigration controls and, as such, in unauthorized identity craft practices.

Taking the person as a unit of analysis, this chapter critically engages with the debate over the constitution of personhood and explores what unauthorized identity craft reveals about the conception of the citizen as a person. Of special relevance for the theme of this book is the consideration of dividualism and individualism as different types of social being in traditional and modern societies, respectively. The development of these ideas in social theory deserves closer examination as they reflect how the citizen came to be imagined as a particular type of person. Moreover, in different conceptualizations of personhood, the symbol of the mask stands central. As this relates to unauthorized identity craft, I pay particular attention to different perceptions of the mask in discussions of how personhood is constituted.[5]

Of Persons and Masks

In the field of anthropology, the debate on personhood was initiated in an essay by Marcel Mauss ([1938] 1985) in which he argued that each society produces its own type of person and that the notion of the person as known in Europe was not found in other societies. In an evolutionary logic, he outlined the development of the category of the person from the time of clan-based "primitive" tribes to that of modern Europe. Using examples from tribal societies in North America and Australia, he emphasized the use of masks in rituals in which mask bearers either reincarnated an ancestor or assumed a particular social role. He then analyzed how the members of those tribal societies obtained their names. The Zuni Pueblo Indians, for example, had a pool of available names, each designating a particular role in the clan. But, as with the Kwakiutl of the American Pacific Northwest, the name of a person was not always permanent and might change every season and as the person grew up and undertook different roles in the clan. Australian Aboriginal people, such as the Arunta, named their children after the name of an ancestor, which determined the rights of the person and the person's position in the clan. Using these examples, Mauss (1985, 5) argued that "the clan is conceived of as being made up of a *certain number of persons*, in reality of 'characters' (*personnages*)" and "the role of all of them is really to act out, each insofar as it concerns him, the prefigured totality of the life of the clan."

Mauss proceeded to the next stage of personhood's historical development, shifting from the American and Australian "primitive" societies to ancient Roman civilization, which he considered more advanced. The Romans were "the people who established the notion of the 'person' (*personne*), the designation of which has remained precisely the Latin word" (Mauss 1985, 14). The term *person* originates from the word *persona*, which, in ancient Rome, referred to the theatrical mask used in performances. Thus, as with ritual masks in the tribal societies described earlier, the *persona* in ancient Rome designated a role, a character, and a state of being in which the mask bearer did not exist in his or her own independent subjectivity. The transition to the notion of the person as we know it today took place over a long period in ancient Rome when the persona "was made the locus of general rights and duties as a legal 'person' and citizen of the state" (Carrithers, Collins, and Lukes 1985, vii). Key moments in this transition were the establishment of individual rights, such as those resulting from the termination of the right of the paterfamilias to kill his children, and the obligation of Roman citizens to have a name that no one else could use. Citizenship, therefore, is the legal basis of personhood and a required condition for the development of individuality (Turner 1986). The person, Mauss (1985, 14) wrote, is "more than a name or a right to assume a role and a ritual mask. It is a basic fact of law." Mauss ended his historical analysis by stressing the role of Christianity in providing a metaphysical quality to the self-awareness of persons in their individual relationship with God. The historical narrative of Mauss, proceeding from "primitive" tribesmen to Roman citizens to Christian individuals "leads from a start in pure role without self to a finish in pure self without a role" (Hollis 1985, 220).

Mauss's conceptualization of personhood was used by subsequent generations of anthropologists not only to analyze how local understandings of personhood, in Africa, Asia and Oceania, are tightly embedded in kinship (e.g., Fortes 1987) but also to contrast these concepts with Western ideas of individuality (La Fontaine 1985). Dumont, for example, described the partibility of the person, which he called *Homo hierarchicus* (1980), in Indian caste society in contrast to the *Homo aequalis* (1979) in European societies, which he claimed to be founded upon an ideology of egalitarianism and equality. In Melanesian ethnography, similar distinctions have been present in the study of personhood and social relations. The notion of dividualism, which became known through Strathern's work, is central in this debate.[6] With that term, Strathern referred to the relational existence of persons in Melanesia in implicit contrast to Western individualism. She construed dividual persons as "the plural and composite site of the relationships that produced them" (Strathern 1988, 13), which has been taken by other anthropologists as the opposite of Western individuals represented as autonomous, thinking, and free-acting entities (see LiPuma 2001, 132–33).

From an empirical perspective, these conceptualizations of modern society as composed of equal and autonomous individuals, in contrast to kinship-based traditional societies in which persons participate in one another's existence, are mainly based on philosophical, legal, and religious sources, rather than the study of practices in everyday life. Scholars who conducted empirical research on people's practices in contemporary European societies have been critical of such a strict taxonomy. Euro-American psychologists and sociologists, for example, emphasized the role of social interaction in the constitution of one's personhood. The psychoanalyst Carl Jung, a contemporary of Mauss, used the notion of persona in his analysis of the individuation process. Similarly to Mauss, he used the Latin word for the mask to describe the roles that people assume in their everyday lives. Nevertheless, for Jung, persona was not used in reference to forms of personhood in earlier, less developed societies but to his contemporary setting. The persona, for Jung (1972, 157), was "as its name implies, only a mask of the collective psyche, a mask that *feigns individuality*, making others and oneself believe that one is individual, whereas one is simply acting a role through which the collective psyche speaks." This is an important observation: the roles people enact daily may give the impression they are self-conscious and autonomous individuals, but their roles are firmly embedded in social relations and society's norms and expectations.

In a similar vein, the sociologist Erving Goffman (1959) stressed the key role of interaction in the production and realization of the self. In contrast to Mauss, who argued that each society has its own conception of personhood, Goffman suggested that the self is constantly produced and reproduced through social interactions. In these interactions persons perform roles. These roles do not mask "true persons," but they make persons. Thus, the performative constitution of the self, according to Goffman, is flexible and contextually bounded because the presentation of the self is adjustable to the audience in question. This approach is particularly useful in understanding unauthorized identity craft practices because, as we will see, the same performance by migrants can elicit different results, depending on the audience: in some cases, the relationship between a document and a person is established; in others, a "genuine" relationship between the two is challenged.

Conceptualizations of subjectivities in Africa offer perceptive takes on personhood and have contributed powerful critiques of related binaries in social theory. The philosopher Kwame Gyekye (1988) critically engaged with the perception that African societies are communalistic, in contrast to individualistic European societies. Gyekye described the social order in African societies as "amphibious" because "it manifests features of both communality and individuality" (31).[7] Amphibious subjects are able to navigate social fields and comply with social norms and expectations while they also pursue individual aspirations and wishes. This skill of adjustability is important in the rapidly changing postcolonial Africa where persons constantly face new conditions. "Subjects in the postcolony," Achille Mbembe (2001, 104) suggested, "have to have marked ability to manage not just a single identity, but several—flexible enough to negotiate as and when necessary." Along similar lines, the Cameroonian anthropologist Francis Nyamnjoh (2017) emphasized the incompleteness of being and described personhood as a permanent work in progress. For Nyamnjoh, persons are incomplete beings that constantly cross frontiers. These conceptualizations of the person by Gyekye, Mbembe, and Nyamnjoh differ from the ideal of an autonomous, self-conscious, and well-defined individual. Of course, the question is whether these ideas of personhood are applicable only for African subjects. For Nyamnjoh the answer is clearly negative: all persons are incomplete beings. Apart from the relevance of these approaches for theoretical discussions over personhood, they provide important insights into understanding West African migrants' engagement in unauthorized identity craft. Crafting alternative identities is a way for West African migrants to adjust in new contexts that are particularly hostile to them.

In a recent essay, Nyamnjoh (2021) elaborated on his ideas about being and becoming African with a reference to an Igbo proverb that appeared in Chinua Achebe's work. As the proverb goes, the world is a dancing masquerade that you cannot understand if you remain standing in one place. The symbolic meaning of this proverb is that you need to keep moving and changing standpoints to better understand and grasp the world. As Achebe explained, "the world is in a continuous state of flux, and we, as inhabitants of the world, must learn to adapt, to change, and to move."[8] West African migrants in Europe not only move and shift their standpoints toward the dancing mask but they also switch positions and wear the mask themselves. They do not only

interact with others from different standpoints, establishing relations of interdependence. They also become others by wearing their masks, that is by
using their identity documents and assuming their social role.

Referring to this Igbo proverb, Nyamnjoh drew a connection between
mobility—in its real and metaphoric sense—and personhood: moving entails
the crossing of new frontiers and a reflexive understanding of the self in relation to others. A link between mobility and personhood is also made by Cole
and Groes (2016a) in their conceptualization of affective circuits: through
mobility migrants try to reposition themselves from the margins to the center
of affective circuits where they can claim valuable forms of personhood. The
metaphors of the dancing masquerade and of the affective circuits essentially
illustrate a process of social becoming in terms of social navigation. In the
case of the dancing mask, spectators move as they follow the ecstatic performance of the masquerade. Through mobility spectators gain knowledge but
also realize the incompleteness of their being. In the case of affective circuits,
migrants move through networks whose size and composition change as well
as the direction and volume of the flows within. Through mobility migrants
could gain social status, authority, and respectability, but they also realize that
they remain dependent on social relations, albeit in different ways.

In the following pages, the story of Jason, a migrant from Ghana, introduces the reader to the struggles of West African migrants to travel and stay
to Europe. I trace Jason's dramatic efforts to follow the dancing masquerade
around the globe. In this adventurous journey, Jason constantly confronts the
violence of the state and attempts to overcome it by wearing masks, assuming
other person's identities. His life story offers a detailed account of his struggle
to obtain documents and appropriate them as his own. But essentially his story
shows how, through all these experiences, Jason manages to reposition himself
to the center of his affective circuit and become the person he aspired to be.

Crossing Borders, Changing Identities?
The Life Story of Jason

In my first visit to Ghana, in the summer of 2011, Reverend James, a Ghanaian
Pentecostal pastor in Amsterdam, gave me the contact details of his "brother"
Jason in Accra and asked me to get in touch with him. When I arrived in
Ghana, I called him, and we arranged an appointment for what I thought
would be a brief and routine visit. Over the phone, he was very kind and followed consistently Christian etiquette (e.g., "God bless you," "Amen," "With
the grace of Lord"). Until we met, I thought Jason and Reverend James shared
common parents. To my surprise, Jason met Reverend James only a few years

earlier in Amsterdam, where he used to live before he was deported to Ghana. With clear excitement, Jason shared with me how he managed to come to the Netherlands, passing through many African, Asian, and European countries and using many different documents and identities. Jason's adventurous life "in overseas" was to some extent similar to the stories of other West African migrants (Zuluaga 2015), especially those with modest economic backgrounds. Many of the migrants I interviewed engaged in some sort of unauthorized identity craft and rarely traveled directly to Europe. Jason gladly agreed to talk to me in more depth about his life, and this resulted in a series of lengthy interviews. In his early forties at the time of the interviews, Jason was a very charming speaker and full of energy. He enjoyed narrating his life and laughed loudly over his experiences, even his most painful failures.

SIX FOR ONE AND ONE FOR ALL: ORGANIZING THE DEPARTURE

Jason Opare was born in the early 1970s and grew up in a small village in southern Ghana. His father was married to three women and had twenty-two children. As a small farmer, his father could not easily support all his wives and children. Jason recalled that he grew up in extreme poverty, which brought shame to his family. That shame, and being inspired by other villagers who migrated to Europe, drove Jason's decision to try his luck outside Ghana:

> The family has no respect. You see that this is a very poor family. We have no respect in the society that we're living there. Because they know our background and these people [say] we are very poor, poor, poor. So, we don't have respect. So, I told them [family members]: "No, we can't be undermined by the society we are living because we are poor, poor and nobody respects us because we are very, very poor. So, there should be a stop to this kind of life that we are living. I must get up and sacrifice [myself] so at least we can bring glory to the family."

Jason started thinking of international migration as a way to realize his personal dreams, succeed financially and support his family. His aspiration was to go to the United States, the United Kingdom, or any other European country. For aspiring Ghanaian migrants, these countries are at the top of a geographic hierarchy as the most desirable destinations. Belloni (2019, 3) calls these hierarchies "cosmologies of destinations" and explains that they are not just geographic imaginaries; they also reflect "a pathway of moral achievements and recognitions." Jason knew that it was difficult to migrate legally to these countries:

Because you would need a visa to go to Europe. And the visa got a lot of requirements and if you are a poor man there is no way you can get those requirements. Because they needed a bank statement. Myself I don't have an account, let alone to get a statement.

Beginning in 1991, he worked in manual jobs and started saving money for his trip. He moved to a small place and lived with his partner Akosua. He did not want to marry her before he had realized his migration plans because marriage would bring children and it would be much more difficult for him to invest his savings in migration. In 1994, Akosua got pregnant. Jason and Akosua kept her pregnancy secret for a few months, and Jason started looking at how and where he could migrate with the money he had saved. His savings from three years' work were not enough to apply for a visa or pay a broker, who at that time charged between US$4,000 and $6,000 for a connection to what he called "an advanced country." Jason followed the example of other Ghanaians he knew and chose to travel to South Africa. His visa application for South Africa was rejected. He decided to travel to Zimbabwe, for which, as a Ghanaian national, he did not need a visa, and to continue his trip to South Africa overland. His intention was to go there, work for a while, make some money, and invest in the next segment of his trip "to a more advanced country." In total, six people, including Jason, contributed their finances to Jason's migration project. Jason, his two sisters, his half brother, and a friend put all their resources together to pay $1,000 for the airline ticket to Harare. He borrowed $200 from another aspiring migrant, promising that once he had entered Zimbabwe, he would send the full amount back together with the refundable return ticket: "Because you can't go to the immigration there and you have nothing to show that you have with you. There is no country in the world that you can pass through the immigration without them asking you if you have pocket money."

Jason directly flew from Accra to Harare, where for the first time in his life he faced immigration control. He waited in line and showed his never-before-used Ghanaian passport to the officer. "The guy looks at me, says my passport is not OK, wants to give me a lot of problems. I say, 'Man! This passport I made it myself.'" With this statement, Jason wanted to emphasize the originality of the document he had obtained by applying in person at Ghana's Passport Application Centre without any involvement by an intermediary. In other words, Jason was enacting the ideal of the citizen as an autonomous person that has a one-on-one relation with the state. He continued:

There was a heated argument between me and the immigration officer because he said he wants to deport me. And remember, we have put a lot of money here [laughing loud] and the whole resources of the family. And the whole family is counting on me with that little investment that I can't even redeem them later. So, if I am not careful and I am sent away from Zimbabwe that means I am going to perish and to pay the family, friends and to pay the other guy who gave me the money. It would be very, very difficult.

Jason calmed down and made an agreement with the officer: he would give him $50 in exchange for an entry stamp. They agreed, and Jason was granted entry. He took a taxi to the city. As he had promised the friend back in Ghana, Jason repaid the borrowed $200 and sent him his return ticket. His friend would reap the refund of return flight in exchange for the risk he had taken in lending Jason money from his own very limited travel budget. In Harare, Jason met other Ghanaian migrants who also intended to go to South Africa, but they were thus far stranded. One of them, from Jason's hometown, was going to try again and offered to take Jason with him when he crossed the border. They made an appointment, but when Jason went to meet him, he had already left for South Africa. Jason talked about this as "a huge disappointment in my life" at a very critical moment. It made him leery of trusting others.

The border crossing would not be as easy as he had thought, and he came to realize that he would have to pay a broker to assist him. He found a "Ghanaian brother" who offered to provide him with a Malawian stolen passport in exchange for $200. Citizens of Malawi could enter South Africa without a visa. But Jason had run out of cash, so he sold his own passport to a Ghanaian who wanted to return to Ghana, as well as his spare pair of jeans. That might seem drastic, but his Ghanaian passport, containing no visa, could be used only to travel back to Ghana. The value of a traveling document is defined not by its "genuineness" but by its scarcity and its ability to grant its holder (legitimate or illegitimate) international mobility. This ability is not contained in the document but is subjected to the global political economy and interstate relations,[9] the level of the document's appropriation by its holder and the setting where the document is used. Jason's Ghanaian passport in Zimbabwe could grant international mobility only to persons who resembled him and wanted to travel to Ghana. In that sense, his passport was of little value to him. Furthermore, the Ghanaian migrant who bought Jason's passport needed it because he wanted to avoid the lengthy bureaucratic procedure at the Ghanaian embassy, not because he was not entitled to a Ghanaian passport. For all these reasons, Jason sold his passport for just $50. He gave everything he had earned by selling his passport and his pair of jeans, which was less than $200, to the Ghanaian brother and took the Malawian passport with the promise that when he would get a job in South Africa, he would send him the rest.

He arrived at the border together with four other Ghanaians who had also bought stolen Malawian passports. As the Zimbabwean officers did not closely inspect the passports, all five individuals passed through Zimbabwean controls, Jason exiting Zimbabwe as Stanley Msonga. However, when they arrived at the South African side, they realized that it would be very difficult for them to pass through the "computerized control" with stolen passports. Jason was intimidated and returned to the Zimbabwean side. He and his fellow Ghanaian travelers then decided to jump over the border fence and entered South African territory.[10]

I asked Jason whether his fellow Ghanaian travelers were Akan, like him, and in what language they communicated. He answered:

> We were many but when we travel we are all Ghanaians. Even if we do not speak one language, once we are Ghanaians we are all together because we have one mission. And our mission is traveling for better purpose, for a better life. We understand each other because we have only one mission. Our goal is get to South Africa, when we get there we can get some job too, and after that job we can travel to overseas.

SOUTH AFRICA:
SEARCHING FOR THE RIGHT PERSONA

On South African territory, a border patrol apprehended them. "Where are you from?" asked the border guard. And they all replied, "We are from Liberia." Before leaving Zimbabwe, others advised them that they could avoid deportation from South Africa by seeking asylum as nationals of Liberia, which was embroiled in civil war. Their preparation in Zimbabwe for this alternative plan included learning not only the legal provisions and rights but also how to present themselves as Liberians:

> We managed to get ourselves some Liberians' names. But at that time people in South Africa they didn't know much about Liberia because you know South Africa was isolated because of the apartheid. We learn some things for Liberia. Some basic things. Their flag, their presidents, . . . they got their independence, their currency. You know those things we call them "ability questions" that they can ask you.

Jason claimed that his name was Alfred Kpoto and applied for asylum. After a few months in detention, Jason was granted asylum as a Liberian and issued a temporary residence permit that he would have to renew in six months. In Johannesburg, Jason met another Ghanaian, Kojo, who helped him find accommodation and work. Before he settled in South Africa, Kojo had attempted unsuccessfully to migrate to Europe through Libya, then moved to Gabon and then to South Africa. Kojo hosted Jason and helped him to set up a small fruit stand. The beginning was difficult for Jason. He had to deal with hostile attacks by other migrants and some South Africans. The very first fruit he bought for his stand was stolen: "I came back home crying, crying, crying. I couldn't understand why life is not fair. Nothing is working."

He started saving money from street vending with the intention of using it to travel to the United Kingdom. A former classmate, already in London, sent £200 in support of Jason's migration plan. With that money and his savings, he bought a Malawian passport and a ticket to London. In September 1995, he unsuccessfully traveled to London as Trevor Chimodzi:

> When I was going to airport my heart was pumping, pumping, pumping. Because I knew I had to take another risk. Because the document is not good but I have no way. It's my picture on it but the document is not genuine. So, I tried. I went there, dressed very smart. I went to the check-in. Try, try, try. Nobody don't give me the boarding pass.

Although he was very disappointed with this outcome ("I have to come and cry again. I can't make it!"), he did not stop trying. He returned to his fruit stand to work and make more money to be able to afford a better strategy. Meanwhile, his temporary residence permit was about to expire, and he had to again face South African authorities. Instead of applying for a renewal of his refugee identity card, he decided to seek anew asylum with his own name, claiming that he was from northern Ghana, which had seen a recent outburst of ethnic violence. It was difficult for Jason to perform constantly, especially in front of authorities, the persona of the Liberian refugee Alfred Kpoto. Many migrants in South Africa manage to secure a legal residence permit as refugees with the assistance of corrupt officers (Alfaro-Velcamp et al. 2017). For as much as $2,000, which is shared between the corrupt officers and the intermediaries that bring migrants to them, migrants can get a refugee status document (Section 24) and a unique registration number uploaded in the national refugee database administered by the Department of Home Affairs. Jason followed a similar route, eventually managing to be granted asylum under his name, Jason Opare, and received the refugee identity card with the thirteen-digit barcode. Although he was from southern Ghana, refugee status as a persecuted northern Ghanaian made him feel more secure:

> I don't feel comfortable with other characteristics. I am not a Liberian. And if I meet a real Liberian, I have a problem. You understand? . . . And I don't

like this kind of life. It is like you're pretending to be Mr. A whereas you are Mr. B. So, I don't like that. [And I had] a Liberian name also, which I don't like. And then, the date of birth and everything. It's is not good. It's not a genuine thing. And I like genuine things! So, when I have everything, a refugee status in my own name, with my date of birth, my country there, I feel comfortable. Because I am a Ghanaian. I can tell I'm a Ghanaian. My name is Jason Opare and I am OK with everything because everything is OK.

After the unsuccessful attempt to travel to London with a Malawian passport, he reconsidered his plan to migrate to the United Kingdom. With money he made in South Africa, he bought a Zimbabwean passport and this time tried to travel to Canada. At that time, nationals of Zimbabwe could travel visa-free to many economically advanced countries, such as the United Kingdom, Canada, South Korea, and Israel. Jason wanted to travel to Canada, where one of his half brothers was living, and he expected this half brother would assist him when he arrived.

GOING TO CANADA, STRANDED IN ASIA

Jason followed the advice of other Africans who had done the same and, instead of buying a direct flight to Canada, he bought a flight first to Kuala Lumpur in Malaysia and a second flight from there to Toronto.[11] He said: "So, I do it like this because my documents are not OK. So, that in case I have problem then I am already in Malaysia. It is better than being in South Africa." On Easter Monday, in 1996, Jason, as Robert Williams of Zimbabwe, flew without incident from Johannesburg to Kuala Lumpur, but he was denied boarding for his second flight to Toronto.

He stayed in Malaysia for seven months, after having easily found a job on a construction site. Jason and some other African migrants worked in different companies with the same work permit of a Nigerian national named Usman Bahari: "We managed to get some fake documents, working permit. This is not good. When we get one photocopy, we make copy for all of us [laughter]." Jason earned a lot from this job and sent money to the family members and friend who had helped him buy his first flight to Zimbabwe. He remitted money to his partner Akosua for their newborn son and sent money for the funeral of his father, who had died that year.

Jason had to leave the country every three months and reenter to extend his temporary stay in Malaysia as a Zimbabwean traveler. For this reason, he traveled twice to Thailand using his Zimbabwean passport. With the same passport, he opened a bank account and started saving. In December 1997, he attempted again to travel to Canada using the same Zimbabwean passport.

He thought, "So, now my passport looks genuine" because it had "a lot of stamps and a lot of entries," and he had a bank account and a credit card with the same name as in the passport. Nevertheless, the agent at the check-in counter did not seem convinced. After a heated argument with him, Jason managed to get a boarding pass for the first leg of his flight to Taipei.

For Jason, the agent's hesitation was not necessarily the result of his Zimbabwean passport's inauthenticity. After all, this was not the first time he traveled with a document that was not his own, and the only time he used his own Ghanaian passport, when he landed in Zimbabwe, he was treated with the same suspicion. His first failure to travel to Canada with the Zimbabwean passport, which he had used to travel from South Africa to Malaysia, was not caused by the passport's not being genuine but by its not looking genuine enough. This time the same passport's authenticity was better established, in Jason's understanding, because a traceable person was contained in the document. The authorities could see in his passport and the attached supporting documents traces of a person who had traveled, opened a bank account, and had economic transactions, and all these had been controlled and certified by other authorities.[12] Contrary to an unstamped passport ("virgin passport"), a passport with visas and stamps indicates frequent traveling, and thus its holder is less suspect as an unauthorized migrant. For the same reason, intermediaries that offer assistance for European visa applications usually place in their clients' passports fake visas and entry stamps from other countries. In this way, they create the impression that their clients are well traveled and increase their chances of being granted the visa. This is another instance that demonstrates the "intriguing coexistence of the inauthentic and the authentic" (Adebanwi and Obadare 2022, 84).

Jason boarded the plane and flew from Kuala Lumpur to Taipei, where he would take his transit flight to Vancouver. While he was waiting at the departure hall of Taipei's airport, two immigration officers approached him and asked to check his documents:

> They ask me what is my name. "You are holding my identity and you are asking of my name?" Then I told them my name [Robert Williams]. They say they want my height. They want to check. . . . So, they asked me to get up because I was sitting so they can check my height. I got up. They checked my height. . . . What am I going to do in Canada? I said I am going for Christmas holiday. They said, "Do you have money with you?" I said, "Yes, I have money with me." They say, "Where is the money?" Then I show them my bank statement. But before then I have already taken the money to buy the ticket [laughter]. . . . Where am I going to Canada? I said Vancouver. "Which address?" I showed them a hotel reservation.

The officers made a phone call to the hotel in Canada, and once the hotel confirmed Jason's reservation, they returned the passport to Jason and allowed him to board the plane. Ten minutes before departure, two officers boarded the plane in search of Robert Williams. They asked Jason to follow them for another control. Jason refused and argued fiercely: "Why? Why don't you want to ask any of them [other passengers] a question? Because I am a black man?" They handcuffed him and took him by force off the aircraft.

He described this incident as one of the most frustrating failures of his life. He recounted:

> That was the day that I cried. Yeah, man. So, I didn't make it again! Another glorious opportunity has gone. And I don't know when I will be able to get another arrangement to get to that far. . . . I was thinking: So how come everybody, I have so many friends, they have managed the same route, they are successful, some have managed to get to the UK, someone in Canada, someone in the US, in Australia. Most of them have managed to get to their destination. I have tried so much and yet nothing is working. I keep on asking, "Hey, is it because I am from a poor family so this poverty is chasing me wherever I go?"

The immigration officers in Taipei's airport asked him to request a letter from the Zimbabwean embassy certifying that the passport was genuine and belonged to him. Jason thought:

> I told myself, "I am not a Zimbabwean. So, how can I go to the Zimbabwean embassy?" I only tell the man, "If you don't value this passport, why do you value a letter?" No, no. I don't need a letter to travel. I need a passport! This is an international passport. You need a passport to travel.

His arguments did not convince the Taiwanese authorities, so Jason had no choice but to give up. He cooperated with them for his "voluntary" return to South Africa, where he had supposedly departed from.

BACK TO SOUTH AFRICA

On December 18, 1996, Jason arrived in Johannesburg and his case was handed over to South African authorities. Since he was carrying a Zimbabwean passport with no valid residence permit, the South African authorities had to arrange his repatriation to Zimbabwe. Jason willingly disclosed the unauthorized identity craft he had engaged in and that he was not a Zimbabwean national, to avoid his removal to Zimbabwe. "So, I said, 'Look, this passport is not mine.' They said, 'Yes?' I said yes." He was transferred to the police station of the airport for further investigation.

There, he saw Calvin, a Ghanaian friend he had met in Johannesburg. They did not talk to each other because Jason heard Calvin saying he was a Liberian and Calvin glimpsed in Jason's folder the Zimbabwean passport. "We can't know each other and speak the same language," Jason told himself. When no one was around, Calvin said to him, "Hey, I thought you are in Canada!" Jason responded, "Yes, and I thought you were in London!" Jason explained what happened and Calvin said he had sought asylum in the United Kingdom but after eight months in detention was deported. In the presence of officers, they stopped talking to each other and each continued with his own performance to authorities.

On the basis of his previously recognized refugee status, Jason managed to stay in South Africa. At the same time, he faced charges for falsification of identity documents and was imprisoned for six months. When he was released, Jason decided to stay in South Africa to earn money and then return to Ghana, where he could either start his own business or prepare a better-funded attempt to migrate to Europe. In the years that followed, Jason worked as a security guard in a hotel in Cape Town. After more than two years of full-time work, he had saved enough and applied for a new passport at the Ghana High Commission.

At that time, Kwesi arrived in South Africa and needed Jason's assistance. Kwesi was the son of Jason's older half brother who had helped fund Jason's trip from Accra to Harare. Kwesi's goal was to travel to the United States, but he still needed money to cover the broker's fees. Jason called the Ghana High Commission, canceled his passport application, and gave Kwesi the $400 he would have paid for the passport application process. "It's a sacrifice for him," he said. Surely—but his savings amounted to $5,000, so he did not have to cancel his passport application to come up with $400. The fact was that Jason had changed his mind again; it was never clear to me why, but perhaps Kwesi's plan had reignited Jason's desire to, as he said, go "overseas." With all the money he'd saved, he thought it would be easier this time.

THE LAST EFFORT:
THE MAKING OF A GENUINE PASSPORT

A local South African intermediary, a "brother," brought Jason to the authorities of a small village and instructed him to request the issuance of an identity card under the guise of a South African who had been exiled during apartheid. He also accompanied Jason to assist in his performance as a South African and vouch for his declared identity:

When I got to the place, I didn't talk to anybody. . . . So, I pretend to understand the language very well, but if you ask me, I talk small-small. I don't make lengthy statements because I will do mistakes. So, when they ask me a question, I answer and then I do not talk again. They told me, "What happened?" I told them I was in exile.

Jason's performance as an exiled South African was successful. He was issued a South African identity card, the first step toward the much-desired "genuine" South African passport:

So when I finish, the idea is to get genuine documents. I don't want any document. Because those documents I used initially, I never survived. So, now I wanted to travel with genuine documents. I don't want to travel with fake documents. So, let me get the passport, so, the passport is biometric. So, that one is OK. [The previous ones] were not biometric. So, I had problem with the immigration and then they say, "Oh, this passport is not good, is not for you" and all these. So, this time I have to try and get genuine thing. Because that's the only way I think I can survive.

With his South African identity card, he applied for and was granted a South African passport. In Jason's understanding, this passport was "genuine" not only because the official South African authorities issued it and included his biometric information but also because the passport belonged to a person who existed beyond this document—not an existing person but one whose life was traceable in other documents, preferably issued by state authorities and at an earlier date than the "genuine" document. The importance of a person's traceability for making a document authentic was the reason that led Jason to apply for a South African identity card, and then for a passport, with the name Robert Williams, the same name that appeared in his previous Zimbabwean passport:

So, that, because I have already traveled a lot with that [Zimbabwean] passport. I have a lot of documents. Even though they have taken the Zimbabwean passport already. But those documents, there is no passport number there and it doesn't say that I am a Zimbabwean. So, I can get a lot of evidence that this name is correct.

The passport's credibility was built on three elements: the official state authorities issued the passport; the biometric information mentioned in the passport corresponded to the person who held it; and the passport belonged to a traceable person. Still, a fourth element was necessary to glue all these elements together and create the document's "authenticity": performance. Jason had to successfully perform the role of the person who was the legitimate owner of the passport, otherwise immigration authorities would doubt the document's authenticity and the relationship between the document and its holder. A successful performance not only is a function of the person's abilities and skills to enact a role but also depends very much on the audience in question.

Although Jason could speak some Zulu, Xhosa, and Afrikaans, a South African could easily understand from his accent that he was a native speaker of none of them. Because of this, it would be very risky for him to depart from an airport in South Africa or any neighboring country. He followed the advice of other people who had done the same and decided to go to Tanzania to take a flight to Europe.

Before doing this, he opened a bank account with his new passport and deposited all his savings. With a bank statement and an airline ticket, he successfully applied for a Schengen visa at the Dutch embassy. Having a South African passport, a Dutch Schengen visa, and about $5,000, Jason departed Cape Town for his trip to Europe in December 1999. He took a bus from Cape Town to Durban to Mbabane in Swaziland (now Eswatini):

> I get out of South Africa now. So, now, nobody can challenge me, my nationality now. Because wherever I am going, I'm only going to speak English. I am not going to speak the local language.

His next stop was Maputo in Mozambique, then Lilongwe in Malawi. On the way to Malawi, the bus he was in had a serious accident. No passenger was fatally injured. But the accident made Jason realize the risk he was taking, and more specifically the perils of unauthorized identity craft:

> Nobody was hurt but I got to ask myself, "If I am to die here . . . ?" I mean, nobody knows me. And this name, the passport I am holding, this nationality. A whole a lot of thing came to my mind. My family can never trace me. Because I am not with my own identity.

The traceable person that Jason had created with such effort was merely a role. If Jason died, as happens daily in the Mediterranean to migrants who are called, ironically, "undocumented," only the bureaucratic person he was performing could be traceable. The Akan proverb *wode nnabraba tu kwan a wudu; na mmom wonsan w'akyi bio* (If you travel with fraud [or based on deceit], you may reach your destination, but you will be unable to retrace your path) can literally describe Jason's fear about this situation (see Inusah and Segbefia 2021, 347). If he were to die, his family in Ghana might never find out whether he was alive or dead.[13] His family could never bury him in his hometown, a manifestation of belonging and valuable personhood, which would be disgraceful not only for Jason but for his family as well (Van der Geest 2000; Geschiere 2014).

After a long and difficult journey, Jason safely arrived in Dar es Salaam, Tanzania. From there he took a direct, ten-hour flight to Amsterdam's Schiphol Airport. At passport control, a Dutch immigration officer took him to a separate room for further investigation that lasted more than half an hour. Jason had learned from his previous experiences and did not panic.

> I knew the man was not quite sure of me. He can deport me. He can refuse me entry. So, I tried to pretend that I am OK. Everything is fine with me. Even though deep down I was having a lot, a lot of thinking going through my mind. My heart was pumping because I knew if that man refuses me, it's the end of my life [laughter]. So, I was, I wanted to be friendly with the man at all cost. Because I didn't want him to . . . like that I am under arrest, or the man will give me problem. I just wanted to create an atmosphere that the man [who] was there [would think,] "No, this guy is a genuine man." You understand? I didn't panic. I didn't show anything that the man will give me a problem. Even though I have similar experience before. I know immigration how they act. So, this time because I have a lot of experience I know how to handle the man.

The officer's first question was why he did not depart from South Africa. Jason was prepared for such questions and replied with "white lies." He said all flights from South Africa to Amsterdam were fully booked in December 1999 and January 2000 (which he knew was true) and that he therefore had traveled to another country to take a flight before his visa expired. The officer asked him why he chose Tanzania and not a neighboring country. Jason told him he wanted to tour some African countries before he continued to Europe and showed him the receipts from all the hotels he had stayed in on his way from South Africa to Tanzania. The officer asked him whether he knew someone in the Netherlands and Jason responded negatively. He then asked him why he chose the Netherlands for his vacation. Jason explained that he was interested in visiting the Netherlands for its historical relationship with South Africa. At that point, he started speaking Afrikaans to illustrate the linguistic connection between the two countries ("So, when I got there I speak some Afrikaans and it's like Dutch and the man was impressed"). However, his main objective was to make him believe that he was a "genuine" South African. While in South African territory, his language skills could betray that he was not a lawful owner of his passport, in Amsterdam, the same language skills strengthened the genuineness of his passport and the relationship between passport and holder. After the officer received satisfactory answers, he left the room. When he came back, he told Jason that someone was looking for him in the arrival hall. Jason reacted:

> I said, "Me? I have already told you that I do not know anybody here. How can someone wait for me outside?" Because I knew he wanted to play with my intelligence.

The officer was bluffing. Perhaps his intention was to check the credibility of what Jason had already said to him. The failed bluff made Jason understand that he was very close to getting the entry stamp:

> This man is searching through the passport, opens all the pages, picking up the stamp, about to stamp it, puts it in the ink and then he suspends it again. Then he gets up again and walks, walks. Then he came back again with the man [another officer]. Then he called me, "Mister!" I say, "Yes man!" Now, he takes up the passport again, with the stamp, and then he put the stamp inside there. He said, "Welcome to Holland."

"THE DOCUMENT IS GENUINE, IT'S THE PERSON WHO'S NOT"

After five years and four months of trying, Jason set foot on what he called "an advanced country." From Amsterdam, he immediately took the bus to London. At Dover Strait, he passed successfully through the French passport control but was denied entry on the British side. As he recalled, the British officers told him that for the duration of his declared UK visit, he should have at least the equivalent of £500. Jason called friends and relatives all over the world to ask whether they knew anyone in France or any nearby country who could host him for a while. Kwesi, the son of his brother who had traveled to the United States via South Africa with Jason's financial assistance, gave him the contact details of Dorothy, a Ghanaian woman who lived in Paris. Jason called her and asked her to temporarily accommodate him. Dorothy replied positively but never came to pick him up or answered his calls. Then Kwesi's wife provided Jason with the telephone number of a Ghanaian woman, Getty, living in Amsterdam. Jason called her and explained his situation. Getty agreed to host him for a short period. Jason returned to Amsterdam and stayed at her place.

After a while in Amsterdam, Jason bumped into John, his former Ghanaian flatmate in South Africa who had also migrated to the Netherlands. Jason and John decided to rent a room together in the Bijlmer. The room had only a mattress on the floor that the two shared without ever, as Jason said, "having any problem":

Because we know our mission, our goal. We have been struggling. When John came to South Africa, he went to South Korea and he was deported to South Africa. He had a problem in South Korea and he was using an Ivorian passport . . . So, it's like we have the same mission, the same problem. So, we understand each other. There was a very mutual relationship with John. We were ok and some time we share ideas, how to make it in life and all those things.

Jason faced difficulties in finding relatively stable employment in the Netherlands. John supported him and encouraged him to attend his Pentecostal church. Jason was very reluctant to attend a church. John explained to him that through his dedication to God, he could see his effort bearing fruit and convinced him to give it a try. Jason recalled his initial reluctance:

> Because the church, they make money from the people. And me, I am struggling. The little money I have, I don't want to go and give it to the church. I am a poor man. . . . So, I went to this church there. I decided. I said OK. I use my brain a lot and not getting resources. I have to stop and then give my life to Christ. Maybe I get resources. Because I thought I am a very smart, thinking guy, doing a whole lot of things, doing things on my own. I never get resources.

Things started getting better for Jason as he managed to find jobs in the manufacturing and construction sectors. He landed these jobs using the work permit of Getty's husband, Justice. Jason introduced himself to his employer and colleagues as "Justice" and performed this role every day at work. "The document is genuine, it's the person who's not genuine," Jason explained to me (see chapter 3). With the first money he earned, Jason bought a secondhand Opel Vectra and sent it to his brother in Ghana. The car was sent to his family not to use or sell but just to keep there. Owning the car in Ghana provided Jason with a sense of security for his life in Europe and was a step toward gaining some autonomy and independence:

> The idea of buying the car, what I'm telling, bring this car down, so that my brother will keep it for me, in case I got deported then I just sell the car quickly and I don't have to go to people for money to travel again or to do whatever I want to do. Because of the past experience I have gone through, I don't want to rely on anybody again. Because sometimes nobody helps me eventually . . . I know what I have gone through before. But I tried to raise money, $1,000 . . . Think about five people [who had to contribute]! I don't want that thing to happen again. So, I always wanted to be self-independent. Even if something happens to me I can be capable of solving my problem without having to go to anybody.

In the years that followed, Jason sent two more cars to Ghana and deposited about €9,000 in a Ghanaian bank account with money he earned as a worker in the Netherlands. In the 1990s and early 2000s, before the onset of the financial crisis, there were many job opportunities for migrants in the Netherlands and one could easily find a relatively well-paid full-time job. During his stay in the Netherlands, Jason worked for three different employers, always using the papers of someone else. His last job was at the construction site of the World Trade Centre's building. In February 2005, the Labor Inspectorate inspected the site. Jason and two other African workers were detained. Although none of them had their own Dutch residence card or work permit and in principle they were all deportable, deportation could not be executed without Dutch authorities establishing their identities. And yet the lack of appropriate documentation is what made it difficult for Dutch authorities to prove the legal personhood of Jason and his colleagues—a necessary step before treating them as citizens with no residence rights and deporting them. Jason and his colleagues were effectively undeportable unless an embassy recognized them as citizens of its country and issued emergency travel documents (Griffiths 2013, 285). The Dutch government exerts pressure on migrant-sending countries to facilitate the repatriation of their nationals who do not have the right to stay in the Netherlands and lack any other form of identity documents.[14] One of the three persons arrested did not disclose his identity and after some months in detention was eventually released (see Kalir 2017). Later, Jason learned that he had moved to Belgium. Jason, however, had already fulfilled his migratory plans and made the money he had hoped to make, so he cooperated with the Dutch authorities for the organization of his "voluntary return." His trip from Ghana to "an advanced country" had lasted more than five years; his return trip from the Netherlands to Ghana took seven hours (fig. 2.1; table 2.1).

BACK TO GHANA:
BECOMING A BIG MAN

When Jason arrived, he had already sent three cars to Ghana and had about $9,000 in savings. He invested that money and opened an extremely successful trading company importing secondhand cars from Europe. In just a few years, Jason became very wealthy, and his life changed dramatically. He married Akosua and had five children. He first built a house in his hometown and then bought a semifinished house for himself and his family (wife and kids) in Accra (fig. 2.2). The Accra house is rather big, with six bedrooms, a large living room and a kitchen. I was especially impressed by the six private bathrooms—one

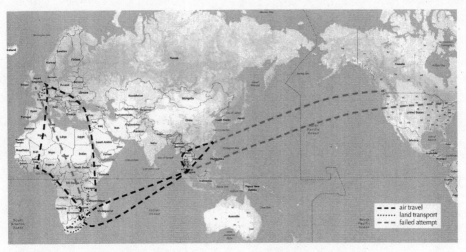

FIGURE 2.1. Jason's journey.

for each bedroom (Jason said he wished to make his home "look decent"). He has also bought a larger piece of land in Accra where he will build his "dream house," using building material he wants to import from South Africa and Europe. Jason financially supported many of his relatives to achieve their goals as well. He has paid the university fees of his nephew, who became a doctor. He supported the migration projects of several other family members. His company employed his nephew and helped teach him about business. Today Jason enjoys the respect and appreciation of his family members and many others. Reverend James, after visiting Jason in 2013, told me, "He is a big man now." Jason showed me a text message in his phone from his brother in Canada. He explained that this brother used to talk dismissively about him before. Jason's eyes got wet as he was reading out the message. His brother apologized for what he thought of him and congratulated him for now helping their family.

In our last interview I asked Jason, "Do you think that you have fulfilled the vision you had when you left from Ghana?"

Yes, yes, yes, yes, yes. Because this is what I wanted. To be recognized. Recognition. That people recognize. OK. That is the . . . recognition. Because I told you, initially, we were not recognized at all. People used to tease us for poverty: "these people, they are poor." But now it's OK. Because I have raised my family.

His economic success and accumulation of wealth changed not only his status among his family and community but also his ability to travel. Today, Jason can more easily travel to Europe and, more important, do so using his

TABLE 2.1. The personae of Jason

Persona	Nationality	Type of identity document	Successful act	Failed act
Jason Opare	Ghana	Passport	Ghana exit Zimbabwe entry	
Stanley Msonga	Malawi	Passport	Zimbabwe exit	South Africa entry
Trevor Chimodzi	Malawi	Passport		South Africa exit (to United Kingdom)
Alfred Kpoto	Liberia	Refugee identity card	South African residence permit	
Jason Opare	Ghana (northern)	Refugee identity card	South African residence permit	
Robert Williams	Zimbabwe	Passport	South Africa exit Malaysia entry (4 times) Malaysia exit (4 times) Thailand entry (2 times) Thailand exit (2 times) Taiwan entry Taiwan exit South Africa entry	Taiwan exit (to Canada)
Usman Bahari	Nigeria	Work permit	Registered employment Malaysia	
Robert Williams	South African	Passport	South Africa exit Swaziland entry Swaziland exit Mozambique entry Mozambique exit Malawi entry Malawi exit Tanzania entry Tanzania exit Netherlands entry (2 times; 1 air, 1 land/no border control) Belgium entry (2 times, no border control) Belgium exit (2 times/no border control) France entry (2 times/no border control) France exit (to United Kingdom) France exit (to Belgium/no border control)	UK entry

(continued)

TABLE 2.1. (*continued*)

Persona	Nationality	Type of identity document	Successful act	Failed act
Justice Owusu	Ghana	Work permit	Registered employment Netherlands (in 2 factories)	Registered employment Netherlands (at construction site, hired but arrested after control)
Jason Opare	Ghana	Passport	Netherland exit Ghana entry	

own passport and name. He does not have to engage in unauthorized identity craft anymore:

> Now I can travel very, very easily. Because now I got all the requirements: I have properties and I have money. So I don't have problem. Do you understand? That is it. Because now if I go to the embassy, whatever they demand I have it. They only demand bank statement and I have a lot of bank statements. No problem! Bank statement is fine. And then they need company registration certificate, which I have. And they want a tax clearance certificate . . . which I pay tax also.

Nowadays, Jason, as a wealthy businessman, does not need to become someone else or rely on others to cross international borders. Because of his wealth he can be granted a visa for almost any country he desires and he can travel with his own name and documents:

> I don't think that now I have a problem with immigration [authorities] if I travel to go to abroad and do my business. No! Because if I go there, it's my own name, my own passport and I have money with me. I have invitation [from companies his business cooperates with], I have everything. So, nobody can tell me he wants to deport me.

Conclusion

For Mauss, the role of the state and citizenship, as he documented it in his analysis of personhood in ancient Rome, was crucial in the transition from a persona, in the sense of a partible social being dependent on others, to a person, in the sense of an independent and autonomous individual. Jason's story shows that his experiences of dependency did not happen in situations

FIGURE 2.2. Jason in front of his home, under construction, in Accra. Photo by the author.

where the state was absent or even relatively absent. On the contrary, Jason was forced to rely on others and perform different personae to overcome the violence of the state's exclusionary politics. The presence of the state did not emancipate Jason from his dependence on others; on the contrary, it reinforced the necessity of relying on others, either existing persons or persons who existed only in the state's records.

After many failed attempts, Jason managed to enter Europe with a South African passport as Robert Williams. The crafting of this identity required years of effort. Jason created the bureaucratic person "Robert Williams" and through an extensive process of kinning managed to embody him. In this process of kinning, Jason laboriously crafted a web of relations that connected persons, objects, and institutions. When Dutch officers inspected Robert Williams's South African passport and Dutch visa, they assessed many of these relations. First, the biometric information contained in the documents corresponded to Jason's body. Second, Jason's performance convinced them that he was a South African traveler and his relaxed interaction with them dispelled any initial doubt. Third, Robert Williams was a person with traceable life: he had a bank account and credit card in his name; he had traveled to multiple destinations, as evident in the stamps in the passport and the hotel reservations in his name. All this proof was at Jason's disposal. Of great significance was that many of the pieces of proof existed before the passport's date of issue, so they were not produced with the passport under inspection.[15] For this reason, Jason had created Robert Williams of South Africa, giving him the same name as in his previous Zimbabwean passport. In that way, he could use earlier proof under the name he had created with the Zimbabwean passport. Jason had evidently become an expert in identity craftsmanship.

The life story of Jason is neither unique nor representative of the life of other West African migrants with whom I spoke. That said, Jason's openness to speak about his own experiences, including detailed descriptions of the travel documents he used, makes his narrative quite different from those of many West African migrants I interviewed. Why did Jason share his life story with me? Why was he so comfortable, even eager, to explain all the identity documents he used, his troubles with immigration authorities, and his failures?

To a certain degree, Jason's openness was due to my relationship with Reverend James, who enjoys his deep appreciation and respect. Another reason was that all the interviews I had with Jason (nine in total) took place in Ghana. In general, the interviews I had in Ghana with returnees and aspiring migrants were more open than those with Ghanaian and other African migrants in Europe. But the most important reason for Jason's openness was that his life story was presented as a story of transformation, as a story of success.[16] Jason's narrative was about the fulfillment of his aspirations and the changes he achieved for himself and his relatives. Migrants' narratives are not simply factual representations of their lives. Their accounts give meaning to their decisions and actions and frame how they understand themselves in relation to others as well as how they want to be seen by others (Olwig 2012; Şaul 2017). The central message in Jason's narrative was clear: against all odds he managed to succeed as a result of his personal efforts, persistence, patience, and intelligence. Jason talked about his life transitions in a quite triumphant tone, beginning from the time he was absolutely dependent on others until the time he became financially successful and started assisting others.

This type of life narrative is common in capitalist societies that place individualism at the center of their ideology. A few decades ago, Lewis (1993) wrote about the individual-as-central sensibility in American capitalism, which explains and justifies success and failure as pure outcomes of individual effort and skill that overcome structural constraints. Narratives of middle-class Americans who started from zero but became wealthy and successful through hard work and effort closely resemble Jason's story. A case in point is the story of Oprah Winfrey, perhaps the epitome of the American dream, who grew up in poverty and managed to become one of the richest and most powerful women in the United States. Winfrey, in multiple interviews and public appearances, has talked about her success, explaining it as an outcome of the full realization of her skills, making the right choices, learning from her mistakes, believing in herself, and being goal oriented: "It's about what you can do. You just need to run that race as hard as you can, you need to give everything you've got, all the time, for yourself!" Jason's narrative is strikingly similar to wealthy Americans' interpretation of success. However, zooming in on Jason's life shows us that the process of becoming successful may involve periods of extreme dependency and reliance on others.

Similarly, the individuality and personal agency at the heart of Winfrey's advice for success was preceded by an earlier life, like Jason's, that was much less autonomous and independent. In a letter to her "younger self," published in *O, The Oprah Magazine*, Winfrey (2012) wrote, "You've spent too many days and years trying to please others and be what they wanted you to be." She recalled "the wounds of your past," such as rape and molestation by family members (see chapter 3 for the negative side of kinship) that "damaged your self-esteem." She referred to a partner she had brought to the first TV station that had hired her: "He's intimidated. You don't know this, though, because you can see yourself only through his eyes. A lesson you will have to learn again and again: to see yourself with your own eyes, to love yourself from your own heart." The differences in the lives of Oprah Winfrey and Jason are obvious; but their early lives, before success, both involved having to see themselves "through the eyes of others" and assume roles that did not please them. The dividuality of their earlier lives, undoubtedly gendered, is constitutive of their current experience.

However, the question remains whether this indicates a shift from dividuality to individuality, similar to the transition described by Mauss from the persona to the person. The narrative of Jason may indeed support such a shift from a life of dependence to a life of financial autonomy and esteemed status. Nevertheless, Jason's current position is still contingent on social relations. The respect and appreciation he earned is a result of his support to his relatives and other people of his social networks. His story demonstrates not only how he eventually managed to help his family to gain "recognition" but also how he repositioned himself to the center of affective circuits and achieved respected status for himself within his family and community (Cole and Groes 2016a). Being at the nodal point of affective circuits implied a transformation of his role from recipient to provider of material resources and gaining of control over the circulation of the various resources within these circuits (see also: Cole 2016; Groes 2016; Kleinman 2016; Vigh 2016). Instead of framing the transition in terms of dividuality and individuality, I prefer to describe it as a change of position within his affective circuits: from recipient of others' assistance and a person who lacked social recognition, to a provider for others, and a person with authority that enjoys the appreciation of his kin.

3

"Working with My Sister's Papers"

The word *abusa* in the Twi language means "in three parts." In Ghana, the term is associated with the cultivation of cocoa, one of the country's major exports, and especially with a crop-sharing arrangement in which the farm owner gives one-third of the cocoa production to the "*abusa man*," usually a migrant, as payment for his labor.[1] The farm owner provides tools and equipment to the migrant laborer, who then takes full care of the farm (Hill 1956, 1963; Robertson 1982; see also Okali 1983).[2] In the Netherlands, this term has obtained a new meaning among Ghanaian migrants, most of whom originate from cocoa-producing regions, and other Africans. Ghanaian and other African migrants use the term *abusa* to describe the loaning of identity documents from a legally authorized to a legally unauthorized migrant worker so the latter can obtain employment under the name of the former. The owner of the identity document, the authorized migrant, usually receives one-third of the salary earned by the unauthorized migrant who uses the identity document (Garcés-Mascareñas and Doomernik 2007; SIOD 2005; Osei 2014; Mazzucato 2008, 209). The term *abusa* denotes the practice of "identity loan," as Horton (2015) has called it, even when the compensation differs from one-third of the salary or when it involves non-Twi speaking African migrants—the latter to a lesser extent.

Document lenders and document borrowers both describe the *abusa* relationship as kinship, with particular reference to siblinghood, and the loaning of identity documents as an act of solidarity and help. However, the practice of identity loan often results in unpleasant and even unpredictable situations. Although the use of kinship terminology may suggest that the practice is indeed based on solidarity and care, in reality it often has destructive effects for both parties. Those who engage in the practice of identity loan expose themselves to significant risks, including disputes over practical matters (e.g., disagreements about the exact amount of payment) and serious existential issues. Migrants' reliance on kinship is a way for them to deal with these uncertainties and feel more secure. But often migrants' expectations are not met as kinship proves unreliable. The role of kinship in identity loan and the use of kinship terminology in this context is the central focus of this chapter. As outlined in the introduction to this book, new conceptualizations of kinship, either as relatedness or as mutuality of being, offer possibilities for the study of kinship that go beyond the ethnocentric divide between biological and social relationships and are inclusive of the various ways persons "participate intrinsically in each other's existence" (Sahlins 2013, ix). These conceptualizations of kinship can be helpful in analyzing how identity loan between authorized and unauthorized migrants results in mutual dependencies and intersubjective participation.

Nevertheless, as explained in the introduction, these new conceptualizations of kinship tend to emphasize egalitarianism and commonality over inequality and the negative aspects of kinship relations. Especially for Sahlins (2013, 24), the intersubjectivity of kinship is strongly associated with solidarity and reciprocity—"I take diffuse enduring solidarity and the like as the corollary subjectivity of mutual being." This idea dates back to 1972, with his concentric-circle model in which generalized or positive reciprocity exists in the inner circle (house, family). As the distance from the inner circle increases, generalized reciprocity turns into negative reciprocity. "Broadly speaking, mutuality of being among kinfolk declines in proportion to spatially and/or genealogically reckoned distance," maintains Sahlins (2013, 53). The association of kinship with reciprocity can too easily imply that jealousy, conflict, betrayal, and violence, to name a few, are anomalies of kinship relations. This chapter shows that these unpleasant practices and emotions are not anomalies of kinship but the dark side of it. This is rarely acknowledged by migration researchers who study kinship (but also often kinship scholars) or by our research participants when asked about kinship. Researchers of kinship should be careful, as anthropologists have known since Malinowski ([1922] 1984), not to conflate discourses and practices of kinship, and rather to take care to question whether and why the way informants talk about kinship is different from their daily experiences. In other words, to answer the question "what is kinship all about?" (Schneider 1972) and understand "what kinship is and is not," as the title of Sahlins's (2013) book puts it, we first have to analyze what kinship does and how (Carsten 2013).

The chapter first introduces identity loan in the Netherlands and raises questions about the usefulness of new ideas in the study of kinship, such as mutuality of being (Sahlins 2013), for the analysis of partible subjectivities resulting from the exchange of identity documents. Then it examines identity loan in a comparative perspective to contextualize *abusa* in the Netherlands. The chapter continues with ethnographic cases that detail how identity loan operated in practice, the dangers it entailed, why people turned to kinship for security, and how they were often disappointed and found themselves in unpredictable situations.

"It's Time to Be My Own Person": Kinship as Intersubjective Participation

Sharon, a fifty-year-old woman from Nigeria, had been in the Netherlands since 1993 but only recently was legalized for family reasons. In 2012, Sharon was my neighbor in the Bijlmer, and I used to spend several hours every week in her apartment talking to her and her partner. Since then we remained in close contact even when I moved out of the Bijlmer. For many years, Sharon earned her living by cleaning the houses of Dutch or foreign middle-class families. In March 2015, holding her newly issued residence card, she came to my apartment in Amsterdam East and sought my assistance to apply online for job openings through staffing agencies (*uitzendbureau*).

We prepared her CV, wrote a letter expressing her motivation, and applied for jobs in the cleaning sector through the online platforms of various employment agencies. Sharon told me she would have preferred to continue cleaning houses and being paid under the table rather than cleaning offices as a registered worker. I suggested that she upload an online ad on an advertising site and try her luck finding new clients there. She liked that idea, and we prepared the text of the ad.

I uploaded the text on a popular advertising website and entered her contact details. The website recommended that users, to increase the visibility of their advertisement, add their photograph. "Shall I put my picture?" Sharon asked doubtfully. After some thought, she decided to do it and justified her decision saying that a nice portrait would be important for her potential clients to choose a trustworthy-looking person. She asked me to open her Facebook profile and go to the album "1,000 Faces of Me." In this album, she had many pictures of herself with very different hairstyles, looks, and clothes. "Shall I put this one where I look like Oprah?" She pointed to one in which she had curly hair and wore a suit. "No," she answered herself, "put this one from the church. I look decent and God-fearing woman." I added the picture of her choice and published the ad online.

A few minutes later, Sharon again worried about the photograph: "Do you think people who know me can see my picture online? I don't want them to

gossip that I'm looking for a cleaning job." I said that this was not very likely
to happen because only people who look for a cleaner would come across
her advertisement. However, I could sense that this was not her concern and
suggested deleting the photograph from the ad. Sharon took a deep breath
and said: "My problem is that my old clients know that my name is Roberta
and I am from Ghana. I don't want them to see now that I try to find a job
as Sharon." "Really? Why?" I asked. Then Sharon told me how and why she
assumed that identity.

In the early 1990s, when Sharon first lived in Amsterdam, she worked for a
cleaning company using the identity documents of a Ghanaian woman named
Roberta. Sharon borrowed Roberta's documents in exchange for a percentage
of her salary. Because Sharon worked in Roberta's name, her monthly salary
was deposited to Roberta's bank account, and Sharon had to meet her regularly to collect her salary, less the agreed percentage. However, Sharon did
not work very long for the company. Many of the company's Dutch clients
appreciated Sharon's hard work and skills and hired her, on an undeclared
basis, to clean their houses. Sharon preferred to clean private houses because
she was less exposed to controls, earned an income that she did not declare
to tax authorities, and most important received payment in full directly. For
these jobs, Sharon did not use Roberta's documents, so of course she did not
have to pay her. However, since she found her clients through her registered
job in the cleaning company, she had to introduce herself as Roberta. Since
then, she found all her clients through the recommendation of an existing
or former client, so they all knew her as Roberta from Ghana. Sharon had
clients who had known her as Roberta for more than fifteen years, and she
had to perform that role constantly. For example, before traveling to Nigeria
for vacations, she told clients she was visiting Ghana, and when she returned
brought them artifacts that she presented as "gifts from Ghana."

As we were discussing her concerns, Sharon momentarily considered
changing her name in the ad from Sharon to Roberta. However, she quickly
discarded this option. She said that every time she started working for a new
client, she was afraid to be asked for her ID, so the client could be sure about
who was entrusted with the key to their house. Although this had never happened, she was prepared to go to Roberta and ask for her ID so she could
show it to her client. She knew that she still needed Roberta and tried to
maintain a good relationship with her. Although her "sister Roberta" was "always nice" to her, Sharon did not want to depend on her forever: "Now I have
my own papers and it's time to be my own person."

The exchange of identity documents between Sharon and Roberta resulted in a dependency that lasted almost two decades, much longer than

the short period during which Sharon actually used Roberta's papers. Neither Sharon nor Roberta had anticipated that a strategy for Sharon to find employment could have such undesirable, long-term, and volatile consequences. Their exchange of identity documents resulted in mutual participation in each other's lives, exactly what Sahlins (2013) described as "mutuality of being" and "intersubjective participation." For Sahlins, however, kinship's mutuality of being has mostly positive connotations. Regardless of her good relationship with Roberta, Sharon's eagerness to be her "own person" hints that Roberta's participation in her existence was suffocating and unpleasantly experienced. The ethnographic material that follows, *pace* Sahlins (1972; 2013), demonstrates that the intimacy entailed by intersubjective participation is also fueled by fear and insecurity. Before examining how intersubjective participation is experienced by those involved in the exchange of identity documents, and especially by those who borrow the documents, it is important to place this practice in a comparative perspective to be able to see the similarities to and differences from practices of identity loan elsewhere.

Identity Loan in a Comparative Perspective

Identity loan in the context of migrant employment is not unique to the Dutch case. Similar strategies to secure a job have been followed by unauthorized African migrants in other countries as well, such as the United Kingdom (Vasta 2011; Vasta and Kandilige 2010), France (Kleinman 2019, 100; Le Courant 2019), Germany, and the United States.[3] *Surprising Europe* (2013), a news magazine about the lives of African migrants in Europe, which also aired on Al Jazeera, referred to the practice of identity loan as "cloning" and explained that "as an illegal immigrant you are not allowed to work. But if you become a legal 'someone else,' you can find a job." The magazine's reporter, a Sierra Leonean who used to work illegally in the United Kingdom, showed on camera how "cloning" works in practice and successfully applied, under the name of another migrant, for a health assistant position in a London care home (fig. 3.1).[4]

A number of studies have documented similar practices in other migrant communities. There as well, kinship is central to the circulation of documents and the management of risks in identity loan arrangements. Mahler (1995, 170), for example, documented this practice in a passing reference to unauthorized migrants from El Salvador in Long Island, New York. She came across cases in which unauthorized migrants borrowed, "often for a price," the documents of "cousins who look somewhat alike" to fill in the Form I-9

FIGURE 3.1. Video stills from *Surprising Europe* (2013) showing the "cloning" process: (A) Sorious (*left*) used the ID of Mohammed (*right*) to apply for a job. (C) Sorious puts on the name tag "Mohammed" on his first day at work.

for employment eligibility verification used by employers to verify the identity of newly hired employees. In her research on unauthorized Mexican migrants in the United States, Del Real (2019, 563–64) observed the sharing of authorized migrants' social security numbers with unauthorized migrants, usually relatives and friends, who wanted to find better-paying jobs that required documents. While these arrangements were often mutually beneficial for borrowers and lenders, unauthorized migrants were exposed to more risks, such as the loss of their earnings and accusations of identity theft. In a different context, in post-Soviet Moscow, Reeves (2013) described the indispensability for migrant workers from Kyrgyzstan to obtain or borrow a Russian passport in order to find employment. The Russian government imposed labor market quotas on migrant workers and obliged employers to pay higher taxes on the salaries of foreign citizens. Reeves's (2013, 512) ethnography showed that Kyrgyz people who obtained Russian citizenship and their "network of kin who borrow their documents" could easier find jobs in the Russian labor market than those who had only Kyrgyzstan passports. In France, Indian Sikh unauthorized migrants "depend on kinship networks to get access to 'borrowed' documents" that they need to apply for jobs (Moliner 2011, 172). Sikh unauthorized migrants usually found documents from other members of their *biraderi*—extended clan network (brotherhood). In Amsterdam, Echeverría came across the practice of identity loan among the Ecuadorian community. He mentioned the case of an Ecuadorian migrant woman who often replaced her "cousin" in her registered work while "her boss didn't say anything" (Echeverría 2020, 200). Vasta's (2011) research on the "paper market" and the strategies of various unauthorized migrant workers in the United Kingdom confirmed that the practice of identity loan also existed there and that unauthorized workers usually used the documents of family members or friends.

The most extensive and detailed account of identity loan is the ethnography of Horton (2015, 2016a, 2016b) on unauthorized Mexican migrants employed as farmworkers in California. More than half of agricultural workers in California are unauthorized migrants, and according to estimates (Horton 2016a, 14; 2015, 57), 50 percent to 70 percent have worked at least once using someone else's documents. The Immigration Reform and Control Act of 1986 penalized employers who knowingly employed unauthorized migrants. Nevertheless, employers are not required to control the authenticity of their workers' documents. It has been quite common across the United States (Mahler 1995; Massey, Durand, and Malone 2002; Chauvin 2010; Ordóñez 2016) for unauthorized migrants to work under a fake social security number. As Horton explained, Mexican unauthorized migrants, upon their arrival in California, did not often have funds to buy a social security card on the black market. They had no other option but to use the documents of family members or persons in their network. Sometimes, they were even expected to borrow the documents of the family members who funded their trip to the United States. For authorized migrants employed as farmworkers, it was quite profitable to have someone else working under their name with their documents because it increased their unemployment payments in nonfarming periods. In contrast to the *abusa* arrangements in the Netherlands, the owners of the documents profited only from the unemployment benefits, calculated on the basis of the total earnings registered in their name, and did not receive compensation from those who borrowed their documents. Often, they even paid unauthorized migrants to use their documents. Legitimate holders of documents paid about $100 for every $1,000 earned by the unauthorized migrant who worked under their name (Horton 2016b, 73). In addition to this extra tip, an incentive for unauthorized migrants to borrow documents instead of buying falsified papers,[5] Horton's study pointed out the decisive role of employers and labor supervisors in identity loan arrangements. Not only did they turn a blind eye to the practice; they often made a job offer "contingent on the perspective employee's acceptance of a document loan" (Horton 2016a, 15). Labor supervisors, who were often relatives or acquaintances of migrant workers, provided them documents from other family members and friends.

As Horton's study demonstrated, kinship was present and regulated the unlawful practice of identity loan. Although Horton (2015, 57) recognized that "reciprocal relations among marginalized groups should not be romanticized," her conclusions, echoing Sahlins (1972), suggested that family and close kinship relations, if not a safe haven, "pose the least risk to the borrower" of documents and that "the risk of betrayal intensifies with social distance" (59). However, these conclusions were mostly based on migrant narratives about identity loan in general and not specifically on their experiences. As Horton said, due to the topic's sensitivity, she did not ask migrants about their own documentation practices and "prefaced each interview by stating that I was interested in narratives about the topic rather than each interviewee's personal practices" (Horton 2016a, 13).[6] Nevertheless, in the five detailed cases she analyzed (Horton 2015), it appears that there was some ambiguity in kinship relations and mistreatment among relatives.

A common point in all studies of identity loan is people's reliance on kinship. Facing the risks that this practice entails, migrants first look for help among people they know or people with whom they can forge relationships regulated by kinship norms. As a Ghanaian migrant explained to me, "It has to be someone that you really know well or someone you can accept as a family." Unfortunately, the previously mentioned studies, with the exception of Horton's work, did not investigate further why kinship was so important in identity loan practices and how precisely it regulated the exchange of documents. Apart from kinship, it is clear that employers also played a major role in this practice. Working with someone else's papers is possible only when employers allow it, either because they do not realize it or because they pretend to not realize it. The latter is more likely, especially in the United States, because employers can avoid the fine for employing unauthorized migrants if they convincingly argue that they have also been deceived about a worker's identity and legal status. Furthermore, in all cases presented here, it is evident that state policies and controls have turned identity documents into scarce resources. Since identity documents became necessary for their employment and survival, unauthorized migrants have had to engage in exchange relations with holders of these valuable objects.

However, there are also significant difference between the cases. We see that the payment arrangements can greatly vary, such as the one-third commission paid by the document borrower to the document lender among African migrants, or the tip paid by the document lender to the unauthorized Mexican migrant. In all known cases, those involved in the circulation of documents shared the same ethnic background. This is not always the case in the exchange of documents among African migrants in Amsterdam. It is possible that documents are exchanged between migrants from different African countries, such as between Sharon from Nigeria and her Ghanaian sister, and even continents (e.g., Surinamese, Dutch Caribbeans). Moreover, the degree of employer involvement in these practices varies. To a significant extent, employer knowledge of identity loan determines the risks of the practice. Another important difference is the spectrum of choices and alternatives to identity loan that migrants have in various settings. It appears that relations between document lenders and document borrowers as well as the price of documents and conditions of exchange are determined to some extent by the degree of necessity for unauthorized migrants to engage in identity loan to find employment and earn their living.

It is thus necessary to contextualize the practice of identity loan and examine the structural conditions in which it emerged and how it developed over time. As I already outlined (chapter 1), in the Netherlands, this practice of identity loan emerged in the early 1990s, when the Dutch government introduced new rules that made it extremely difficult for unauthorized migrants to work without documents. At the time, African migrants in the Netherlands were mostly from cocoa-producing regions of Ghana. These migrants, both authorized and unauthorized, were familiar with the crop-sharing arrangement of *abusa*, which gave the name to the practice of identity loan and its logic of exchange.[7] Identity loan was quite common until the late 2000s, when the Dutch government introduced a high administrative fine for employers who hired (knowingly or unknowingly) unauthorized migrants. But in the same period, openings for flexible jobs decreased drastically with the effects of the global financial crisis, and employers preferred to hire newly arrived migrant workers from Europe's periphery. These developments have almost displaced unauthorized migrant workers from the formal labor market and led to a decline in the practice of identity loan. Today, identity loan for employment purposes still takes place among West African migrants in the Netherlands but to a much lesser extent.

The remainder of this chapter returns to ethnographic material and examines how identity loan operated in practice, the risks that it entailed, and why migrants involved in it appealed to kinship to frame the relationship between document lenders, document borrowers, and intermediaries.

"As Brothers We Love One Another":
Kinship and the Risks of Identity Loan

Ikenna, originally from eastern Nigeria, had lived in Amsterdam for two decades. He studied business administration at an American Ivy League university and worked in a nongovernmental organization that raises funds for education projects in Africa. He was also a junior pastor and prayer group leader in a Pentecostal church in the Bijlmer. I met him for the first time in 2008, when I visited his church, and stayed in regular contact. One day, in 2012, he called and asked whether I could assist his "brother from Cameroon" to find a job. Ikenna knew I was working in a large fast-food restaurant and asked whether I could refer his brother, who did not have a residence permit, to my employer. I replied that this was difficult and risky. I also said that I had already tried it with someone else and was not successful. He insisted that it would be useful for the three of us to meet and discuss it. I agreed, and we met in his apartment in the Bijlmer.

When I arrived, Ikenna, as always, ran up to me, hugged me, and exclaimed, "My brother! Thank you Lord! What a grace!" He introduced me to "brother Henry," who was already there. Before we did anything else, Ikenna suggested we all pray together. We made a small circle, held our hands, and let Ikenna lead the prayer:

> Holy Father, we are so thankful to you. Thank you for the gift of good health.
> It's awesome, Lord. Father, we often take for granted your graces but when we

see our fellow human beings, just like us, whose bodies have been tortured and destroyed by the devil, then we see how wonderful your grace is upon us with good health. Father, there are many things that we do not have and desire. Father, we often forget the innumerable, the uncountable blessings, the things that we have, the things that you blessed us with.

Ikenna mentioned some quotes from the Bible that he knew by heart and continued:

Father, this afternoon, we are not counting the things we don't have but we are blessing you for the things we have which all come from you Lord. And we say thank you. Thank you for my brother Apostolos.

Ikenna narrated how we met and how thankful he was to God that he met me. He continued:

As brothers we love one another and work for the kingdom of God. Thank you for brother Henry. Oh, God! What an amazing grace Lord! Thank you for the gifts that you are giving to us to help one another and to help others who are less privileged than us. Father we give you thanks. In Jesus mighty name. Amen.

After the prayer and some ice-breaking talk, Ikenna opened up the topic that I was invited for: "Brother Henry . . . He is looking for . . . He doesn't have his own papers and is looking for . . . Well, tell yourself!" Henry explained that he used to work in an Amsterdam restaurant kitchen. He worked there many years using someone else's papers but that person had left the country and Henry could not continue working with his papers. Henry asked if I could help him get a job in the restaurant where I worked. I told him that this would be difficult because my boss would not hire someone without documents. Henry said, "I also can do it with a church brother who is mostly busy with business and he is not working. He told me that if I get a good job, I can contact him and he can give me the passport to use it."

I explained how I had tried to help someone who did not have his own document to get a job at the restaurant and how it had not worked out. I suggested connecting him with a Nigerian friend who worked in a company that distributed newspapers. This friend had told me that there were quite a few unauthorized migrants working in that company, and his boss did not seem to care about it. Henry showed some interest and asked for my friend's contact details. About an hour later, Henry warmly thanked me ("thank you my brother!") and left.

Later, I met Henry a couple of times. In all our communications, he consistently addressed me as "brother," even in very brief text messages. Henry

did not proceed with the newspaper job because the brother who had promised him his passport did not want to do so for a part-time job. He thought
two or three hours of work a day was not worth the risk. Henry also told me
that the reason he stopped working at the restaurant was not because the
person who gave him his documents left the country, as he had originally told
me, but because of a dispute between them. Henry had agreed to a commission of 20 percent of the salary, which was a relatively good deal:

> The only thing I was always having issue with was that he was taking the holi-
> day money. He wanted it all . . . And on the top of that, he would take *belasting*
> [tax refunds]. I never asked *belasting* money from him. Because you know
> when you work, at the end of the year, *belasting* is paid for. I never, I would
> never ask him. I would never ask him to give it. So, he was taking *belasting*, he
> wanted all the holiday money and the 20 percent.[8]

The disagreement over payment matters eventually led them to terminate
their cooperation and made Henry reconsider how he thought of him:

> In the beginning, you are brother. But when you start behaving [like this] how
> can I call you a brother? It's like you try to tell me, "It's a business relation-
> ship?" How can I call you a brother? A business relationship is a business
> relationship.

Fearing the loss of his full-time, permanent job, Henry kept trying to find a solution and kept addressing him as "brother." The appeal to brotherhood, however, did not resolve their issue. The person who loaned his document to Henry
not only did not give him the holiday allowance but also asked for his document back. It is interesting that Henry continued to frame in kinship terms
(*brother*) his relationship with the new person who would give him his document and those who promised to help him find a job—Ikenna and myself. The
unpleasant experience with the first person who loaned him his documents
did not make Henry reconsider his ideas about kinship and brotherhood in
particular. On the contrary, to Henry the problem was that the other person
saw their relationship not as kinship but as a "business relationship." If both of
them had, according to Henry, thought of their relationship as a brotherhood,
there would be no tension between them and all would have gone smoothly.

It is important to reiterate Henry's point of view that it was not the economic element that made the relationship with his document lender a business relationship. For Henry, the commission of 20 percent in exchange for
identity documents was compatible with what he thought was brotherhood
because he understood that the relationship should be mutually beneficial.

Thus, what transformed their relationship from brotherhood to a business relationship was the market logic that the other person's actions demonstrated. Henry suspected that the lender asked for his documents back to give them to someone who would not complain about the holiday allowance and tax refund and would perhaps pay a commission of 33 percent, which had become more or less standardized. In other words, his former brother's actions seemed to be motivated by profit maximization, not by his concern for the well-being of both of them.

All unauthorized migrants involved in identity loan fear the kind of problems Henry faced with his former brother, and many end up experiencing them. For example, Emanuel, originally from Uganda, used the papers of Prosper, a Ghanaian naturalized migrant, whom he found through a friend of a friend. Emanuel worked in a cleaning company with Prosper's papers and experienced many problems in receiving the agreed-on percentage of his salary. Not only Prosper did not give him the holiday allowance; he also spent Emanuel's whole salary, deposited in his bank account, to transport goods to Ghana. After Emanuel narrated this frustrating story to me, without referring to the Ghanaian migrant not even a single time as "brother," I asked whether he considers him a brother: "No. Because if you call yourself a brother to someone, you can't treat him bad. It's painful. . . . You work for nothing." However, Emanuel added that they used to address each other as brothers until the moment they started having problems. Similar to Henry, Emanuel said that if both had kept their word about the agreement that they made, they would have continued to be brothers.

Both Henry and Emanuel conceived brotherhood as a relationship of solidarity and care. It is remarkable, however, that they both addressed their document lenders as "brothers" from the very beginning of their contact, before they experienced any caring behavior (Nave 2016). The appeal to brotherhood was used to elicit a behavior that would comply with an idealized perception of what it means to be a brother. Both of them stopped thinking of the relationship as kinship the moment they realized that the behavior and motives of their document lenders were not what they had originally projected by addressing them as brothers.

Afua's story, which follows, will help us understand how relations of siblinghood are successfully established and maintained when experiences and practices correspond to kinship norms. Afua's case also highlights the importance of intermediaries, who, like Ikenna and myself in Henry's case, become kin members. Furthermore, her story will help us see the risks of identity loan beyond any anticipated tensions over financial arrangements.

Three Personae, Two Identity Documents,
One Laborer: The Case of Afua

In 1997, Afua traveled from Ghana to the Netherlands on a visitor's visa to join her husband, Kofi, who was already in Amsterdam. Afua overstayed her visa and remained in the Netherlands without a residence permit for eight years. Upon her arrival in Amsterdam, Afua had learned from her Ghanaian circle that controls for unreported employment (*zwartwerk*) were very rigorous, and for unauthorized migrants to get a job, they had to use someone else's identity documents.

"You cannot use a white person's paper," Afua said and started laughing. Migrants had to find documents of persons who physically resembled them. This automatically limited their search to Amsterdam's black population (mostly Africans or Afro-Caribbean Dutch citizens).[9] However, most significant in the search for documents was to find, as Afua stressed, "a trustworthy person." After all, the salary you would earn using someone else's documents was deposited to the latter's bank account, and you had to be sure you would receive your salary according to the agreed-upon arrangements. Afua said:

> Because some people, when you work, to give you your money, it's a problem. There were so many things going on. People who use their paper to work and then they would refuse to give you the money. Or they would be giving it to you in bits. And it's messed up.

I asked her, "So how can you make sure that someone is trustworthy?" "It all depends on who introduced you," she responded. Afua's husband Kofi informed his brothers and sisters in his church that his wife wanted to work and asked them to help her if they could. Benjamin, another Ghanaian migrant, and Kofi's (church) brother said the cleaning company where he worked was hiring. Benjamin suggested that Afua use his wife Barbara's documents and apply for the job, which was provided through a staffing agency. Benjamin talked to his supervisor ("chef") about Afua and made him understand that she would work there using someone else's papers. His supervisor agreed and Afua was hired as Barbara.

Before Afua started working, she agreed with Barbara and Benjamin on the percentage she had to pay to Barbara in exchange for the documents: "Others who were also doing the same thing were collecting one-third of the money from those who were using their papers. But she was taking a quarter . . . She just wanted to help."

Afua started working as Barbara in the same company with Benjamin. Every month she seamlessly received three-quarters of her salary from Barbara.

Afua and Barbara addressed each other as "sisters" and acknowledged that the one was helping the other. Afua later learned that Barbara and Benjamin benefited from the arrangement not only because Barbara received one-quarter of Afua's salary. The most important thing for Barbara, who worked as a part-time cleaner, was that official records showed she worked more hours than she actually did. With the introduction of a minimum salary requirement for family reunification, Barbara could not meet the minimum standards to be entitled to legalize her husband Benjamin's presence. Afua's hours, registered under Barbara's name, eventually helped Barbara meet those requirements and apply for the legalization of her husband's stay.

Every day, from six to nine in the morning, Afua worked as a cleaner, and everyone addressed her as Barbara, including Benjamin and another Ghanaian colleague who knew that her real name was Afua. When she finished this work, she continued with her housecleaning job. Afua managed to find many clients who paid her under the table. Every day, after her morning job, she cleaned one or two houses where her clients addressed her as Afua.

Afua's income from two jobs was not enough for her to cover household expenses and save money for her own legalization. She was happy with her relationship with her sister Barbara and knew that Barbara could not give her documents for another job because she was also working part-time in the evening. So Afua talked to her church pastor, who in turn asked the women of his church to help Afua. One church member, Gertrude, approached Afua and told her that her sister Mariam had landed a job in a staffing agency and was looking for someone to work in her name. It was an evening job in a small food production unit in Amsterdam. Afua and her husband Kofi met Mariam to discuss the job and make all necessary arrangements. Initially, Mariam did not find necessary to discuss in advance the conditions of payment and suggested to have this discussion once she receives Afua's salary in her bank account. Afua protested:

> I said, "No. This is an agreement. You have to tell me how much you are going to take. If the money comes and then you say I am taking half of the money, what will I do?" She said, "No. You know everybody takes one-third. So, you let the money come." So, that was the agreement.

The next day, Afua went to work at the food production company. She did not take along Mariam's identity document, because her formal employer was the staffing agency, which had a photocopy of Mariam's passport. At the company's reception, Afua's photograph was taken for a pass required to enter the workplace.

Afua worked daily in three jobs and was living a triple life:

> So, one time I'm called Afua, another time I'm called Barbara. Another time
> I'm called Mariam. So, I always in the morning [laughter] I have to be alert
> that I'm called Barbara, in between I'm called Afua and then in the evening
> I'm called Mariam.

Afua's relationship with Mariam was not as good as her relationship with
Barbara. Afua did not have regular contact with Mariam, and she usually
received her salary from a man whose relationship to Mariam was a mystery
to her:

> She was not always around. She was living with a man. She called him her
> husband but I do not know whether they were truly married. It was the man
> who had to give me my money. He had to withdraw the money from the lady's
> account and then give it to me. And then he took more than necessary.

Afua met Mariam in person only twice. Because of this and her man's skim-
ming off her salary, Afua was disappointed in Mariam. They did not address
each other as sisters, Afua told me, and their lack of contact meant that no
relationship could develop.

The final blow to their relationship came five months later, when Afua
learned that Mariam was allegedly "a prostitute." She heard this rumor from
other Ghanaians. This was something that Afua could not take. How could
a Christian, like Afua, assume the identity of a "prostitute"? Using Mariam's
identity documents implied that Afua had been *becoming*, rather than pretending to be, Mariam every day. In the beginning, Afua might have thought
that identity loan, or more generally unauthorized identity craft, was just a
strategy to get a job. She had not anticipated that using someone else's identity
documents could create such an existential problem for her. That Mariam
might be a sex worker made Afua panic; Afua worked every day and socialized with others as Mariam. And Mariam partially sustained herself from
Afua's work and income. Their identities were intertwined.

Afua thought she was lucky to learn the "truth" sooner rather than later;
it would have been more difficult to dissolve their collaboration as time went
on. She informed Mariam that she wanted to quit her job and terminate their
cooperation. She was not explicit about the reasons and did not confront her
with what she had heard. She received her last salary payment from Mariam's
man. Afua never again heard from Mariam or her sister Gertrude. In contrast, when she stopped working with Barbara's papers, she maintained a very
good relationship with "her sister," even after Barbara left the Netherlands:

I was helping her, she was helping me. And it was so easy for me at the end of the month. Because they [Barbara and her husband Benjamin] would pay every four weeks, when it's time for me to get my money. They never gave me problem. They just gave me my money . . . We kept the contacts even when I stopped working with her paper after three years.

In 2005, eight years after her arrival in the Netherlands, Afua received her own papers. The first thing she did with her Dutch residence permit was to give it to a Nigerian sister from her church. She knew that she and her Nigerian husband had a very difficult life in the Netherlands: "The husband had to use another Nigerian man's papers to work and every end of the month there was always a problem with the money . . . So, the lady said, OK, then she will also find something to do." At the time, Afua was earning her living exclusively from housecleaning and did not need her papers to work. With Afua's papers, the Nigerian woman found a part-time job as a cleaner. Afua told me she did not ask for a commission and turned over the full salary every month: "Because I knew they were having a lot of problems with the man and they really needed money. So, as it is, what that little money . . . what would that do to me?"

At the same time, Afua's husband, Kofi, tried to help the woman's husband claim a greater salary percentage from the person who gave him his documents—not surprisingly by appealing to kinship norms and relations. Kofi knew the Nigerian who was lending his document and knew his wife even better because they attended the same church. This is how Kofi recounted the story:

> The guy distributes newspapers from 3 a.m. till 6 a.m. with the bicycle and that's risky. And then the whole money is €500 a month and the person who gave him his book [passport], who is a very rich person and has a very big, big company of his own, he takes €250 out of the €500! This is criminality! *Your brother is in need!* €500 is so small . . . I told to the guy (who used the document) to go back to the wife (of the person who owns the document). Because when they talk to the wife, the wife talks to him . . . So he gave him €150 more. He gave him €400.

Afua's story is indicative of how the system of identity loan, or *abusa* in Twi, operates in daily life and the various possible arrangements. Identity loan entails mutual dependence; the two main participants become part of each other. Their "intersubjective participation," however, is fueled by fear of unpredictable consequences. The appeal to kinship is an attempt to regulate these consequences and make those participating in identity loan feel more secure. Document lenders and document borrowers are not the only ones who participate in the exchange of documents. As we have seen in this section, intermediaries, who also participate in webs of kinship relations, often are matchmakers and participate in the negotiation of the price and the loan conditions. They may intervene as well if something goes wrong.

Witchcraft as the Other Side of Kinship

"The intersubjectivity of magic may be coercively introjected, in which respect it is not the same as the mutuality of kinship. Moreover, magic need obey no principle of amity but may indeed be malevolent," states Sahlins (2013, 59), making even clearer his positive approach to kinship. Sahlins concludes that, because he is "concerned with what kinship is, I reserve these issues for other occasions" (60).

However, for many Africans—and not only Africans—witchcraft and kinship are interconnected (Geschiere 1997, 2013; Apter 2012; Daswani 2015, 141–42, 113–15). Those who are close to you and are part of your life have tremendous power over you and can be very harmful precisely because of their social proximity. To emphasize the link between witchcraft and social closeness, Ghanaians often say, "It is the insect inside your clothes that bites you" (Dzobo 1992, 97; Van der Geest 2013, 61).

Mama Clara, a Ghanaian woman in her fifties who had been naturalized in the Netherlands, told me that she had never given her documents to someone else: "Because I do not want to die." I did not understand what she meant and asked her to explain. First, she said, if her documents were used by another migrant woman, whatever happens to that woman also happens to her. For example, she said, if at work the person has an accident or dies, she will also die administratively in the records of the Dutch authorities. What Sahlins (2013, ix) wrote about relatives, that they "live each other's lives and die each other's deaths," describes very well those consequences of identity loan's intersubjective participation that discouraged Mama Clara from participating.

Second, she said, legally unauthorized migrants are usually dissatisfied with the percentage of salary kept by the document owner and do not understand that they save part of that money to pay lawyers in case they are caught by police.[10] According to Mama Clara and other African migrants I talked with, because unauthorized migrants cannot seek the help of authorities (e.g., police) to resolve their disagreements with those who give them their documents, they exercise or threaten them with witchcraft. The pastor of a Ghanaian Pentecostal church told me: "Most cases would use voodoo. Not just in any case. Most cases. They will threaten if you cheat me, I will put the voodoo curse on you." Thus, becoming part of each other in the context of identity loan creates potential not only for kinship solidarity but for conflict as well. Mama Clara said there had been many Ghanaian migrants in Amsterdam who died unexpectedly, and she suspected that their deaths were caused by witchcraft attacks. A few weeks after our conversation, the *African Bulletin*, the most popular monthly newspaper for Africans in the Netherlands, published the article "Alarming Death Rate in Ghana Community in NL," which seemed to confirm Mama Clara's claims about unexplained deaths. The article mentioned that in the previous three months in Amsterdam, at least eighteen Ghanaians had died from sickness, minor illnesses, or unusual death and that a traditional priest had predicted that in total thirty-five Ghanaians would die that year.[11] Mama Clara stressed that, for those who want to rent out their documents, it is of utmost importance that they find someone whom they can trust to not practice witchcraft if he or she is dissatisfied. "That's why," she continued, "it's important to find a good Christian." According to Mama Clara, Christian faith not only will deter a person from practicing witchcraft but will also protect the person from witchcraft attacks.

In one of my visits to the Pentecostal church where Mama Clara and her daughter were dedicated members, Pastor Benny gave similar advice to the congregation about how to protect themselves from witchcraft. Although I had heard that Pastor Benny was occasionally involved in identity loan arrangements, his advice about witchcraft protection was more general and did not exclusively address those participating in identity loan. That day, a Ghanaian migrant asked Pastor Benny and the members of the church to pray for him because he was afraid that his family members in Ghana wanted to bewitch him. Pastor Benny gave the microphone to the middle-aged man and asked him why he believed that to be so. The man said his family was angry with him because he had stopped sending remittances after he had lost his job (for similar cases, see Sabar 2010; Cohen 2018). Pastor Benny asked the congregation to pray for him and reassured him that since he was a "strong prayer," he had nothing to be afraid of. Pastor Benny turned to the other church members and said that as born-again Christians, they should not worry about witchcraft: "You are spiritually sealed and no evil spirit can harm you."

The same message was conveyed by a Nigerian witch doctor in a video I came across on Facebook, shared among my Amsterdam-based Nigerian friends. The witch doctor, holding an allegedly demonized pigeon that was pacified with anointing water, was brought by his family for deliverance to the well-known church of T.B. Joshua in Lagos. Before his deliverance by T.B. Joshua himself, the witch doctor explained how he killed people by sending the pigeon to the house of the person his clients wanted to harm. He said that the pigeon was not an ordinary bird but a demon—and indeed, he had

sent it from Nigeria all the way to Italy and the United Kingdom. A woman
in the audience asked whether the pigeon could kill born-again Christians.
T.B. Joshua asked the audience to clap for this question and turned to the
witch doctor for his answer: "With born-again [Christians], it's quite different. Some people go to church but they [also] go to [the] herbalist's house.
But if it is a true Christian, the pigeon will come back and say it does not have
the power to kill that person."[12]

Religion, like kinship, provided those involved in the exchange of identity
documents some sort of security and protection from the evil of witchcraft.
However, this sort of security, also like kinship, was quite ambiguous and
uncertain. An important question was how someone could be sure that he
or she were "spiritually sealed." The prayer group leader in Pastor Benny's
church explained to me that every time a person sins, even if smoking a ciga-
rette or drinking alcohol, he or she is exposed to evil spirits that can enter the
body through "openings" and possess it. But even when someone meticu-
lously follows the word of the Bible, it is still possible to be possessed by spirits that enter the family because of the sinful behavior of a family member.
For example, a woman I met in another Pentecostal church told me that the
health problems she was facing were caused by a spirit that entered her family
through her deceased mother because her mother used to practice witchcraft.
This spirit, she said, passed from her mother to her, and in turn she unwillingly passed it to her son, whose mental health became unstable. Therefore,
although becoming a born-again Christian, praying, and following the word
of God could strengthen someone against the threat of witchcraft, no one can
be absolutely sure of being "spiritually sealed."

Cooperating with a born-again Christian in identity loan, either as borrower or as lender, may provide some protection to those participating in
the exchange of identity documents, but it does not guarantee that they are
protected from occult powers. After all, it is difficult to tell whether someone
is a "good" and "true Christian," and African migrants in Amsterdam who
practice witchcraft, or more precisely those who are accused of practicing
witchcraft, are most of the time Christians and churchgoers. In 2015, a few
years after my conversation with Mama Clara about the importance "of finding a good Christian" for identity loan, I learned from her daughter, who had
recently been diagnosed with cancer, that they had had an argument with
Pastor Benny and left his church. She lowered her voice and told me that
she had witnessed firsthand that the anointing oil Pastor Benny used in the
church was sent in a parcel from Ghana. "Don't you understand?" she asked
me. "Why does he import anointing oil from Ghana and doesn't make it himself? Why don't you make your own anointing oil, if you are a man of God?"

Thus, Mama Clara's daughter implied, Pastor Benny did not have the spiritual gift necessary for using anointing oil. But she went even further and expressed her doubts over whether the oil was sent to Pastor Benny by another pastor. Was it in fact sent by a fetish priest? she wondered. The suspicion that even Pastor Benny himself practiced witchcraft raised the question of the boundary of trust—a key concern, as we have seen, in identity loan. How can you be sure that a fellow church member will not use witchcraft against you when the pastor of your own church is allegedly involved in witchcraft? How can you be sure that those who become part of you through identity loan will not act malevolently toward you? Can you control the undesirable consequences of the intersubjective participation that identity loan entails? These are torturous questions that West African migrants in the Netherlands cannot answer with certainty.

Between Fiction and Reality

The existential dangers inherent in identity loan are well portrayed in works of fiction, such as in the novel *Greener from a Distance* by Charles Nfon (2013), a Cameroonian migrant in Canada.[13] In this novel, Nfon narrates the story of Befe Mboma, an unauthorized Cameroonian migrant in the United States who used the identity document of another Cameroonian migrant, Chefon Mola, to find work. When Mola got sick, he returned to Cameroon where he could afford the treatment of his illness with the money that Mboma paid him for using his documents in the United States. With his health condition deteriorating, Mola anticipated his death and wrote a letter to Mboma: "I want to thank you for all your help. You changed my life the day you arrived the USA; the cleaning, the cooking and especially my regular portion of your salary. You have faithfully respected our arrangement. If not for this illness, I would have lived like a king in this country" (Nfon 2013, 58). Mola expressed his gratitude to Mboma whose money, for using the documents, made Mola's life in Cameroon "less painful than it would have been otherwise." "As a token of appreciation," Mola wrote, "I am sending all my documents and certificates to you. I believe these will help you fully become me, if you so desire" (58). Mola hoped that his paperwork would help Mboma to have a less precarious life in the United States and finally start visiting his wife and children in Cameroon.

Indeed, after Mola's death, Mboma fully appropriated his identity and got naturalized as an American citizen in Mola's name. In his new life, everyone knew him as Mola, including his new wife and daughter, who did not know anything about his other wife and children in Cameroon. When his daughter in the United States became an adult, she traveled to Cameroon, without her parents' knowing it, and discovered the secret of her father's identity. Upon her return to the United States, she confronted her father with what she learned and informed her mother about it. Mola's wife in the United States lost her trust in him and, echoing the fears of Mama Clara, insinuated that he might have killed his friend: "From what I know now, I won't be surprised if you poisoned your friend in order to inherit his identity" (Nfon 2013, 61). Overwhelmed with what seemed to her a betrayal of trust, the wife had a heart attack and died. After her sudden death, the daughter wanted to report her father to police. Mola asked her to consider the consequences of his possible imprisonment for his family in Cameroon with whom she had just connected. The appeal to kinship convinced the daughter to change her mind and continue living with her father's secret.

The story ends with the remarks of a Cameroonian migrant who learned the story of the person he knew as Mola: "If you ask me, I think Pa Mboma is a more appropriate name for that man. He looks like a python aka mboma that has just swallowed a goat" (Nfon 2013, 64). The comparison with a snake that has eaten a goat is powerful and implicitly makes an association with witchcraft, as witches are believed to gain their mystical power by eating their relatives (Geschiere 2013; Awedoba and Hahn 2014, 49). The metaphor of the python that swallows a goat points to the intersubjective consequences of identity loan. Indeed, for those involved, their "lives are joined and interdependent." (Sahlins 2013, 21). Yet this closeness does not entail only safety but danger as well.

Conclusion

After several interviews with Jason, the Ghanaian deportee whose adventurous life appeared in the previous chapter, I asked him what the word *brother* meant to him. In our interviews, Jason had used *brother* to also refer to other black migrants who lent him their identity documents that enabled him to either work or travel. Jason answered:

> For me, I consider the word *brother* [as] somebody [who] I can count on in times of difficulty. When I'm in trouble, the person that will be next to me, he is the one I consider a brother. Somebody who cheers me up and says, "Look, guy, you can do it," or somebody who can help [me] out of my problem. I consider him more brother than my own siblings or my half brothers, or my extended-family brothers.

Jason's definition of brotherhood papered over all the negative and unpleasant experiences he had passed through and framed brotherhood in a positive

way. Such a positive conceptualization was very common among African migrants when they talked about kinship and especially siblinghood. Nevertheless, this did not imply that Jason and other West African migrants suffered
no negative experiences or emotions in these relationships. While the positive framing of brotherhood could make unequal relations more bearable,
in practice, they could be abusive and filled with negativity. Discourses of
kinship may not directly reflect practices of kinship, but they still have a performative effect. A positive conceptualization of siblinghood had an impact
on how unequal relations between siblings were experienced and negotiated
in everyday life. As described earlier, for instance, the exchange of identity
documents entailed a high level of risk both for borrowers and for lenders.
Those who participated in the exchanges framed their interdependency as
siblinghood, projecting their expectations of caring, loving, and altruistic behavior that corresponded with the accepted norms of siblinghood, of how
brothers and sisters should behave toward each other. By appealing to the
code of siblinghood, borrowers and lenders of documents attempted to mini-
mize the risks and dangers associated with their exchange.

The newly formed kinship relations among West African migrants in
Amsterdam, apart from being framed positively, required a necessary degree
of force and inflexibility to have their scope fulfilled. Just after Jason had offered his definition of brotherhood, I asked whether he had many brothers.
Seemingly annoyed with my question, he pulled from my folder the paper
on which I had drawn his genealogy diagram, pointed to it, and said, "I've
already told you." Certainly, the idiom of siblinghood used among African
migrants under precarious circumstances is associated with conceptions of
siblinghood deriving from shared parenthood. Such an association does not
mean that the term *brother* is used metaphorically. A metaphor requires the
existence of two separate and clearly defined domains (Lakoff and Johnson
2003; Sapir 1977). Can we indeed make a separation in which one domain,
perceived as real kinship, lends its vocabulary to the other? It is important
that migrants do not make such a sharp distinction. As is evident from the interaction with Jason, the two meanings of brotherhood, one a strong bond of
social relations and the other a product of shared parentage, are intertwined
and used interchangeably. Moreover, the distinction between real and metaphoric kinship would automatically disqualify the reason African migrants
use kinship terminology to describe relationships crucial to their survival in
Europe. The analysis of the ethnographic cases here shows that relationships
that regulate access to scarce resources in highly ambiguous and unequal settings require a stabilizing force. The appeal to siblinghood among the document lenders and borrowers in Amsterdam denotes a sense of obligation that

is more difficult to renounce (see Baumann 1995). To make these relationships fulfill their expected function, they need to be, on the one hand, framed
positively in a language of support and solidarity, and on the other, they require such a degree of inflexibility that the obligations stemming from them
cannot be easily dismissed.

Furthermore, the ethnographic cases of this chapter show that siblinghood in the context of identity loan is closely interrelated with other forms
of kinship and embedded in a wider network of kinship relations constituted
by different means. In the detailed case studies of this chapter, the siblinghood of lenders and borrowers of identity documents overlapped mostly with
kinship in a Pentecostal church context. However, in other cases of identity
loan, siblinghood between lenders and borrowers of documents overlapped
with other forms of kinship, such as siblinghood based on shared parentage, transatlantic black brotherhood, and "tribal" kinship that crossed religious boundaries (e.g., Yoruba brotherhood between a Yoruba Christian and
a Yoruba Muslim). Beyond these overlaps, broader kinship relations regulate
siblinghood between borrowers and lenders of identity documents. "It all depends on who introduced you," Afua said, and as we have seen, the persons
who brought into contact authorized and unauthorized migrants are often
involved in the exchange of documents and step in if something goes wrong.
To some extent, therefore, siblinghood in the context of identity loan is vi-
talized by other kinship relations onto which they have been grafted. The
relationships between borrowers and lenders of identity documents that exist
in isolation from other social relationships can dissolve relatively easier than
siblinghood embedded in a wider network of relationships. As we have seen,
for example, the troublesome relationship between Emanuel and Prosper,
who lacked common contacts, lasted for a short period, after which Emanuel
stopped considering Prosper his brother. On the contrary, Afua and Barbara,
whose husbands were church brothers and initiated the identity loan between
the two women, collaborated for many years and have remained sisters even
after Afua stopped using Barbara's papers. The relations that surrounded the
exchange of documents gave life to the sisterhood between Afua and Barbara.
Nevertheless, their relationship also helped sustain the surrounding relationships. After all, Afua's hard work with Barbara's papers enabled her to afford
the cost of her legalization in the Netherlands and enjoy a family life together
with her husband. Additionally, the hours registered under Barbara's name
helped Barbara to meet the minimum income requirements and apply for
the legalization of her husband, Benjamin. Therefore, the intersubjective participation of borrowers and lenders of identity documents can affect and be
affected by the wider network of kin.

4

Dying Relations?

"We are not brothers and sisters anymore," concluded Linda, my Nigerian flatmate, after she mentioned that some Nigerian and Ghanaian migrants in Amsterdam had been treated badly by Dutch Afro-Caribbeans, especially Afro-Surinamese. Linda was not the only African migrant who shared with me stories of tension and conflict between Africans and Afro-Caribbeans. Since 2008, when I carried out my first ethnographic fieldwork in Amsterdam, I had heard many similar stories from West African migrants. These stories emphasized their distrust and even fear of Dutch Afro-Caribbeans and also betrayed some jealousy about their privileges, namely Dutch citizenship and migrant legality.[1] In 2008, a Ghanaian pastor told me:

> The Ghanaians are very hardworking people, working about fourteen hours a day on average. The Surinamese don't like to work. And the Ghanaians wouldn't like to work. And they say, you know, "Well, we came here, we don't have papers, residence permit, work permit, and we rent somebody's book [i.e., passport] to work, share to three the money and you [Surinamese] got it free and you don't go to work?"

However, unlike Linda's conclusion, these stories rarely denied the kinship link between Africans and Afro-Caribbeans—what I call transatlantic kinship. The African migrants I spoke with in the context of my 2008 fieldwork did refer to Dutch Afro-Caribbeans as "brothers and sisters." "We are the same blood. They are brothers," said a Ghanaian informal taxi driver (*snorder*), explaining the historical relationship through transatlantic slavery: "They are Africans. They are Ghanaians. They moved as slaves from Africa." "Every black person is a brother or sister," insisted Evelyn, a Nigerian woman married to an Afro-Caribbean man from Curaçao.

What I came to realize in my previous fieldwork was that if someone was denying that African and Afro-Caribbeans are "brothers and sisters," they were usually the latter. "There are some who don't want to admit it. But most of them know that they came from Africa and this is a fact," continued the same Ghanaian taxi driver. Alex, another Ghanaian migrant, appealed to brotherhood when three black men, Surinamese according to him, tried to rob him in the elevator of a building in the Bijlmer in the 1990s. Trying to appease the one who demanded his money, Alex asked, "Brother, why do you treat me that way?" The invocation of brotherhood did not result in different treatment, as Alex hoped, but irritated the robber. "Brother? Your people sold us!" he responded, referring to the selling of relatives in the transatlantic slave trade. Interestingly, the remembrance of transatlantic slavery could provide links for the establishment of unity between African and Afro-Caribbeans, but it has also raised thorny issues that risk rupture (Balkenhol 2021; Oostindie 2005; Holsey 2008; Schramm 2016).

Despite the tensions, Africans and Afro-Caribbeans lived in the same neighborhoods, especially in the Bijlmer, visited the same churches, and cooperated in several activities, such as identity loan and marriage. As Dutch citizens, Afro-Caribbeans loaned their documents to unauthorized African migrants who resembled them and assisted them in getting legalized through marriage. These observations from my 2008 fieldwork led me to examine, in this study, how exchanges between Africans and Afro-Caribbeans in identity loan and marriage resulted in new forms of belonging expressed in kin terms and how successfully the idiom of siblinghood regulated the tensions and risks entailed in these exchanges.

Nevertheless, in recent years these forms of cooperation have declined remarkably. New laws on family reunification have made it very difficult for unauthorized migrants in the Netherlands to get legalized through marriage to a Dutch citizen. This has, in turn, negatively affected the number of new marriages with Afro-Caribbeans, who are predominantly Dutch citizens, and made unauthorized African migrants look for other possibilities. According to data from the city of Amsterdam, there is a significant decrease in the new marriages of Nigerian and Ghanaian migrants to "Surinamese" and "Dutch Caribbeans." For the period 1996–2000, the percentage of marriages to Surinamese and Dutch Caribbeans was 27 percent for Nigerians and 6 percent for Ghanaians; for the period 2006–2010, it dropped to 11 percent and 2 percent (see tables 5.1 and 5.2 in chapter 5). Moreover, as explained earlier, the practice of identity loan has almost disappeared because of stricter controls for unauthorized labor and unequal competition for jobs with legal but precarious migrant workers from Europe's periphery. An Afro-Surinamese person who worked as a recruiter in various employment agencies told me that, before 2004, "a lot of passports and work permits circulated" between Africans and Surinamese, and employers knew it. A Nigerian migrant told me:

> In the past, it didn't really matter. Nobody was asking anything. And the chef [manager] was not going to get into trouble. He would take you even if he knew that this is not your real document. But now you get into trouble. So, they check very well.

Today employers are highly reluctant to hire a worker who presents an identity document with a Surinamese name and can hardly speak Dutch.

As African migrants became less dependent on Afro-Caribbeans, the idiom of black siblinghood lost some of its currency, and I increasingly heard comments similar to Linda's conclusion. "How can they be brothers and sisters [laughter] when they don't mean any good for you?" said a Nigerian woman in 2014. "We shop with them, we greet them, we are friends but to a limit."

This chapter examines the problems of creating transatlantic kinship between two groups, legally precarious West African migrants and Dutch Afro-Caribbeans, that share common history and experience the exclusionary consequences of hegemonic whiteness in the Netherlands (Wekker 2016). But members of these groups also have different access to rights and a different structural position in the Netherlands. The chapter explores the process of making and unmaking of this kind of kinship in relation to legislative changes that have affected the forms of exchange between Africans and Afro-Caribbeans in the Netherlands. More specifically, it focuses on how the devalorization of Afro-Caribbeans' civic resources has affected their marriages with African migrants and examines the wider implications for their in-between social relations and common belonging.

New approaches to the study of kinship challenged the previously dominant structural-functionalist model that considered kinship static. Instead, the newer generation of anthropologists examine the kinship-making process (Carsten 2004; McKinnon 2016). If kinship is something that is made and not given, then it should be possible to undo kinship. The processual analysis of new kinship studies has mostly focused on the making of kinship and, to a certain extent, has neglected the unmaking of kinship.[2] The ethnographic analysis of this chapter contributes to the study of kinship as a process and shows how kinship between Africans and Afro-Caribbeans is made and unmade in the context of changing legal barriers to migration. For this reason, the chapter is structured around two extended ethnographic cases of African and Afro-Caribbean couples in different time periods and looks into not only how the law regulated their intimate life but also its consequences for their forms of belonging.

A Transatlantic Reunion? A Ghanaian Migrant Marries His Surinamese Sister in Amsterdam

COMMON DEPARTURE, UNCOMMON TRAJECTORIES

Jack was born in the late 1960s in Sekondi, a small Ghanaian coastal town where he lived until he finished secondary education. Ghana, formerly the Gold Coast, has a long history of European presence, dating to the sixteenth century. A major landmark in Jack's hometown is Fort Oranje, built by the Dutch West India Company in the seventeenth century and later sold to the British. The fort is located on top of a hill next to the harbor and is visible from all over Sekondi. It was used as a slave-trading post, as were most other forts and castles along the coast, and today serves as a lighthouse and a base for Ghana's Ports and Harbors Authority.

Along the coast, there are many Portuguese, Dutch, British, and Danish establishments that had been used in the gold and slave trades. Enslaved people temporarily stayed in these European forts and castles before they were forced onto ships and transported across the Atlantic. Enslaved Africans who departed from the Gold Coast and survived the crossing ended up working in plantations in the Americas and the Caribbean. A significant number of them, but certainly not the majority, were shipped to Suriname. The Dutch historian Alex van Stipriaan (2000, 13; see also Oostindie 2005, 63) estimated that about 30 percent of all enslaved persons brought to Suriname departed from Elmina, a town just a few kilometers from Sekondi that has an impressive and well-maintained castle (St. George). The castle, built by the Portuguese and later seized by the Dutch, is today a major attraction for tourists, especially those who visit Ghana as a pilgrimage to the land of their ancestors. In recent decades, a growing number of African Americans, Black British and, to a lesser extent, Netherlands-based Afro-Caribbeans have traveled to Ghana and visited the numerous slave forts and slavery-related monuments. Ghana has become a popular destination for slave-roots tourism and has been attempting to establish itself as a motherland of the African diaspora (Bruner 1996; Oostindie 2005; Schramm 2016).

Although Jack had heard about the history of slavery, it was of little interest to him while he was in Ghana. For him, as he said, the most important concern was how he could make it "overseas." His father had fourteen children with different wives, and it was hard for him to take care of all of them. His mother died when he was still young. He grew up with the mother of his other siblings. His mother's sister took care of Jack's school fees until he graduated. After Jack finished school, he started thinking of migration abroad as a way to effectively deal with his life's hardships. Two of his brothers had migrated to Greece but advised him it was not a good place for him to migrate to. Jack was a good student at school, and it would be better for him to migrate to a country where he could continue his education. His aspiration was to go to the United Kingdom and study law. He did not apply for a British visa because he knew that he did not fulfill the requirements. After consulting with his brothers, he decided to travel to the Netherlands, where he knew some friends of his brothers and at a later stage could try to move to the United Kingdom. In 1991, he traveled to Germany on a temporary visa and a few weeks later moved to the Netherlands.[3]

WHAT IF YOUR BROTHERS CAN'T HELP YOU? REDISCOVERING KIN FROM THE OTHER SIDE OF THE ATLANTIC

Soon after his arrival in the Netherlands, Jack realized that the situation was more difficult than he had expected. Without being able to move to the United Kingdom, he found himself trapped in the Netherlands. His aspiration of university education collapsed, and finding a low-skilled job became imperative for his survival. He moved to the Bijlmer, stayed with other Ghanaians, and did the menial jobs that most Ghanaians were doing at that time. His uncertain legal status made his situation even more stressful.

Although in the early 1990s the Netherlands was already implementing policies that made migrant life more difficult, they were not as strict as they are today. Nevertheless, Jack's frustrations were heightened because no one from his social environment could help him improve his life:

> Actually, you don't know about stress when you're coming from Africa. You do not know stress, what stress is. Because life is easygoing. You know. Easygoing. If you don't have, someone will help you. You can always find means for all sources. But here, the lifestyle here is only stressful. No support from friends. Nothing. But there you help each other. You advise each other. You go with each other. But here it's not like that.

When Jack arrived in Amsterdam in 1991, he knew a few friends of his brothers and socialized with them and other fellow Africans he met in the Bijlmer. Most of the people in his social network were not unwilling but simply unable to help him. In the early 1990s, the small number of Ghanaian migrants living in Amsterdam had only recently arrived, were very poor in terms of civic resources, and had not widely established access channels to other resources such as formal and informal employment. In 1992, only 18 percent of the 5,106 registered Ghanaians in Amsterdam were Dutch citizens; by 2013, this had risen to 40 percent and the total number doubled to 11,602.[4] Nigerians had a slight presence in 1992, with just 336 people registered in Amsterdam; that number quintupled to 1,766 in 2013.[5]

It did not take too long for Jack to understand that he could not expect much support from other African migrants who were more or less in the same situation as he was. Yet in the Bijlmer, "a country within a country" in Jack's words and "the black neighborhood of Amsterdam" to the Dutch, Africans were not the only residents. African migrants lived in high-rise blocks with other migrants from Suriname and to a lesser extent from the Dutch Caribbean. Preceding and following the 1975 independence of Suriname, a vast wave of Surinamese migrants arrived in the Netherlands, and the government placed many of them in the newly built estates in the Bijlmer that were originally intended for middle-class families. Since they were born in a constituent territory of the Dutch Kingdom, they were Dutch nationals and could receive state welfare. Thus, Surinamese had resided in the Bijlmer since the 1970s and had a more privileged legal status than their African neighbors. A great number of the Surinamese residents of the Bijlmer, maybe the majority, were descendants of enslaved persons who had been brought to Suriname from Africa. For African migrants in Amsterdam, the African origin of black Surinamese and the history of transatlantic slavery could establish new connections between them and the relatively better placed Afro-Surinamese. But contrary to what Jack expected, his appeal to a common origin with Afro-Surinamese was rejected by those he approached:

> Most of them, at that time, when I talked to them, they didn't want to accept [it]. Some of them, most of them, they won't say that they have African backgrounds. They didn't want to hear that. They say, "You're African." I say, "You're also African." And you tell them . . . They kept arguing!

In the late 1980s and early 1990s, other Ghanaian migrants had similar encounters with Afro-Surinamese in the Bijlmer. But Afro-Surinamese reluctance to acknowledge their African ancestry changed considerably in later years. In all my interviews and talks with Afro-Surinamese people, no one ignored that their ancestors came to Suriname as enslaved persons from Africa.[6] The politicization of the history of slavery and the beginning of a postcolonial debate about the role of the Dutch in the Atlantic triangle shed more light on the connections between Africa and the Dutch colonies in the Caribbean.

The remembrance and commemoration movement in the Netherlands, led primarily by Afro-Surinamese activists, emerged and thrived in the 1990s. The first public manifestation was on June 30, 1993, an evening vigil at Surinameplein by a few hundred Surinamese who gathered to commemorate the abolition of slavery and recall the involvement of the Dutch in the Atlantic slave trade. Since the mid-1990s, Sophiedela, an Afro-European women's organization, has organized living-room talks (*huiskamergesprekken*) with Afro-Surinamese migrants to discuss problems related to Afro-Caribbean communities in the Netherlands and the legacy of slavery. In 1998, Sophiedela and another organization, Stichting Eer en Herstel, Betaling Slachtoffers van de Slavernij in Suriname, submitted petitions to the Dutch Parliament requesting the establishment of a monument to commemorate the victims of slavery and the Dutch legacy in transatlantic slavery (Balkenhol 2021; Nimako and Small 2010). Debates over the monument and its location followed, and in 2001 the National Monument for Slavery was erected in Oosterpark. Surinamese, and to a lesser extent Dutch Caribbeans, were the main participants in the debates over the monument, but Ghanaians participated as well. The ambassador of Ghana participated in the monument's inauguration ceremony, which was attended by Queen Beatrix, Prime Minister Balkenende, and other important figures of Dutch political life (Oostindie 2005, 60–61).

Throughout the 1990s Jack's contacts with Afro-Surinamese people multiplied, and he noticed a gradual shift in the way they positioned themselves in relation to Africans:

> They are more flexible now. I see that when they talk about Africa they take it easily. Even some of them say, "I'm also from Africa," "My parents were from Africa and through . . ." I don't know. The blacks seem to know that all . . . they have African background. But previously it was not like that . . . I think in the beginning they didn't have a good concept about Africans. Because they did not have much information. What they knew about Africa was "they live on trees," "they are poor," this is what they used to think about us.

The 1990s was an important decade for the exploration of the connections between Africa and the Caribbean and the Dutch role in the Atlantic triangle. Having different motives, African and Surinamese migrants in Amsterdam became more interested in each other. Learning more about transatlantic slavery brought African and Surinamese migrants closer together. Nevertheless, in addition to building bridges, slavery's history also raised difficult issues. One was that kidnapping by Europeans was not the only means of slave recruitment, as was often portrayed. A great many enslaved Africans had been sold or pawned to European slave traders either directly by their relatives or with the involvement of African chiefs (Kopytoff and Miers 1977; Piot 1996; Perbi 2004).[7] In June 2002, cooperation between African chiefs and European slave traders was remembered during an official visit to the Netherlands by Ashanti King Osei Tutu II. The Afro-Surinamese chairwoman of Amsterdam Zuidoost District Council, Hannah Belliot, refused to shake his hand until he apologized. She stated:

> This entire mission should not have taken place. The descendants of African
> slave traders, too, have to offer their excuses, as a symbolic gesture. In the
> Netherlands, many of the descendants of slaves have only just become aware
> of their history. The relations (between Ghana and the Netherlands) are based
> on the slave trade. You can't simply sanitize that![8]

In all my interviews with Afro-Caribbeans and African migrants in the Bijlmer, the issue of African involvement in the slave trade either was absent from their narratives or they attached scant importance to it or even misinterpreted it. For example, a Ghanaian woman who arrived in Amsterdam in 1988 explained the change of attitude of Afro-Surinamese toward Africans: "In the beginning Surinamese did not like us. Dutch people were saying to them that we sold them! This is who the Dutch are! But now Surinamese learned that this is not true." This statement, which certainly does not reflect historical fact, was made during a chat in front of her young Dutch Caribbean "daughter" who silently waited for us to finish our talk about slavery so she could tell us about her Nigerian boyfriend. In our discussions about slavery, Jack did not bring up the issue either.

JUDITH: "WHERE DO I BELONG?"

Judith was born in Paramaribo in 1969, when Suriname was still part of the Dutch Kingdom. One year before Suriname declared its independence in 1975, Judith's parents moved to the Netherlands with their three daughters. They settled in the Bijlmer, where they remain. Judith was four years old when she left Suriname and has no memory of the country of her birth. She still has a few relatives in Paramaribo but has never visited them.

Judith grew up in the Bijlmer socializing with other Surinamese, white Dutch people, Dutch Caribbeans, and children of Turkish and Moroccan migrants who came to the Netherlands a bit earlier than she and her family did. She was baptized in the Evangelische Broedergemeente, like many Afro-Surinamese, and until the age of eighteen she attended the predominantly Surinamese church in the Bijlmer together with her parents. As an adult she stopped attending church regularly because she did not like the preaching of pastors. The beginning of her adult life was marked by the loosening of her bonds with her church community. She started questioning her Christian faith and considered other religions, such as Islam. It was also a period of job instability and uncertainty. She worked in several different places as a shop assistant or office assistant.

The changes of the 1990s described earlier—the emergence of transatlantic slave trade remembrance and commemoration movement and the growing presence of African migrants in Amsterdam—found Judith in a period of personal exploration. Her sister became very interested in "Black history." Judith was also interested in history. Learning more about the colonial past of Suriname enabled her to see more clearly the connections between her place of birth and Africa, which some Surinamese neglected or even denied.

When Judith talked to me about the identity crisis she experienced at that time, she used a vocabulary of identity and belonging that demonstrated how familiar she was with that terminology. However, her "identity crisis," as she described it to me, was a mixture of ethnic and personal concerns. The questions she was asking herself—such as "Where do I belong?"—did not have only cultural connotations; sometimes in our conversations she interchangeably asked, "What kind of person am I?":

> One time I was standing on the balcony and I was looking down. And I was like . . . seeing people walking. And in the way we are raised, we are not raised in the typical Suriname way. So, the language [Sranan Tongo], I don't really talk. And sometime when you hear the people talk and you think like . . . No, it's very rude and impolite . . . So, looking down, I was like, I don't belong this way . . . I wasn't the outgoing type, the smoking-drinking type, the type . . . So, I was like . . . No, I can't fit in this group. I can't fit in that group that always sit at home and don't work. So, I don't fit in this group. I am not in the group of, you know, sometimes you have some groups of Suriname women who you can hear them from miles coming. I don't belong to that group. So, I was like, OK, where do I belong?

In 1996, one of her Surinamese friends advised her to visit the Holy Blessings Church, saying that the senior pastor was Ghanaian. Judith thought about it and out of curiosity attended the Sunday service. It was her first time in a Pentecostal church. The pastor's lively preaching, the people speaking in tongues, the loud music, and the gospel songs shocked her: "Oh my God! What is this? I'm having a headache! I said I'm not coming again." She was very sure she would never go back. However, for a reason she could not explain, the following Sunday she changed her mind just a few hours before the service and went to the church. Since then, she has become a loyal member of the Holy

Blessings Church. In 1998 she was baptized again and became a born-again Christian. The Ghanaian pastor told her that after her first visit, he prayed for her to return and become a church member. This gave her an explanation for her reconsideration of not visiting the church again.

By that time, Holy Blessings Church was still a medium-sized church with approximately twenty to fifty attendees, a balanced mixture of Afro-Caribbeans and African migrants. Before Judith became a member, all her contacts with African migrants were limited to mutual greetings with her Ghanaian neighbors. In the church, Judith had the chance to meet African migrants, and talk with them and get to know them:

> I've grown up with Hindus. I know Muslims. I know Dutch people. Christian people. No. But not Africans. Yes, OK, Moroccans. But not Africans like Nigeria and Ghana and all those things. And I really started to talk to them, at least in church. They were very nice people. Really. Very humble, very soft and all that. For me it was not difficult to relate.

Beyond the Sunday service, Judith participated in church activities (e.g., Bible study group) with other members. She showed dedication to the church and its evangelical mission and gained the appreciation of church members and the pastor. She also volunteered for the church and took on responsibilities in the choir. In the church, Judith had the chance to come in contact with other church members of different ethnic backgrounds and get to know them better. The relationships she developed were framed in a language of sibling-hood (*brother*, *sister*). In her private conversation with Pastor Benedict and his wife, Judith addressed him as "papa" and his wife as "mama" and they both referred to her as their "daughter":

> It also has to do with what they do for you. Not that they do things for me but you know, when we talk, you know, they put themselves in that, like, you know, the mother would have talked to you or your father would have talked to you, sit you down and talk to you. And that makes them the mother or the father.

In April 2000, after a church service, Pastor Benedict introduced "sister Judith" to "brother Jack" who at that time was working in Eindhoven and did not regularly attend Holy Blessings Church.

A FAST DECISION: DEALING WITH UNCERTAINTIES

Although based in Eindhoven, Jack started attending on a weekly basis the Sunday masses of Holy Blessings Church. Judith and Jack met every Sunday before or after the service. It did not take long for their first date, just a few weeks, and a bit more time for the church members and pastor to learn about it. Since it was the pastor who introduced them and their first meetings were at the church, it was impossible to keep their relationship secret from the church community. The pastor and some other church members blessed and prayed for their relationship, expecting them to formalize it and marry as soon as possible. This was particularly stressful for Judith, who was not used to what she called "the Pentecostal way":

> But people were telling me: "If you start getting involved then this is gonna happen, that is gonna happen. And before you know you cannot . . ." I was like "Oh my God!" [laughter]. You understand. You're like, oh my God, too soon, too fast! And how do I know, how do I know that I make the right choice? Because I had that mentality that I need to take my time to get to know you . . . But the Pentecostal way is not that I take two years, three years to know you. It's not the Pentecostal way.

Three months later Jack and Judith went for a walk in the Bijlmer, the neighborhood Judith had lived in for decades. Jack proposed. Judith recalled that she was so overwhelmed with emotion that she could not even recognize the area they were walking through:

> I live there all my life and I was in the place . . . "Oh, I don't recognize that one." He said, "No, don't worry." And we walked. And he just held my hand and I was like . . . "Hey, I don't feel jumpy, you know, I don't feel anxiety." So I was OK. I was really . . . By that time I was then really relaxed. Coming down from the . . . you know, all the emotions . . . And I said OK. And then I said to myself, "Why not? If he comes, why not take that opportunity or that chance to trust and to be trusted?"

Judith's decision to marry Jack surprised her family and friends, but they did not seriously object to it. Similarly, Jack's friends and family in the Netherlands received the news well. However, some Ghanaians warned him that he should think carefully about his choice. Jack recalled: "There were people saying to me, 'Suriname, it's very difficult.' They said that they are very troublesome."

Judith was present in my interview with Jack and seemed to understand why his Ghanaian friends were biased toward Surinamese women. She explained the difference between a Ghanaian woman and a Surinamese woman and expressed her dislike of Ghanaian women's "submissive behavior" toward their husbands:

[Ghanaian women] are submissive but not in an upright way. You know, they are always, "You have to submit to your husband," and then in the inside of them they really want to care for the man. Whatever. We are outspoken. And I wanna tell you something that I don't like. It's that they are going to keep quiet, keep it here, keep it here [points to her heart], be sorrowful, be painful, swallow everything. But that is not the Suriname woman. That is the Ghanaian woman. Is that healthy? No, I don't think so. Because you're a human. You have feelings here [points to heart]. You have something to say. They have a voice. God never tells you to be submissive and to take everything so that means that the man can do anything he likes and you are also inside, you are crying, you are not happy, you are not . . . That's not nice. I call that forced submission to your husband.

BACK TO GHANA, BACK TO ROOTS?

A few months after the marriage proposal, Judith and Jack traveled to Ghana to marry. Although this was not necessary for Jack's residence permit, it was faster and easier to marry in Ghana, and it was also a good opportunity for Judith to meet Jack's family and visit the places that some of her ancestors had possibly passed through. Jack's family received her very warmly. Judith had only nice things to say about the way they treated her. She said that they made her feel "at home." However, Ghana's history of slavery, as Jack said in an interview, had affected the welcoming behavior of his family toward Judith for a rather different reason from what Judith perceived. Jack recounted:

I said from the beginning I'm coming from a very liberal family. There are some families they don't accept it sometimes, unless you marry from your own tribe . . . You're a Ghanaian of this tribe, you see another Ghanaian from another tribe, they don't accept it. You have to marry from the same tribe. But I'm coming from the coast. My ancestors, they have encountered with the white people so, you know, they are very liberal. So, it doesn't matter . . . as long as you are happy that's what they want.

According to Jack, Judith was warmly received not as a lost kin from the other side of the Atlantic but as a foreign woman who was welcomed because of his family's progressive stance against tribalism, which supposedly originated from their contacts with European slave traders, merchants, and missionaries.

In Ghana, the term *obroni*, usually translated as "white (person)," does not have the same meaning as the Dutch racial category of *witte*, or "white." Skin color is not the only criterion for the categorization of someone as *obroni* and sometimes skin color and phenotype are irrelevant. Ghanaians call *obroni* those persons whose mannerisms indicate a privileged position but not necessarily white skin color (Schramm 2009; Darkwah and Adomako Ampofo 2008). Although Judith would unquestionably be a black person (*zwarte persoon*) in the Netherlands, she was categorized as *obroni* in Ghana and certainly not in the same category as other Ghanaians and Africans. Darkwah and Adomako Ampofo (2008), in one of the rare studies on binational marriages in Ghana,[9] observed that non-Ghanaian wives of Ghanaian men were usually well received by the man's family, but *obroni* wives enjoyed even more favorable treatment and benefits than wives from other African countries.

Their trip to Ghana was also an opportunity for Judith to learn more about the land of her ancestors and the history of slavery. They visited the Elmina and Cape Coast castles near Jack's hometown. Their tour of the slave dungeons and other rooms was informative and very emotional for Judith. When I visited these castles, I had the chance to talk with the accredited tour guides. They said their narrative depends on the audience; they are more sensitive with African American and Afro-Caribbean visitors for whom their visit to the castles is often emotionally intense. Indeed, they told me that they would not place a white visitor in a group of African Americans, fearing that a disrespectful comment from the white person could trigger a conflict with people on a pilgrimage to the places of their ancestors' suffering. They even mentioned the case of a mixed marriage between a "Caucasian" and an "African American" that ended after the couple's visit.

In Ghana, Jack and Judith had a civil marriage, then, back in the Netherlands, they married at Holy Blessings Church. They made sure to take photographs of their wedding in case Dutch authorities, who would assess Jack's residence permit application, questioned the authenticity of their marriage. The bureaucratic procedure to apply for Jack's resident permit was not as pleasant and quick as they had hoped, but at least they did not face any serious obstacle. Judith's part-time earnings were sufficient to reach the requirement of 70 percent of minimum salary, and in those days Jack did not have to sit for exams in Dutch language and culture as migrants are obligated to do now.

Jack and Judith remained in the Netherlands and soon had two children. Today they are still married and plan to soon make a small investment in Ghana and open a business there. The story of Jack and Judith is illustrative of how the emerging ideology of transatlantic kinship and black unity in the 1990s brought them into contact and, to a certain extent, facilitated the formation of their family. Their marriage did not face significant legal barriers, despite Judith's unstable job situation, and it provided Jack with a long-term residence permit and later Dutch nationality. A decade later, Kelly, another member of Holy Blessings Church, would have a rather different experience

of immigration regulations, an experience that would lead to a different outcome for transatlantic kinship.

Chronicle of a Failed Marriage: Kelly and Sam

During a visit to the home of my Ghanaian friend Elisabeth in December
2011, I had the chance to meet Kelly, a young black woman who was born
on a Caribbean island and grew up in the Netherlands with a white adoptive
family. Kelly was twenty-seven and had two kids, a four-year-old daughter
and a nine-year-old son. I could immediately tell that she was a very beautiful
woman, even though the day I met her she did not seem to have taken care of
her appearance. She had no makeup, her hair was covered with a headband,
and she wore an old tracksuit that was ripped and dirty. Kelly was fluent in
Dutch and spoke English very well; she spoke the two languages interchangeably with Elisabeth. The first thing that Kelly ever talked about with Elisabeth
was Tyler Perry. I did not know Tyler Perry, so they both explained to me
that he is an African American comedian who performs the character of Madea, an old African American woman involved in funny incidents that always
end with a gospel song and a Christian message. Then Elisabeth revealed her
large collection of Tyler Perry DVDs and chose one for us to watch. Kelly
and Elisabeth knew the script by heart and competed with each other for
who would first recall Madea's words. It was more than obvious that they had
watched that particular episode many times. Yet they were laughing loudly
with Madea's jokes as if they had heard them for first time.

When the film finished, Elisabeth went to the kitchen to prepare food
for us. I asked Kelly about her relationship with Elisabeth. Kelly referred to
Elisabeth as her "big sister" and talked with great appreciation and admira-
tion of her. They had been friends for only a few months, although Kelly had
known of Elisabeth for a longer time as a member of her church. At church,
Elisabeth was known to everyone as "the pastor's daughter." The two wom-
en's first interaction was in March 2011, when Kelly approached Elisabeth in
church to tell her she had dreamed that Elisabeth was pregnant. Elisabeth had
recently learned she was pregnant and had not shared the news with other
church members. For Kelly, this was a prophetic dream that led her to talk to
Elisabeth and eventually become her "younger sister." They started meeting
to study the Bible and pray together. Elisabeth helped Kelly to understand the
Bible and learn more about her religion. Elisabeth's counseling role was not

only limited to religious guidance. Kelly was heavily indebted by loans that her ex-husband took out in her name. Elisabeth counseled her and assisted her in making arrangements and setting a schedule to pay off the debt.

When Elisabeth returned from the kitchen, Kelly said that everything was set for her upcoming trip to Ghana. In a few weeks Kelly was traveling to Ghana alone—it would be her first time abroad in her adult life. I asked about the purpose of this trip, and she briefly explained that she was going to meet a guy she had been dating online. When Kelly left, Elisabeth told me Kelly was going to Ghana with welfare money she had received to pay her children's school fees. She had advised her not to spend it on her vacation in Ghana because welfare authorities could monitor how she used the funds, and she could get into serious trouble. Nevertheless, Elisabeth believed that Kelly needed some rest, especially after the latest, very turbulent period of her life. Kelly had just divorced her Surinamese husband, who physically and financially abused her. Elisabeth hoped that Kelly's vacation in Ghana and Sam, the man she had met online, would give her some peace of mind.

I asked Elisabeth what she knew about Sam. How safe was it for Kelly to travel to an unknown country, without any travel experience, and meet an unknown man she had found on the internet? Elisabeth's reply was anything but reassuring. Elisabeth herself had a profile on the dating website BlackPlanet.com whose users were predominantly African American, with smaller numbers of Africans who lived all over the world. Through Black-Planet, Sam contacted Elisabeth and they started chatting. As Elisabeth clarified to me, she rarely responded to men based in Africa. She told me several times, mentioning hilarious examples, that most profiles from Africa-based users were from men who wanted help migrating or younger men who would eventually ask for money. Elisabeth made clear to Sam that she was not interested in continuing the chat because she could not see anything they had in common. So she ended the online relationship, but in the meantime, Sam had added Elisabeth as a friend on Facebook and sent friend requests to some of her Netherlands-based friends. Kelly was among Elisabeth's friends whom Sam approached on Facebook and the only one who started chatting with him.

Elisabeth said that she had already asked Jeremiah, a friend in Ghana who I also knew well, to find information on Sam, and he responded that Sam was "OK." But a couple of months later, in summer 2012, when I met Jeremiah in Ghana, he had a far-from-neutral opinion of Sam. He had indeed confirmed to Elisabeth that Sam was an existing person who lived in Accra. Jeremiah told me that he had also warned Elisabeth that Sam was a "cheater." According to Jeremiah, Sam was not a Ghanaian, as he claimed, but a Nigerian who was trying to travel to Europe through Ghana. Apart from Jeremiah, I also asked a friend of mine in Ghana to offer his assistance to Kelly if she needed anything while she was there.

Kelly's trust in an unknown man she met on the internet was worrying. How could she take such a risky decision to spend her welfare money for a trip to meet a stranger she dated online? Why did she have to go all way to Ghana to find a partner? I could not answer these questions until I learned more about her life and past experiences with men. After our first meeting at Elisabeth's place, I visited Kelly at her apartment and gave her the contact details of my friends in Accra. We met a couple of times before her trip to Ghana, and when she returned, we started meeting on a regular basis. It did not take her a long time to open up and tell me about her life, and her relationship with Sam and other men.

BORN IN THE CARIBBEAN AND RAISED IN THE NETHERLANDS: THE LIFE OF AN ADOPTEE

Kelly's social housing apartment was large, simply furnished and full of children's toys. She had the absolute minimum furniture because she feared that collecting agencies (*incasso*) would confiscate her property for unpaid debts. Her apartment was decorated with drawings of her kids, religious posters, and photographs of herself with her adoptive family. Her parents had made posters and calendars using various family photographs from Kelly's youth to the present day: family gatherings, school festivities, vacations with her parents, and many other happy occasions that gave me the impression that her parents were attentive and caring. In all of the pictures, from small family dinners to large wedding parties and school events, Kelly was the only person of color. Kelly grew up in a predominantly white Dutch social environment. While I was silently looking at these images, her little son felt that he had to clarify what he probably thought I had in my mind: *Mijn moeder is geadopteerd* (my mother is adopted).

Kelly was born in 1984 on a Caribbean island. She did not have memories of the island and knew nothing about her biological parents. "What I do know is that my mother left me"—her only comment about the woman who gave birth to her. She was nine months old when she was adopted by a white middle-class family in the Netherlands.

Contrary to all of Kelly's siblings, who continued their education and later became successful professionals, she completed only compulsory education. She told me that she had a very troublesome relationship with her adoptive parents and ran away from home many times. Nevertheless, Kelly acknowledged that her parents were caring and supportive, and she attributed her problems to the fact that she was adopted:

> It is scientifically proven that people who are adopted, they experience . . . they are afraid the people will leave them or they are afraid to bind to people. . . . I can be friends with anybody very fast but I am not good to hold them because at a certain time I am going to claim them. But that is just something because somewhere in my subconscious mind I have a record of being left by someone. So, that is what is affecting my lifetime here . . . Also, what they say is, they say that like 90 percent of the adopted people cannot get along with adoptive parents.

At eighteen she left home and soon got pregnant. Her boyfriend and the father of her child was a young man who earned money selling drugs. Soon after the birth of their son, her boyfriend was arrested and imprisoned. She had been living in a shelter; as a young single mother, she moved with her baby to another shelter. She was not in contact with her parents and had no other friends to support her. In that phase of her life, the only people around her were Ali, her new boyfriend, and Katja, a woman she met through Ali. Kelly was in love with Ali and happy with her new relationship. After a while, Ali proposed that Kelly take advantage of her beauty and make money from it. More precisely, he asked her to become a sex worker and work for him in Amsterdam's Red Light District. Kelly accepted. She did not explain to me her motivation. She did say she discussed her concerns only with Katja, who was in favor and in general supportive of Ali. When I asked Elisabeth why she believed Kelly so easily accepted Ali's proposal, I expected Elisabeth would show some understanding for her younger sister's choices, but she more or less blamed her for being a very "impulsive person."

For about four years, Kelly worked behind a window in the Red Light District, offering her sexual services to ten to fifteen clients per day. She gave all her earnings to her boyfriend Ali, who returned to her a small portion to pay her expenses (e.g., rent, babysitter, clothing). As she said to me, she had the freedom to choose her customers: "I didn't take blacks. I didn't want them. It takes too long with them." Although Kelly, and probably Ali, had sexual contact with many people, the erotic and emotional attachment with Ali was supposed to be exclusive. In 2006, after a four-year romantic but not sexually exclusive relationship, Ali started dating a young Moroccan woman. Kelly felt betrayed. She stopped working for him, quit sex work, and reported him to police. Kelly said that police estimated that she had given Ali around €500,000 earned through her sex work. The case ended up in court with Ali charged with human trafficking. But it was difficult for Kelly to prove that all her earnings were given to her boyfriend, and Ali was acquitted.

Once away from Ali and sex work, Kelly tried to start a new life. She moved to a new social housing apartment in Amsterdam and started looking for a job. In the meantime, she became pregnant by a man who disappeared before she even gave birth. In that period of her life, Kelly told me, she felt very disappointed about the choices she had made.

BORN AGAIN TWICE:
BECOMING CHRISTIAN AND BLACK

Kelly had been baptized a Protestant but stopped attending church after she left her parents' home. One day in 2006 she received an invitation to a Pentecostal church in her neighborhood:

> I received a flyer and in the beginning I didn't want to go. And I was doing the dishes and the Holy Ghost . . . like . . . I think it's the Holy Ghost. Now I know it's the Holy Ghost. That time I didn't know. It was pushing me and pushing me. Like "Go. Just go!" So, like five minutes before the service started I was on my bicycle and go to the church.

That was her first time in "what Dutch people call black church," she said. The pastor was a white Dutch person, and the congregation was mostly Surinamese and Dutch Caribbeans. Kelly was warmly welcomed in the church, where she found the peace she was looking for. In the months that followed, she learned more about Pentecostal doctrine, started speaking in tongues, got baptized again, and eventually became a born-again Christian. She stayed in that church for two years, after which she moved on to Holy Blessings Church on the advice of a Surinamese friend who was enthusiastic about the preaching of its senior pastor from Ghana.

By the time that Kelly joined these "black churches," she had limited contacts with other black people and saw them in the same stereotypical way as other people of her social environment did:

> That time I didn't like black people. I put them far from me. Also, the bad report, what you hear for them all the time [that] they cheat, they never gonna stay with a woman, they don't take showers, they smell and they don't look good, they talk strange. That's why I kept myself far away from them.

Although Kelly shared the same skin color with "black people," it was their perceived cultural practices and social behavior that made her think that she was different from them: "I didn't consider myself Black. I considered myself more white than a white person." Her contacts with Afro-Caribbeans and Africans in a church setting made her reconsider her view about black people and find similarities with her own way of thinking and behaving. She embraced a black identity, which was mostly culturally informed but some of which she attributed to genetics:

> I am different due to my own DNA. . . . I am more related to the family of Elisabeth. How they are and how they think and the way that they handle things. Dutch families are not like that. They are very strict. I am used to it, of course, because I was raised with them. I understand it.

"THE FIRST BLACK GUY I DATED AND THE FIRST GUY I MARRIED"

Kelly's participation in "black churches" gave her the opportunity to interact with Africans and Afro-Caribbeans. In this new phase of her life as a born-again Christian, Kelly made several African and Afro-Caribbean friends and for the first time entered into a relationship with a black man. In the office of the welfare department, Kelly met Justin, originally from Suriname, and exchanged phone numbers. In less than a week, Justin had moved in with Kelly. Kelly asked Justin to attend her church: "I think that he turned Christian to satisfy me. Because it was very important that my husband is Christian." Some church elders were quite judgmental that Kelly and Justin lived together without being married. She recalled: "I was very concerned about what people are thinking about me and about how God is standing in the marriage and I was also, like, thinking, like, I won't find any other man. So, I was like, 'This is the man that God has for me and this is it.'"

Pressured by her fellow church members and fearing that this was her last opportunity to get married, Kelly quickly decided to marry Justin even though she had already realized that Justin was "very, very aggressive."

Kelly hoped "that maybe after the wedding everything will get better" with Justin. Contrary to what she wished, the nice days after their wedding did not last long. Justin could not control his anger and behaved violently toward Kelly more and more often. Furthermore, he exploited her financially by draining her small income and taking out bank loans in her name. Kelly started thinking about divorcing Justin already during the first month of their marriage. Yet she delayed the decision for ten months: "I was afraid that if I got divorced I will go to hell. Because the Bible says that God doesn't like divorcing."

The last two incidents of Justin's physical abuse were quite violent, and Kelly reported them to the police. It was clearer than ever to her that she could not continue her marriage. She decided to separate from him. Justin moved out of Kelly's apartment and left her alone to pay off the loan he had taken out in her name. Again Kelly found herself financially and emotionally insecure. How could she go on with her life? Was Justin the man God had chosen for her? Would any other man want to marry her? How could she re-habilitate her life and the life of her children? These were some of the pressing questions that Kelly was asking herself after her divorce.

Around that time she received Sam's friend request on Facebook. She thought he was a handsome African guy around her age, so she accepted his request and they started chatting. That was the beginning of an online affair that would bring Kelly to Ghana and almost make her marry a second time.

"IF HE CAN'T COME TO EUROPE, I'LL GO TO GHANA"

Sam flirted with Kelly and said he was planning to migrate to the Nether-lands. Kelly became interested in him, and felt the interest was mutual, and began envisioning a relationship with him, given his scheduled relocation to the Netherlands, as realistic. She talked to him about her life, her previous relationships, the jobs she had had, including sex work, and the concerns she had for her future. Sam showed understanding for the problems she had faced and continued to face.

By that time, Kelly did not know how difficult it was for Africans to get a visa for the Netherlands. Sam explained to her that he needed to make a lot of "traveling money" before he applied for a visa, otherwise his request would be turned down. Sam did not ask Kelly to financially help him, which she in-terpreted as proof of his genuine interest in her. But she came to understand it would take months, if not years, for Sam to earn the money. In November 2011, just a few months after their first chat, Kelly was already tired of waiting. It was very easy for her to get a Ghanaian visa in her Dutch passport, so she decided to travel to Ghana and meet Sam.

Kelly posted on Facebook a very excited message about her trip to Ghana. She did not specify the reason for the trip, and when her sister asked her twice about it, she replied that she was going to Ghana to meet friends "and also to visit a church." After Jeremiah, Elisabeth's friend in Ghana, told Kelly that Sam was not a Ghanaian but a Nigerian, Kelly confronted Sam, who ex-plained that he was indeed a Nigerian Igbo by his father but his mother was Ghanaian and through her he had gotten a Ghanaian passport. Additionally, a Dutch friend and neighbor of Kelly had her Nigerian Igbo husband to talk with Sam on the phone to prove his story.

Kelly arranged to leave her children in the care of her parents and also Elisabeth and her mother. "When she calls you sister you cannot say no," Elisabeth told me. One day before her flight, Kelly brought her children to her parent's place and returned home to pack her bag. There I visited to give her a gift for Jeremiah. Kelly called Jeremiah for the final arrangements. Jeremiah said that he was looking forward to meeting Kelly, and they agreed they would go out at night to a dance competition. But Jeremiah's condition for going out dancing with her took Kelly aback: as long as Sam was not with her. "He is a Nigerian and I don't like to hang out with Nigerians," he said, reflecting a widespread negative perception about Nigerians in Ghana (Darkwah 2019). "What are you saying? What does it matter? What I know from my church is that we are all brothers and sisters," Kelly replied.

"I AM IN GHANA AND I LOVE IT"—
SIX PEOPLE LIKE THIS

During her stay in Ghana, Kelly kept all her Facebook friends informed about her time there and how her relationship with Sam was developing. Here is a selection of the most relevant posts:[10]

17 December 2011, 9:37 p.m. I'm in Ghana and I love it. But also missing my kids. Big time but they are in very good hands. Aaaah I wanna stay here. I have so much fun..... so much. I JUST LOVE IT.

21 December 2011, 2:03 p.m. Ooh, I have so much fun here. I don't wanna go back. Ghana is great. The people are great. @ tawala beach.

21 December 2011, 2:19 p.m. I am soooo happy going to shop now yeeeh.

21 December 2011, 7:28 p.m. My man. [Comment on photograph of Sam wearing a gray suit.]

21 December 2011, 8:45pm. I love my life. Goshhh feeling so new. Aaah I love my hussy and yeaaah I feel peace finally . . . So anyone who wants to destroy it, please I beg you . . . shut up. Thank you. Going out to beach. Have some nice dinner.

22 December 2011, 12:19 p.m. My husband said this morning: Love is like a butterfly. It pleases where it goes and it goes where it pleases.

22 December 2011, 4:51 p.m. In the bus to Kumasi. My hussy is sleeping and I am full of stress. Wiebel bus goshhhh. Hihihi. Totally happy with my life. Thank you God.

23 December 2011, 10:14 a.m. Soo in love. [Comment on a selfie of herself.]

23 December 2011, 10:19 a.m. I am in Tingtangto or in other words Kintampo and it is sooo local here. I miss Accra. @don't eat for 3 days.

23 December 2011, 5:09 p.m. At waterfall in Kintampo with my husband. [Comment on a selfie of Kelly and Sam in front of Kintampo waterfall.]

23 December 2011, 8:25 p.m. She posted a picture of herself with Sam standing in front of Kintampo waterfall. Their feet are in the water. Kelly's clothes are wet, and Sam has removed his T-shirt. Sam holds Kelly in his arms with his hands around her waist. Kelly has folded her hands around his neck and kisses his left cheek.

23 December 2011, 8:27 p.m. PS I have a great, wonderful, glorious, marvellous TIME here and I love myself haha and my children and my hussy aaaa am so happy. Thank you God for this All . . . thank youuuu.

23 December 2011, 8:28 p.m. I loveeeeee it here and Sam is more than great. I am sooo happy that I am here. . . . Soooo happy.

24 December 2011, 9:09 a.m. Merry X-mas to my lovely hussy yeah. [Comment on a photograph of a brand new silver watch in its box.]

25 December 2011, 6:54 p.m. On my way to Tamale. Had a nice time in Kintampo . . . @ driving very fast . . .

26 December 2011, 3:39 p.m. I am gonna move to Ghana in Kintampo haha I love it here. @ dinner with my lovely hussy.

26 December 2011, 6:55 p.m. I am soooo happy finally. I found myself back. I can't wait till 2012 because that is going to be my year. Full of joy and favour. Believe me! It is going to be a great new beginning for my kidz, my hussy and me! And I thank God for the super grace he has on me. I couldn't be happier. Amen. @ Tamale, chilling and dancing with myself. Whahaha.

27 December 2011, 3:50 p.m. Aaa merry X to me. Yeah. [Comment on a photograph of a new ring in her right hand.]

1 January 2012, 12:35 a.m. Happy new year. This is my year 2012 with my family. @ Tawala beach with my husband!!!!!!! Soooo happy. [Comment on a full-length photograph of herself in a colorful, shiny short dress. Sam comments "U re hottie baby."]

1 January 2012, 8:30 p.m. Kelly changes her relationship status from "in a relationship" to "engaged to Sam."

1 January 2012, 8:51 p.m. This is the best vacation ever. In 3 days getting home for a while!!! Because I will move to my Hussy. Yeaaaah 2012 is the perfect year.

2 January 2012, 10:08 a.m. I just woke up. In about 2 days getting home to very cold country. But for now I will enjoy Ghana with my lovely husband Sam. I had a wonderful time. Sometimes you just know somebody is the one. I am more than happy . . . I thank God for his grace and that I woke up. Have a blessed day ya all.

3 January 2012, 12:11 p.m. Goshhhhh!!! Goshhh just one day left and then back to Holland. I am going to miss my hussy sooo much. Yet I will see him in a few months and then I will be complete again. . . . Some things in life you just know are right.. He is one of them. . . . So, I don't care what anyone says I will be myself and stay free. After all I serve God . . . not men.

BACK TO THE NETHERLANDS

After almost three weeks in Ghana, Kelly returned to the Netherlands. She continued to share her news about Sam with her Facebook friends and added a profile photograph of herself and Sam kissing. Some days later, I came across Kelly by coincidence in the train station, and we had a brief chat about her vacation in Ghana. She liked the country very much and its people for "the way they are, how friendly they are, how they refer to you as a sister." I asked why she was addressed as a sister. She replied: "I believe sister means by color. This is what I hear. Because we are the same color." She looked very happy and excited about her trip, and especially about Sam. He had proposed marriage and she gladly accepted. The problem, however, was how they could live together, since it was difficult for Sam to get a visa to come to the Netherlands. The major obstacle for Sam to a family reunification visa was Kelly's income. Although she had a part-time and unstable job and had just started a small online business selling hair products, her total income was not sufficient to meet the income requirement. But even if she managed to earn as much as the minimum requirement, she would have to prove stable income over a year and a half to the immigration authorities. In addition, Sam would have to relocate from Ghana back to Nigeria and participate in the civic integration examination at the Dutch embassy in Abuja: "Maybe in the past days when you marry somebody you could pick him up. They don't buy it anymore here in Holland. They don't buy it. Even if you're married you still need to do some rules."

Kelly explained this to Sam and made clear that if he wanted to marry her and live with her in the Netherlands, he should get a visa and residence permit on other grounds and by his own means. Sam agreed and returned from Ghana to Nigeria, where he would try to find another way to get a visa to Europe.

Some weeks later, I visited Kelly at her place and we talked in more detail about her relationship with Sam and their plans to have a family. I asked Kelly why she was so excited and what was it in Sam that attracted her so much. Without giving a thought she replied, "The caring! Taking care of people, not only of me but also people around him . . . [Also] he listens very well. If he is angry, if he is really very mad, he doesn't hit, he doesn't beat me." I felt numb when I heard this and said that she should not consider it an asset. In an emotionless tone, she commented that she could not recall ever having a boy-friend who did not beat her. This made me understand better why she was so excited with Sam, as her incredibly enthusiastic Facebook posts showed.

Nevertheless, her time with Sam in Ghana was not as rosy as she wanted her Facebook friends to believe. When Kelly was in Ghana, she checked Sam's mobile phone and found out that he had been chatting with 435 women from all over the world:

> I find out that the time that we were dating, when I was not yet in Ghana, he was also talking with other girls at the same level as me but he was telling me that I was special. Then I found out this. What? You do the same thing with other girls. I was not special. You were just looking which girl will come or not. I was just the stupid girl that came. But no problem. He said he doesn't do it anymore.

Sam promised Kelly he would not chat again with other women and gave her his Facebook password so she could check his account whenever she wanted. Kelly logged into his account regularly and replied to messages he had re-ceived from women, mentioning that she was his wife. She also used his ac-count to compliment and "like" photographs on her own Facebook profile.

Furthermore, Sam told Kelly that he chatted with so many women because he was playing a game with the purpose of making them fall in love with him and then leaving them without starting a relationship or even having sex with them. Therefore, he told her, Kelly was not like the other women because Sam was in a relationship with her, and they had already had multiple sexual interactions. Sam told Kelly he played this "game" because of a trauma from his youth. When he was a pupil, a group of girls had raped him. Many girls had placed ice on his genitals to make his penis hard. Kelly saw I was not con-vinced and told me she also had some doubts: "[But] I believe him because when I saw him telling it, I saw the pain in his eyes and anger that they did that." The presence of emotions, and indeed very strong emotions—sadness ("he was crying, he was very emotional about it"), anger, and hate ("he told me how he hated women through that")—persuaded Kelly that Sam was telling the truth.

DYING RELATIONS: MARRIAGE AND SIBLINGHOOD IN INFERTILE GROUND

In the following months, Kelly and Sam continued chatting online every day. I had the chance to be present for one of their Skype video calls and talked briefly with Sam. Kelly did not want to be in a long-distance relationship and was tired of waiting for Sam to find a way to come to Europe. Sam was planning to use the passport of his "brother," who had traveled to Germany, and for him it would be easy to again get a Schengen visa. Kelly told him that if he would not apply for a visa by May and come to the Netherlands by June she would break up with him, because she did not want to wait. Once he was in the Netherlands, he could stay at Kelly's place and she would help him get a job—if necessary, he could work with her papers. I asked her if it was possible for a man to work under a female name. She said that the Nigerian husband of her white Dutch neighbor was also working under his wife's name as a newspaper distributor.

Sam wanted to apply for a visa and travel to Europe as soon as possible, but as long as he did not have enough money for the brokerage fees he would have to wait. He explained this to Kelly and asked her to help him financially if she wanted him to come to the Netherlands. Kelly erupted: "I was getting so angry the time that he asked me for money that I cursed him to death. I say to him, 'Can you do me a favor?' 'What my wife?' I said, 'Do me a favor and die!' I was veeery angry!"

Kelly's reaction was significant. Both marriage and money, under certain conditions, could enable Sam to migrate to Europe. She was very happy with the marriage proposal but enraged by his request for financial support. Certainly, marriage to someone with modest finances, such as Kelly, did not entitle Sam to a family visa. Nevertheless, if Sam could get a visa solely through his marriage to Kelly, any calculation might seem at least a little less apparent than by merely taking advantage of her finances to realize his migration plans. Both money and marriage can provide access to international mobility, but marriage involves emotions, sex, and a caring relationship that blur any instrumental motives.

Sam did not manage to apply for a Schengen visa, and his relationship with Kelly ended before summer. About a year later, Sam uploaded on Facebook photographs of himself in India, which was probably the destination he

could afford. Kelly also added some photographs of an African pastor introducing him to her Facebook friends as her father. She also changed her family
name in her profile to the family name of that pastor. When we next met, she
told me he was a pastor based in South Africa whom she had met online; they
chatted about religious matters. I could not hide my surprise over the ease
with which she called a stranger her "father" and changed her name to his.
She had a different concern: "The only problem is that he is half-Nigerian."
I wondered why this would be a problem and recalled what she had said a
year earlier to Jeremiah, who did not want to hang out with Nigerians ("we
are all brothers and sisters"). Her comment was sharp and brief: "I don't like
Nigerians."

On Facebook a couple of weeks later, she changed her family name back
to her own.

Conclusion

The stories of the two couples in this chapter took place in two periods when
different laws on family and migration applied. Today Jack would certainly
face more obstacles to getting a residence permit through his marriage to
Judith. Her income from part-time work would not qualify her to sponsor a
family reunification visa, and Jack would have to learn some basic Dutch to
pass the Dutch exams. Likewise, in an earlier period, Kelly's modest and unstable income would not have been a barrier to Sam's visa for the Netherlands.

In these two studies, it became evident how transatlantic kinship, which informed the making of black subjectivities, contributed to bringing Africans and
Afro-Caribbeans closer together. The success and failure of these two relationships, which to some extent were determined by state policies and laws, resulted
from different considerations of belonging and transatlantic kinship. The two
cases suggest that exchange relations between Africans and Afro-Caribbeans
have been vital to the process of making and remaking transatlantic kinship. In
these exchanges, citizenship was an important resource for circulating through
marriage among black kinsmen from either side of the Atlantic. At least in the
previous two decades, since the turn of the century, state policies and legislation have systematically and increasingly devalued citizenship by diminishing
the rights of its holders, such as the right to family life, or by making it more
difficult for citizens to claim those rights. The devaluation of civic resources has
in turn affected exchanges between Africans and Afro-Caribbeans, which has
further consequences for their cooperation in everyday life.

In her book *Fragmented Ties: Salvadoran Immigrant Networks in America*,
Cecilia Menjívar (2000) argued that the limited resources available to recently

arrived Salvadoran migrants in California resulted in conflicts and tensions within their migrant families. The lack of resources, such as migrant legality and social networks, prevented migrants from properly performing their kinship roles; they could only "share poverty" with their relatives. Menjívar's (1995) research showed that, in contrast to Salvadoran migrants, Vietnamese refugees, who had access to welfare assistance, and Mexicans, who, despite their unauthorized status, had access to jobs through their extended networks, did not experience similar tensions within their families. Menjívar's research, in other words, reveals material conditions as the main factors that determine whether migrants are able or not to comply with kinship norms.

To some degree, Menjívar's research is useful for analyzing the process of transatlantic kinship between Dutch Afro-Caribbeans and African migrants in the Netherlands. However, it is insufficient to look only at material conditions. The ethnographic analysis of these two cases shows that the process of transatlantic kinship is also influenced by other conditions, not necessarily material, such as the politics of slavery commemoration in the Netherlands and Ghana as well as other forms of kinship that emerged in the Netherlands, especially in the Pentecostal churches in the Bijlmer. Although we can safely conclude that the devalorization of Dutch Caribbeans' civic resources had consequences for their relations with African migrants in the Netherlands, it is too simplistic to suggest a simple causal relationship between the materiality of citizenship and the process of kinship making and unmaking.

The analysis of the legal shifts in the field of marriage and migration demonstrates that the gradually more exclusionary character of the Dutch state has negatively affected forms of collaboration between West Africans and Afro-Caribbeans in the Netherlands. However, the two groups continue interacting and collaborating in other domains of social life than marriage. Urban popular culture, for example, offer possibilities for persons of West African, Afro-Caribbean, and other origins to work on new versions of black identity (Guadeloupe 2022). Even if their parents may no longer be closely related to Afro-Caribbeans, children of West African migrants craft new forms of belonging with persons of Afro-Caribbean backgrounds that signal Afro-politan horizons (De Witte 2019). As for marriages involving West African migrants and Dutch Afro-Caribbeans, there is indeed a clear decline in their number in the Netherlands. But Dutch Afro-Caribbeans, as Dutch citizens, are also EU citizens. The moment they move out from the Netherlands to another EU country, they can claim protection of their family rights as EU citizens. In that way their Dutch citizenship is revalorized as EU citizenship.

In November 2012, the Dutch Police and the UK Border Agency, in a large joint operation, arrested twenty-three Dutch Caribbeans in the Netherlands and eighty-one Nigerians in the United Kingdom on the charge of participating in or facilitating a sham marriage.[11] As described in a BBC report: "the scam allowed Nigerians to stay in the United Kingdom because they married a European with a right of residence, who were all Dutch nationals, many originally came from the Dutch Antilles in the Caribbean."[12] According to the charges, female Dutch citizens of Afro-Caribbean descent traveled to the United Kingdom and, in exchange for €5,000, fashionable clothes, perfumes, and mobile phones, married unauthorized Nigerian migrants who gained, through the marriages, long-term residence permits in the United Kingdom. A UK Border Agency officer commented, "[The marriage register] absolutely takes off in 2009 . . . There's a huge amount of marriages involving Nigerians marrying Dutch nationals."[13] More recently, a marriage broker was arrested for arranging marriages between Dutch Caribbean women and Nigerian men in France. According to a report by a Dutch Caribbean newspaper in St. Maarten, the marriage broker "recruited vulnerable women in the Netherlands, mostly of Dutch Caribbean descent. He accompanied the women to France where they married Nigerian men whom they never met before . . . Investigations in France and Great Britain show an increasing number of fake marriages in order to directly access European Union (EU) rights. In most of these cases it concerned Nigerian men and women of Dutch Caribbean descent who are in possession of a Dutch passport."[14]

Although restrictive Dutch immigration policies devalued the civic resources of Dutch Afro-Caribbeans in the Netherlands, their Dutch citizenship was valorized as EU citizenship outside the Netherlands. This opened up possibilities for the development of new exchange relations with West African migrants outside the Netherlands and directed legally precarious African migrants toward other forms of kinship with EU citizens. The shift in West African migrants' marital practices fueled authorities' suspicion that these marriages are "sham." Thus, immigration authorities subjected these marriages to further scrutinization. The next chapter deals precisely with these issues.

Marriage, Love, and Inequality

In June 2009, Tim, a Nigerian migrant in Amsterdam and friend of mine, urgently asked me to meet his cousin Kevin. He was not clear about the reasons but said Kevin became interested in talking to me when Tim told him that I was Greek, and at that time, I was working as a housekeeper in a Dutch hotel. The three of us arranged to meet in a central location in Amsterdam. I was the first to arrive. With some delay, Tim and Kevin arrived together. Kevin was in his early thirties, tall, a little bit fat, very talkative and loud—the very opposite of Tim, who was short, slim and had a voice you could hardly hear. Tim introduced his cousin Kevin as his "brother," and for the rest of the conversation they addressed each other as brothers. Kevin also addressed me as "brother Apostolos" and started explaining the reasons he wanted to meet me.

He said his temporary visa would expire soon. For this reason, he asked me to help him find a woman who would want to, if not marry him, have a cohabitation contract with him.[1] This would enable him to extend his legal stay in the Netherlands. He emphasized that he was particularly interested in a European, but not Dutch, woman and asked me to search among my Eastern European hotel colleagues and my Greek network. "She can be from Greece or from Poland," he explained. "It doesn't matter. But not Dutch." It was the first time I met someone in the Netherlands who wanted to obtain a residence permit on the basis of marriage or cohabitation with a foreign EU national instead of a Dutch citizen. Why? He replied vaguely that "it's better" with a non-Dutch European. What would make it "better," and why was he keen on a woman from Greece or Poland?

"I will make your pocket smile, my brother," Kevin told me. Although he did not mention anything about him paying the woman, I assumed that he would be prepared to offer something to her as well. Before we finished our conversation, I asked him, quite hesitantly, if his search for a European partner was limited only to women, and I explained that a same-sex marriage or partnership in the Netherlands could grant him the same rights as a marriage or partnership to a woman. Dutch immigration authorities tend to investigate more carefully heterosexual cross-border marriages in which the "sponsor" is the female spouse. Often assuming that these women are naïve, gullible, and in need of protection, immigration officers inquire into the motives of migrant men to marry them (De Hart 2003, 126–27; 2022, 39). If Kevin was interested in a "marriage of convenience," I thought, a same-sex marriage might be a better option because immigration authorities would less likely suspect it as "sham" (on benevolent sexual culturalism, see Chauvin et al. 2021). He knew this and without a second thought rejected it as an option. Without calling me "brother" again, he said, "Mister Apostolos, I'm talking to you seriously!" His switch from "brother" to "mister" immediately imposed a formality between us and made more apparent our unequal positions—no matter that I was few years younger than him, he had approached me to help him with my assumed connections. Our meeting ended without reaching an agreement or my promising to find what he was looking for.

By that time, other West African migrants in the Netherlands had been legalized, and later naturalized, through marriage to a Dutch national—often originally from Suriname or the Dutch Caribbean islands (see also Van Dijk 2004, 453–54). Why did Kevin prefer a non-Dutch European? In 2008, just a year before our meeting, the European Court of Justice made a groundbreaking decision in the Metock case that effectively obliged all EU countries to grant residence permits, without imposing any onerous requirements, to foreign spouses of EU citizens who had relocated to other EU counties.[2] This applied also to those whose foreign spouses had not previously resided legally in any EU country. It seems that Kevin wanted to benefit from the generous migration rights conferred to spouses of EU citizens. But if EU citizenship was all that mattered, why did he focus on Greek and Polish women, especially when there were more European women from neighboring countries?[3] Why did he not mention, for example, German and Belgian women? In what regard are spouses from Europe's east and south "better," to recall Kevin's enigmatic statement, than spouses from northern Europe who are present in larger numbers in the Netherlands?

In the years that followed, I realized that Kevin was not an exception. During my fieldwork in Amsterdam, I came across and talked with several other West African migrants, mostly men, who were looking specifically for non-Dutch EU citizen partners. As data from the municipality of Amsterdam show, the percentage of marriages or registered partnerships between West Africans (e.g., Nigerians, Ghanaians) and native Dutch, Surinamese, or Dutch Caribbeans—the vast majority of whom are Dutch citizens—has been gradually decreasing. In the period 1996–2000, 67 percent of all marriages registered in the municipality of Amsterdam involving at least a Nigeria-origin spouse and 26 percent involving at least a Ghana-origin spouse were to native Dutch, Surinamese, or Dutch Caribbeans. Fifteen years later, in the period 2011–2015, the percentage of marriages to native Dutch, Surinamese, and Dutch Caribbeans dropped to 31 percent for Nigerians and 13 percent for Ghanaians. For the same two periods (1996–2000 and 2011–2015), the percentage of marriages to migrants of Western origin (*westerse allochtonen*) nearly tripled from 13 percent to 36 percent for Nigerians and from 3 percent to 9 percent for Ghanaians (figs. 5.1 and 5.2; tables 5.1 and 5.2). "Western-origin migrant" (*westerse allochtonen*) is a statistical category referring to those originally from Europe, North America, Oceania, Japan, and Indonesia.[4] However, as other set of data along with my ethnographic observations indicate, these marriages are mostly to European citizens, especially Greeks, Spanish, Polish, and other Eastern European nationalities.

From the conversation we had, it was clear Kevin wanted a relationship with a European woman, as he intended to secure a long-term residence permit. Was that his only objective? If he was interested in a "marriage of convenience" that would allow him to extend his stay legally in the Netherlands, why reject from the beginning other possibilities such as a same-sex partnership or marriage that would help him to obtain a residence permit following the same legal route? Perhaps Kevin would feel uncomfortable pretending that he was in a romantic relation with another man in front of immigration authorities. Was that uneasiness the only reason for his reluctance? Was he also looking for an emotional connection with a European woman? If that were so, wouldn't it be a "marriage of convenience" as I originally thought?

This encounter also raised questions about my understanding of Kevin's search for a partner. Why did I immediately assume that a marriage that would provide access to migrant legality for Kevin had nothing to do with emotions and particularly love? Why did I understand Kevin's motivation only as an instrumental action? Reflecting on this event, I realized that, to a certain extent, I made the same assumption as the state authorities. The state's distinction between "sham" and "genuine" marriages derives from the assumption that interest and emotions are separate domains of social life that are not and should not be in contact with each other. Indeed, migration authorities establish the authenticity of a marriage by assessing the existence of emotions, in particular love, and the absence of other "ulterior motives"

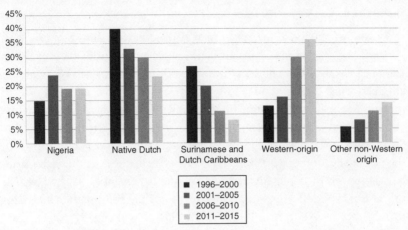

FIGURE 5.1. Marriages and registered partnerships of Nigerians in Amsterdam according to partner's ethnic origin. *Source*: Unpublished Onderzoek Informatie en Statistiek data; see table 5.1.

TABLE 5.1. Marriages and registered partnerships of Nigerians in Amsterdam according to partner's ethnic origin

Period			Origin of partner		
	Nigeria	Native Dutch	Surinamese and Dutch Caribbeans	Western origin	Other non-Western origin
1996–2000	15%	40%	27%	13%	5%
2001–2005	24%	33%	20%	16%	8%
2006–2010	19%	30%	11%	30%	11%
2011–2015	19%	23%	8%	36%	14%

Note: Total marriages 1996–2015 = 247.

Source: Unpublished Onderzoek Informatie en Statistiek data.

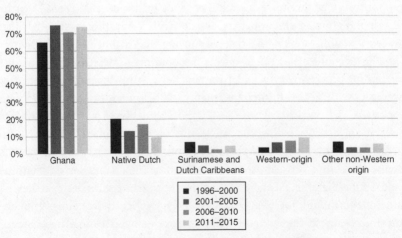

FIGURE 5.2. Marriages and registered partnerships of Ghanaians in Amsterdam according to partner's ethnic origin. *Source*: Unpublished Onderzoek Informatie en Statistiek data; see table 5.2.

TABLE 5.2. Marriages and registered partnerships of Ghanaians in Amsterdam according to partner's ethnic origin

Period			Origin of partner		
	Ghana	Native Dutch	Surinamese and Dutch Caribbeans	Western origin	Other non-Western origin
1996–2000	65%	20%	6%	3%	6%
2001–2005	75%	13%	4%	6%	3%
2006–2010	71%	17%	2%	7%	3%
2011–2015	74%	9%	4%	9%	5%

Note: Total marriages 1996–2015 = 502.

Source: Unpublished Onderzoek Informatie en Statistiek data.

(Eggebø 2013; De Hart 2017a; D'Aoust 2013). Often, scholars and migrant support organizations have unwillingly reproduced the assumption behind the categorization of marriages as sham or genuine, including those who are critical of the exclusionary effects of such categorizations. They do so, for example, when they criticize how the fight against marriages of convenience has exclusionary consequences for "real" couples and "loving" partners.

In this final chapter, I focus on the marriages of unauthorized West African migrant men with women from Europe's periphery. I examine the various forms of exchange that take place in these marriages and investigate the reasons for the shift in the marital practices of West African migrant men. Certainly, changes in the legal framework have made marriage with an EU citizen a much easier and faster way for unauthorized male migrants to legalize their status than marrying a national citizen. This condition is important but not sufficient to explain why these marriages are particularly with women from Europe's periphery and not just any EU citizen. The motives of West African migrant men are not only to get legalized through marriage. Aware that legalization on the grounds of marriage will effectively make them dependent on their wives, they seek alternatives to build a future in which they will not be subordinate to their wives. Recall the advice of Jack's friends to avoid marriage with Judith because Surinamese women are "very troublesome," and also Judith's reaction that Surinamese women are not "submissive" as some Ghanaian men would like (chapter 4). As is well documented in the literature (Menjívar and Salcido 2002; Liversage 2013; Brettell 2017), legalization through marriage enhances the vulnerability of the migrant spouses by making them dependent on their spouses who petitioned for their residence permit. Specifically for men, their dependency on their wives is experienced as an undermining of their authority and a compromise in their ability to fulfill ideals of masculinity, a condition that eventually makes them "unhappy husbands" (Charsley 2005; Hoogenraad 2021; Gallo 2006). In marriages with women from Europe's periphery, who are also migrants and in a similar socioeconomic position in the Netherlands, legally precarious West African men benefit from their wives' civic resources, but they can also assist them in ways that the women value. In such a manner, West African migrant men try to deal with the power inequalities in marriage that spouses' differentiated legal status often generates.

Because these marriages provide relatively easy access to legalization for migrants, they are usually suspected by immigration authorities to be shams. Examining all the different type of resources (e.g., money, emotions, sexual pleasure, civic status) that are exchanged between spouses in these marriages, I do not simply aim to show the entwinement of emotions and interest and the falseness of the sham-genuine distinction—this has been well established by other scholars studying intimate relations generally (Zelizer 2005; Medick and Sabean 1984; Thomas and Cole 2009) and cross-border marriages specifically (Fernandez 2013; Maskens 2015; Constable 2003; Piot 2019; Salcedo Robledo 2011). Instead, the chapter examines the implications of such dichotomy, between interest and love, for the exchanges that take place in the context of marriage and, as a result, the effects on the relationship between two spouses. Contrary to immigration authorities that police cross-border marriages in the name of protecting women (De Hart 2022; Bonjour and De Hart 2013; Carver 2016), the ethnographic material in this chapter shows that the state-imposed romantic love ideal may undermine the bargaining power of women in marriage. Migration researchers risk neglecting these implications when they rely on the state categorization of cross-border marriages as either sham or genuine.

The State of Emotions: Romantic Love and the Marriage of Convenience

In the Netherlands, as in other European countries, the regulation of cross-border marriages became a key concern for the national politics of belonging. State authorities closely inspect cross-border marriages for two main reasons. First, cross-border marriages enable a significant number of foreigners to enter the national territory as "family migrants." Second, state authorities fear that cross-border marriages threaten the cultural reproduction of the nation and its social regeneration. By regulating cross-border marriages, and marriage more generally, the state attempts to define and produce the society it envisions (Moret, Andrikopoulos, and Dahinden 2021).

In that effort, state authorities differentiate between acceptable marriages that will result into "good families" and acceptable marriages that the state tries to prevent from taking place. The Dutch government has justified the introduction of more restrictive policies for cross-border marriages as measures to protect women and ensure gender equality (Bonjour and De Hart 2013; De Hart 2022).[5] All categories of unacceptable and undesirable marriages (e.g., sham, forced, arranged), framed by the state as bad for women, have a common opposite: the love-based marriage. The romantic love ideal has become the means for state authorities to control the gender dynamics in cross-border marriages and prevent undesirable outcomes—both for women and for society in general.

The Dutch state construes sham marriages as those marriages contracted with the "sole purpose" of enabling the migrant spouse to obtain a residence permit and often involve the monetary compensation of the citizen spouse (Immigratie en Naturalisatiedienst n.d.). A genuine marriage is understood as the opposite: a relationship based on and sustained by love.[6] The state categorization of genuine, love-based and sham, interest-based marriages is informed by a modernist ideal of romantic relations that Giddens has described as a "pure relationship." According to Giddens (1992), a pure relationship is a relation of equality and mutuality between two autonomous individuals. It is a relationship of emotional fulfillment in which what one offers to the other is not motivated by the expectation of something else in return. The ideal of marriage as a pure relationship is arguably the norm according to which cross-border marriages are assessed by European states (Wray 2015; Eggebø 2013).

The Marriage of Love and Interest

State's conception of love as a disinterested emotion is dominant across Europe precisely because it stems from a Christian ideal of love opposed to instrumentality. Nevertheless, such a conception of love is not universal and may differ from daily practices. It is important, therefore, for migration researchers and other scholars, to "approach love as an analytic problem rather than a universal category" (Thomas and Cole 2009, 3) and carefully treat the state's conception of love. Problematizing love implies that we pay close attention not only to what love means in particular settings but also to how love is expressed and demonstrated.

Ethnographic studies (Rebhun 1999; Cornwall 2002; Hunter 2010; Constable 2003) have documented how local conceptions of love encompass material interest and how interest may strengthen affection and desire instead of erasing them. In rural Madagascar, for example, the local concept of love, *fitiavina*, refers both to affective qualities and to acts of material support and care. Rural Malagasy express their love by sharing their resources and spending on their beloved ones (e.g., sharing food, buying clothes, paying school or medical fees). For example, "in male-female relationships, a man makes fitiavina through gifts to the woman, and the woman returns the favor of fitiavina by offering her sexual and domestic services, and labor" (Cole 2009, 117). But the teaching of Christian missionaries during the period of colonialism insisted on the separation of love and money and promoted a meaning of love that is selfishless and interestless. To some extent, this contributed to the emergence of a new understanding of love, as "clean *fitiavina*," which, at least normatively, is unrelated to material exchanges (Cole 2009). Similar transformations in the meaning of love have been observed elsewhere and usually are attributed to the spread of Christianity, the emergence of capitalism, and the influence of a globalized Western notion of romantic love (Hirsch and Wardlow 2006; Padilla et al. 2007). This does not mean that love has indeed become disengaged from material exchanges but rather that a new norm emerged that projects emotions and interest as "hostile worlds" (Zelizer 2005). Even in societies of Europe and the United States, where the romantic love discourse originates, love continues to be deeply entwined with material interest but in less explicit ways (Zelizer 2005; Illouz 2007).

Who Fears Love? Gender Inequality and Romantic Love

"A marriage of convenience is not as innocent as it may seem. Sometimes they claim victims, as they may involve people smuggling or human trafficking. This is why the government is taking preventive measures," declares the Immigration and Naturalization Service on its web page (Immigratie en Naturalisatiedienst n.d.). The fight against sham marriages and the policing of other marriages construed unacceptable (e.g., forced, arranged, polygamous) in the Netherlands and many European countries have been presented as measures to protect women (Block, 2021; Muller Myrdahl 2010; Carver 2016). In the Netherlands, marriages to Dutch women are more likely to be suspected by immigration authorities as sham than are marriages to Dutch men (De Hart 2003; Kulu-Glasgow, Smit, and Jennissen 2017).[7] To ensure that migrant men do not take advantage of women, immigration officers inspect the marriage motives and assess as genuine those marriages motivated by love. As Giddens (1992) associates the "pure relationship" with the "democratisation of private life," immigration authorities take for granted that the ideal of love marriage—the common opposite to all marriages classified as unacceptable by the state—protects the position of women and contributes to the establishment of gender equality.

Studies on the historical transformation of marriage, from a relationship pragmatically arranged to a relationship based on romantic love, show that love does not automatically entail gender equality (Collier 1997; Rebhun 1999). The transformation of the meaning of love toward a new normative definition that excludes interest and exchange did not liberate women and often resulted in them losing resources and becoming more dependent on men. However, despite these ambiguous outcomes, many women welcomed the ideals of romantic love and companionate marriage. For them, these ideals contribute to gender equity in marriage and less involvement of (extended) kin in their intimate lives. Quite often these expectations did not realize, and the romantic love ideal turned against the interest of women (Thomas and Cole 2009; Cole 2009; Smith 2009; Cornwall 2002; Kringelbach 2016).

To understand the complex dynamic of love in gender relations, it is important to consider the gendered aspects of the norms of love. There is no doubt that both men and women fall in love. But they are expected to express and demonstrate love differently. These culturally constructed differences are not only a matter of bodily expressions (e.g., kissing, display of affection). When love is demonstrated as care for the other, it often implies altruism, self-sacrifice, and suffering. Arguably, such manifestations of care are more central to norms of how women ought to express and demonstrate their love—with the exemplary case of maternal love, which to some degree informs women's love for other family members (Paxson 2007; Collier 1997). If love has different implications for men and women, the presence of it in a heterosexual marriage cannot by itself improve the position of women.

Gender Dynamics in Cross-Border Marriages

The literature on cross-border marriages has almost exclusively focused on marital relations between migrants and citizens whose ethnic origin was either the country's ethnic majority (Cole 2014b; Constable 2003) or the same as the migrant's ethnicity (Charsley 2013; Williams 2012). Although this body of literature has focused primarily on marriages between migrants and national citizens, and especially female migrants to citizen men, it has offered insights that can be particularly useful for the analysis of marriages in the Netherlands between West African male migrants and peripheral European women.

First, this literature points out that the legal dependency of the migrant partner on her (and rarely his) citizen partner restricts her freedom and makes her more vulnerable and exploitable in the marital relationship (Menjívar and Salcido 2002; Williams 2010; Charsley 2005; Brettell 2017; Liversage 2013). Second, the literature offers important insights about gender inequality and the tenacity of patriarchy in these marriages (Constable 2010; Liversage 2012; Salcido and Adelman 2004; Riaño 2011; Suksomboon 2011). However, we should take into account that, in most cross-border marriage studies, the marriage migrant is a woman whose subordinate position in marriage is amplified by her legal dependency on her citizen husband.[8] Studies on cross-border marriages in which the marriage migrant is the male spouse (Charsley 2005; Charsley and Liversage 2015; Gallo 2006; Partridge 2008; Hoogenraad 2021; Fleischer 2011) show that migrant men feel disempowered by their dependency on their wives. In his work on black male migrants in Germany who are legalized through marriages to white German women, Partridge (2008) builds on the concept of "street-level bureaucracy" (Lipsky 1980) by applying it to the discretion that German women have when they choose partners and essentially decide who will be granted legal residence and citizenship. Noncitizen men, in the dance clubs where Partridge conducted his fieldwork, hypersexualized their black bodies in the effort to seduce white German women who, as "street bureaucrats," could open the door to a residence permit (see also Fleischer 2011).[9]

In his autobiography, Ssuuna Golooba, for many years a Ugandan unauthorized migrant in Amsterdam, describes how he came to learn about the possibility of legalization through marriage and what other African male migrants advised him to do. One of them, Livingstone, warned of the downsides of marrying a "white woman":

> From my experience they want too much sex, but the worst thing is they will treat you like a baby in their houses with no freedom to do anything you want. She can even order you to let the dog out and after the dog makes his business you have to collect the dog shit in a plastic bag and not leave it on the streets. Surprisingly, a white woman can also tell you to sit in the back of the car while the little ugly dog sits on the front seat. They are not afraid of stating their own opinions, not like our African women . . . In Africa, women are supposed to respect their husbands, more than that, they are the ones entitled [sic] to do all the household chores and the like, but that does not seem to be the case in Europe. A white woman treats a man like a house helper: a man to do the laundry and cook—on top of marital obligations—and you will never feel like an African man. (Golooba 2016, 59–60)[10]

In Livingstone's advice, the subversion of gender roles in marriage, especially the downgrading of male authority and the husband's involvement in household activities, stems from a dynamic interplay of racial and civic inequality. The fact that migrant men depend on their wives for obtaining and extending a residence permit undermines the power that they wish for.

At Holy Blessings Church, the Ghanaian senior pastor addressed the same issue, emphasizing the legal aspect, in a Sunday sermon on the topic of fear:

> That was that woman that was married to a man and it was through that woman that the man got his stay permit. Every day the woman had this [the pastor imitated a feminine and authoritative voice]: "You! You got it! I will go to the police. I'm going to tell the police to send you back to Africa." And the man started shaking. One day the woman misbehaved like usual. The man told the woman off. He said, "Whatever you want to do, you can do it." And after the man had spoken to the woman, he went to the room and took his passport. He came and said, "I think you'll need this. Take it to the police" [the Surinamese woman who translates the preaching from English into Dutch starts laughing]. You know, she did not do anything! See! Why? The man confronted his fear! [Cheers from the congregation: "Amen," "Yeah!," "That's it."]

Civic inequality escalates, and often reverses, the power asymmetries of gender relations in the marriages that enable legally precarious African migrants to secure a residence permit in the Netherlands. The question that requires more scholarly attention, however, is how migrant spouses experience and negotiate their subordinate position in cross-border marriages and the strategies they employ to balance or overcome their unequal position. The answer to this question is complex, because there is no common way for all legally precarious African migrants to deal with these issues, and the practices are different for male and female migrants.

For female West African migrants, the subordinate position from their reliance on their husbands for papers is not experienced as an anomaly of marriage. Husbands are expected to provide for their wives and, in return, women offer them care, love, and sex. In Amsterdam, the African migrant women who shared their views with me did not challenge the dominant position of men in marital relations and considered the husband's responsibility to ensure the legal status of his wife an additional task to his role as provider. Although they realized that migrant women who get their papers through marriage are more dependent on their husbands than others, they saw this form of dependency as an extension of the already-existing gender inequality in marriage. Furthermore, some African migrant women who shared stereotypical ideas similar to Livingstone's concerning (Western) Europeans saw marriage to a white Dutch man positively, expecting that Dutch men are more egalitarian husbands (for similar imaginaries in other migration settings, see

Riaño 2015; Cole 2014a). "I'm done with African men!" a Nigerian woman who was searching for a husband on dating websites told me. "Now I look only for Dutch men. A Dutch treats you with respect and won't make my life a mess!"

In contrast, for most African male migrants, the reliance on their wives for papers placed them in a subordinate position in marriage and did not allow them to symbolically articulate the role of provider. This was experienced as a stressful and frustrating situation which went against their ideas about marriage and masculinity (Smith 2017; Cornwall 2002). In the hope of avoiding a marital relationship in which they could not assert authority because of their legal status, many West African migrant men started looking for spouses who, on the one hand, hold the necessary civic resources, namely EU citizenship, and, on the other hand, are in a more or less similar position to them as economic migrants.[11] Migrant women from Europe's periphery are considered ideal marriage partners not only because they are EU citizens, but as working-class migrants, they are in a less privileged position than other European women in the Netherlands (e.g., German, Belgian, Scandinavian).[12] Many times African men, despite their lack of legality, had access to other resources that they could share on a more equal basis with their partners, and in that way they could achieve a more balanced marital relationship. For example, West African migrants have access to transnational networks, which can be useful for their partners to migrate to and find jobs in Western Europe. One such story follows:

> Maria, a Greek woman, and Sunny, a Nigerian man, met in Greece, married and moved to Amsterdam. In recent years their marriage had had ups and downs. In one of our chats, we discussed the recent divorce of Natasha, another Greek woman in the Netherlands, from Segun, her Nigerian husband. Maria supported the decision of Natasha, who was a good friend. In front of Sunny, Maria said that Natasha was facing the same problems as Maria faced with Sunny, which she collectively called "the huge cultural gap between us." Maria said that Natasha was annoyed with Segun because he was saving and sending all his money to his family in Nigeria and that their life in the Netherlands was very miserable. They didn't go out for a drink, they didn't go on vacation together. Sunny was listening to Maria and from his facial expression I could see that he had objections. When Maria finished, Sunny said in a derogatory tone that Natasha "is a woman who likes clubbing." Maria did not like Sunny's comment and asked him how he could comment about Natasha's character without even knowing her well. Then Sunny confronted Maria with a question that took me aback: "If Natasha would not marry him, would she be here [in the Netherlands]? Would she have this job?" Although Natasha

was very young and had only a high school diploma, she found a well-paid job in an international company in Amsterdam with the referral of Segun's brother's wife. "What would Natasha do in Greece now?" Sunny wondered. "If Natasha wouldn't marry Segun, would she be in the Netherlands? And would her other two sisters follow her here?"[13]

Sunny blamed Natasha for being unappreciative of her and her sisters' mobility in the Netherlands that, according to Sunny, was achieved due to her marriage to Segun. These concerns were often at stake in the marriages of African migrants with peripheral Europeans. Women from Europe's periphery assisted their African male partners with their residence permits, and African migrants helped their partners in other ways. In the following ethnographic case study, these forms of exchange appear more clearly.

"If He Can Find Her a Job, Then She Might Do It without Money"

In one of my visits to Christina (Greek) and John (Nigerian) in December 2010, I mentioned to Christina the failed attempt of a migrant colleague, at the fast-food restaurant where I worked, to get papers through marriage to a Surinamese woman in exchange for €15,000. When John joined us in the living room, Christina asked me to repeat the story. While she often tried to speak in Greek with him, to help him to improve his language skills, this time she asked me to narrate the story in English because she wanted John to fully understand it.

When I finished, John said, "Fifteen thousand is too much."

"He didn't have an alternative," I said.

"Why doesn't he go to Poland to marry one or to Slovakia? There it will cost four thousand to six thousand. I have many friends who did it!"

I asked John to elaborate. He said that my colleague should go to Poland, book a room in a hotel, and go out clubbing. He should flirt with women, pay for their drinks, and talk to them nicely. If a woman responded, he could explain his situation and ask her for help. He could offer her around €4,000. He should propose to the Polish woman, bring her to Amsterdam, and offer her free accommodation and help finding a job. "And if he can find her a job, then she might do it without money!" John laughed.

John was not the only person of his family in Europe. He had one brother in Greece, one brother in Spain, and another in the United Kingdom. He and his brother in the United Kingdom had residence permits on the basis of marriage to an EU citizen (both Greeks). His brother in Spain was unauthorized, and his brother in Greece had been legalized in an amnesty program.

When I visited Greece during Easter 2011, I met John's brother, Jim, and we went together to his Pentecostal church. Jim was the oldest brother, in his early forties. He was married to a Nigerian woman who was living in the United Kingdom and worked as a nurse in a hospital. After the service, Jim introduced me to Camelia, a young woman in her late twenties from Romania whom he presented as his sister. We left the church and went to Jim's apartment, where we spent the rest of our day. From what they told me, Camelia and Jim met on the internet, and after they had been chatting for a long time, Camelia decided to come and meet Jim in person.

Later in the evening, Camelia told me that she was looking for a job, preferably in Western Europe. Jim asked if I could help her find a job in the Netherlands. I explained to her that Romanian citizens needed a work permit in the Netherlands due to the transitional period requirements after Romania joined the European Union. She was aware of that but seemed very interested in finding ways to overcome that legal barrier. For the time being, Camelia asked Jim to help her find a summer job on a Greek island. Greece did not apply the same restrictions to Romanians as the Netherlands did, so she could enjoy her right of free movement, settlement, and employment in Greece as a full European citizen.

A few months later, when I returned to the Netherlands, I learned from Christina that Dennis, the brother of Jim and John who lived in Spain, had moved to Amsterdam. To my great surprise, Dennis had married Camelia, who had also moved to Amsterdam. "Well, it's for papers," Christina commented as she was giving me the news. Camelia hoped that Dennis and his brother John would manage to find a decent job for her in Amsterdam. To her disappointment, however, the legal barriers due to her Romanian citizenship did not allow her to work. In the meanwhile, Camelia got pregnant by Dennis. So their relationship was not only on paper and at least involved sexual relations. Dennis and John, unable to find a job for her in the Netherlands, mobilized their transnational networks. Their brother Ugo, who lived in the United Kingdom with his Greek wife, offered to help Camelia. Ugo worked as a supervisor in a cleaning company and made the necessary arrangements to hire Camelia as a cleaner on an undeclared basis. Camelia accepted the job offer and started working there. However, she was very disappointed with this job and threatened to divorce Dennis. As I learned from John and Christina, Camelia accused Dennis of not finding her a good job while his brother John had found a good office job for his Greek wife. Camelia regretted having left Romania and asked Dennis to relocate with her to her hometown. Dennis considered this possibility because his legal status was tied to his marriage with Camelia. John and other friends strongly advised Dennis not to go to

Romania. Nevertheless, Camelia insisted that she wanted to give birth there so her mother could help her. Dennis was left with no choice than to follow Camelia to Romania, where, after quite a long period, he managed to get a Romanian residence permit. A few years later, Dennis, Camelia, and their child moved to the United Kingdom, where they still live together.

Although Camelia held the scarce civic resources required for Dennis's legalization, she relied on her husband and his connections to fulfill her own migratory aspirations in Western Europe. Their marriage was mutually benefi-cial, and each spouse contributed to the other. The multiple forms of exchange t_king place in their marriage created a reciprocal dependency between the spouses. There are similar reciprocal dependencies in other binational cou-ples in which the African migrant men could be legalized or maintain their residence status through marriage and their European wives could benefit from their husbands' networks and resources. It is important to stress that the resources African migrant men had at their disposal likely appeal only to women with a low socioeconomic position in Dutch society, such as many peripheral European migrants.

In the relationship of Dennis and Camelia, the wishes and preferences of Camelia, a migrant herself, were taken seriously by Dennis. Would Dennis show the same commitment to satisfy Camelia if his own personal gains were not at risk and if Camelia's assistance for his legalization was motivated only by (romantic) love? The answer to this question can only be hypothetical. But the next case is about a Greek Nigerian couple for whom the woman's assis-tance to her husband is driven by the romantic love ideal that she embraces. How does the ideal of companionate marriage impact the flow of resources between spouses, and how do they understand these transfers? What are the consequences of the separation of love and interest for the relation between the man and the woman in this marriage? In the following section, I delve into the life story of a Greek Nigerian couple and examine more in depth the process of valorization of the various resources exchanged in their marriage, such as money, legality, emotions, and sexual pleasure, and how the understanding that interest and love are separate has affected gender dynamics in their marriage.

Emotions, Interest, and Sex in the Marital
Life of a Greek Nigerian Couple

In December 2011, I met Frank and Kyriaki in the house of Chima and Ka-terina, another Greek Nigerian couple, with whom they shared an apartment. Frank and Chima are Nigerian Igbo men, and both had lived in Greece be-fore they came to Amsterdam. Chima was the first to marry a Greek woman,

Katerina, and move with her to the Netherlands. Frank followed him in February 2011 with his Greek wife, Kyriaki. Long before I met Kyriaki and Frank in person, I had heard about them. Katerina, for example, gossiped that Frank married Kyriaki "for his papers" and Kyriaki was taking advantage of him. According to Katerina, after Kyriaki married Frank, she stopped working and expected Frank to assume the role of breadwinner and take care of all the household costs.

My first impression of Kyriaki was not positive. In our first meeting, when I said I was doing research on West African men and their relationships with European women, her reaction shocked me. Kyriaki talked in a highly derogatory and dismissive way not only about her husband but about West African migrant men in general:

> They [West African migrant men] leave from hunger, thirst, dirt, and miserable life. You give them your kindness, you take them out to the light to see how normal people live, and in the end they fuck you up psychologically. Well, fuck off in the end. And he is not only one. Apostolos, it's a great percentage of them!

Although Kyriaki had quite an interesting life, she seemed a difficult person to deal with, and I initially decided not to involve her in my research. However, as my research was going on in the Bijlmer, Kyriaki approached me on her own and asked to share her life story. From 2012 until 2015 we had a number of interviews focusing on her life and marriage to Frank. I also recorded the conversations we had on a friendly level about ongoing developments in her relationship with Frank and especially their three attempts to divorce. Additionally, Kyriaki shared her marriage diary in which she wrote in Greek about her experiences and feelings, especially in the first period of her marriage with Frank. In this diary, Frank also wrote a few entries in English. Although I talked more with Kyriaki than with Frank, I gained the appreciation and trust of both of them to the extent that they wanted me to be present and help with translations in their meetings with lawyers regarding their divorce.

UNDOCUMENTED LIVES ON THE DANCE FLOOR

Frank was born in 1980 in Nigeria to a middle-income family. In 2004, the year of the Summer Olympic Games in Athens, he migrated to Greece with the tourist visa of a look-alike Nigerian. In the first six months of his stay, he lived in Athens, where he worked as a street vendor of pirate CDs, as the vast majority of Nigerian migrants earned their living in the city at that time (Andrikopoulos 2017, 226–30; see also Andrikopoulos 2013, 76–78). His good friend Chima worked in a small factory in Thessaloniki and helped Frank get a job in the same factory. Using the papers of another African migrant, Frank relocated and started working there.

As Kyriaki and Katerina told me, both Chima and Frank were attractive and particularly successful with women. Chima was open about his legal status to the women he flirted with and asked every woman he dated to marry him to get a residence permit. Frank was less direct with women and felt uncomfortable telling them about his legal status. He flirted with Greek women in Club Mo, which played rhythm and blues and was a hot spot for Nigerian men in Thessaloniki. On an evening in January 2007, Frank saw a blonde, overweight Greek woman dancing alone. He approached and danced with her. She was Kyriaki.

Kyriaki was one year younger than Frank (1981). She was born in Thessaloniki to a very poor family. She referred to her parents as irresponsible persons, "not worthy of having kids." At the age of seven, her parents went to prison. Guardianship of Kyriaki and her two brothers was undertaken by her aunt, on her father's side, and her aunt's husband. Her aunt and uncle were also poor and earned their living working as cleaners and street vendors. They already had thirteen children, and together with Kyriaki and her brothers had sixteen children to take care of.

When Kyriaki was born, her parents neglected to declare her birth in the state's records, which created many problems in Kyriaki's life. When her school requested that her parents submit her birth certificate, Kyriaki recalled, her parents stopped sending her to school. As an illiterate person who had been schooled for only two years, Kyriaki did not know how to resolve the problem of her bureaucratic nonexistence even when she became an adult. She was a truly undocumented person (in contrast to Frank, who at least used the papers of other migrants). Without papers, she could work only in jobs that did not require her to register, such as cleaner, assistant in a fast-food restaurant, and *consommatrice* (women paid to keep men company in bars).[14] At the age of twenty-five, her first boyfriend helped her to sort out the issue of her papers and finally get an ID and passport. He also helped her register in a second-chance school, where she learned how to write.

When her relationship with this boyfriend ended, she traveled for first time with her new passport to Germany, where her cousin lived. When she came back, she went out clubbing with her female friends, one of whom was interested in dating black men and so led them to Club Mo. Kyriaki went on the dance floor and started dancing alone. She remembered that some men approached and danced with her. Her attention, however, was captured by a guy who was "discretely macho," did not touch her body, and made her feel comfortable dancing with him. At the end of the night, after hours of dancing, he said his name, Frank, and asked for her name and number.

LOVE IS IN THE AIR

Frank started calling Kyriaki and in his poor Greek asked questions about her daily life: whether and what she had eaten, how well she had slept. She liked that Frank was showing interest in her and agreed to meet him again. They dated a few times, and Kyriaki appreciated that Frank did not push her to have sex. One day she invited Frank to her apartment. Frank went to her place and brought a bottle of wine and marijuana. After they smoked a joint and drank the wine, Kyriaki said she had back pain. Frank offered to give her a massage and removed her clothes. Kyriaki recalled:

> Later he said to me that the first time we had sex, he wanted to impress me. So, he tried to put all his mastery to really impress me. He said that he wanted to fuck me very rough. Not because he wanted me to feel pain. He wanted me to really enjoy it and stay with him. And he did it!

They had sex regularly. Frank considered Kyriaki his girlfriend, but Kyriaki was not sure whether she wanted to go further. After a few months, when Frank started staying at Kyriaki's place regularly, Kyriaki felt things had become serious too quickly and decided to end their relationship, but Frank said he loved her. Kyriaki became furious. Greek language has two words for love, *agapi* and *erotas*—these refer to two different emotions but are both translated into English as "love." *Agapi* refers to an emotion that does not only exist between partners but can be felt in other settings as well (e.g., toward your parents or very good friends); it develops gradually and is expressed in different ways as care and dedication. *Erotas* exists only between lovers. It is a strong attraction expressed through sexual intercourse. *Erotas* can also refer to the act of sex (e.g., to make love, *kano erota*). As Kyriaki explained, although *erotas* or passionate love and *agapi* or love are different emotions, they are interrelated and *agapi* in a couple can be complete only with *erotas*:

> So, I said to him, "That's it. End. I cannot anymore. I feel drowned. How else to explain it." And he responded, "But why, my baby? I want you! I love you [*s'agapo*]!" "When did you have time to love me [*na m'agapiseis*]? Fuck off." Well, yes! Is that possible? *Erotas* and *agapi* are different feelings. You can't say, *S'agapo* to someone in just three months. I can't believe that. *Agapi* comes when certain things happen that bond two people. We must differentiate these two. *Erotas* is a different thing than *agapi*. *Erotas* will fade away at some point but *agapi* will stay. So, *agapi* cannot come at first sight like *erotas*. They are two

different things. With *erotas* you revive, you do this, that, you feel good, you fly. [But] in reality its *agapi* and how the other will stand next to you, how he will talk to you [that matters] . . . As long as you are young, *erotas* is necessary. Certainly. Without *erotas*, *agapi* cannot be complete.

Frank and Kyriaki stayed apart for a while, but at Frank's insistence they soon reconnected. As they spent most of their time together, Frank suggested Kyriaki move in with him. In the beginning, Kyriaki was not enthusiastic, but she decided to give it a try because it would be cheaper for her—and she was indeed spending most of her time with him. Now, however, Kyriaki has a different understanding of Frank's motives:

He wanted to show me his good side until I decide to stay with him. And then he thought that little by little marriage would come closer. Because that's the issue. They [African men] try to convince their girlfriend to stay with them, so she will get used to them and will be easier convinced. Because they think, "If we spend the whole day and night together, I will fuck her like crazy, I will treat her nicely, I will take her with me to my friends, so at some point I will convince her." And this is exactly what Frank did with me.

With Frank and Kyriaki, as with most couples, sex played quite a significant role in their relationship. Especially during the early days of their relationship, Kyriaki described their sex life as very intense. She believed her pleasure in having sex with Frank affected many of her important decisions about their relationship, and that Frank manipulated this dynamic: "He had understood my weakness in sex. He felt that whatever bullshit he does, but really whatever, I would forget it after a good fuck. And indeed that worked."

JUST FOR YOUR INTEREST?

Kyriaki and Frank moved to their own small apartment in Thessaloniki and started to share life as a couple. Most of their free time was spent having sex, which Kyriaki said lasted hours, or going clubbing and dancing. A few months after they moved in together, Frank told Kyriaki that the papers he used would expire, and he had to find a way to get new ones. He presented two possibilities. The first would require him to leave from Greece for a couple of months and then return with someone else's papers. The other was to marry Kyriaki and on that basis obtain a residency permit in his own name. Kyriaki did not feel ready to marry him, but she did not want him to get his papers through the first possibility because she would have to stay alone for a couple of months and it would not be a permanent solution. After serious consideration, she decided to marry him.

Kyriaki's friends advised her to reconsider and warned her that Frank was with her only for the sake of the papers. Kyriaki felt confused by his motivations and thus confronted him with the following proposal:

> I said to him before we marry: "Frank, if you want to marry me just for your papers, because I know how it is, I promise you that I will marry you and we will do your papers under an agreement: If there is love between us, we continue with our lives. But if there is no love and you marry me just for your interest, . . . we keep the marriage, each of us continues his and her life and in exchange I want you to help me with the fees of my vocational school." How much was it that time? Was it €2,000? So, each of us would give €1,000. This is what I asked him in exchange. And he insisted, "No, I love you!"

Kyriaki's understanding of love and marriage was strikingly similar to the pure relationship ideal. Once she was assured that her relationship with Frank was based on love, she could not think of any material exchange taking place between them. She could have claimed a payment only if it were not a love relationship. It is noteworthy, though, that love in marriage would erase only Kyriaki's material benefits; Frank could get a marriage-based residence permit either by paying Kyriaki or by loving her. Frank opted for the cheaper choice.

Frank and Kyriaki went to a lawyer in Athens to give them legal advice regarding their marriage and Frank's legalization:

> The first question the lawyer asked me as a Greek woman was: "So, why do you marry him? For money? Does he pay you or it's because of love?" And I replied, "Love and only love" . . . Because she [the lawyer] wanted to know how to speak to us. She wanted to know if it's a professional agreement so in case something goes wrong between us how we deal with it. And if it was because of love, how much would you do for this love?

A marriage motivated by romantic love meant that Kyriaki would not materially benefit from it and that she would have to do the best she could for her partner. The female lawyer asked Kyriaki how much she loved Frank so as to know how much she was prepared to do for him. According to cultural norms in Greece, the love of a woman for her family is proven not just with the denial of personal interest but ultimately by self-sacrifice and suffering.[15] Love (*agapi*), as Paxson (2007, 128) observed in reference to maternal love in Greece, "makes suffering a virtue." The lawyer explained to Kyriaki that because love was the motivation for their marriage, the best option for Frank, and the most difficult for Kyriaki, was to marry in Nigeria and apply together for a visa at the Greek embassy there. Kyriaki found this plan very complicated and started crying in the lawyer's office. However, she loved Frank and was committed to helping him get his papers. In January 2009, almost after a year together, Frank and Kyriaki went to Nigeria to marry and arrange Frank's legal admission to Greece.

TRAVELING TO NIGERIA TO MARRY

Frank borrowed the passport of a look-alike Nigerian and traveled with Kyriaki to Lagos. Exiting Europe with someone else's passport is much easier and less stressful than entering, Frank said. Kyriaki stayed in Nigeria for about a month; Frank stayed two. Kyriaki, and to a lesser extent Frank, kept a detailed description of their trip and their wedding in their marriage diary.

08.01.09

I am on the plane. I drink wine and eat nuts. My baby watches a movie and relaxes and I enjoy the moment because it is unique. I feel wonderful. I am curious to see Nigeria because it's the place where I'll marry the one I want very very very much . . . Frank is a very nice boy, at least so far. He takes care for me. He loves me. He behaves tenderly and now that he's not stressed he is such a sweetie.

They arrived in Lagos and stayed in a hotel. Kyriaki wanted to meet Frank's family, but Frank told her his family lived far from Lagos, and he did not even tell them that he was around because they would expect gifts from him and money. In their diary, you can find entries for the first few days like the following:

09.01.09

We woke up in the morning around 9 and we made love. It was very beautiful because Frank was very loving . . .

Nevertheless, as the day of their marriage approached, Kyriaki had panic attacks:

12.01.09

Then I felt sad, depressed. I thought everything was wrong. For a long time I didn't talk at all. When we went to our room something happened to me and I cried for quite some time. I couldn't stop. My baby did everything for me to feel better but it was impossible. When I felt better he asked me what happened and I explained that I miss my friends and Greece. He said that I should make a phone call to feel better. And I said that I already feel better just because I see him. And it was true. Then we played a little bit and around 8 we went to the lobby.

A few days later, Kyriaki and Frank married:

15.01.09

> Thursday. It's a weird day but also a very happy day. It's the day of our wed-
> ding. We woke up in the morning, had coffee and then his friend and our
> best man came and brought him a suit. It was the first time I saw him in suit.
> I can only say one word: Oh, fuck. He looks great. When I dressed up, he saw
> me, looked at me and said how beautiful I am and hugged me. He was really
> very, very, very sweet. Then we went to City Hall, which was, let's say, OK. We
> waited and finished some paperwork. Then our wedding took place, which I
> didn't really understand. Then we took pictures and left. Frank had something
> to do. Then we bought food and cigarettes and went to our hotel room and ate.
> Then I gave him a nice gift [Kyriaki explained to me later that *gift* referred to
> oral sex]. Then my baby wanted to sleep.

Now in possession of a marriage certificate, they traveled to Abuja, where they
applied for Frank's visa. They were afraid to say that they had met in Greece
since Frank's presence there was unauthorized. They said, as other couples I
interviewed did, that they met online and that Kyriaki met him for the first
time in person in Nigeria. Kyriaki returned to Greece and sent to Nigeria some
additional documents that needed to accompany the application. Almost a
month later, Frank returned to Greece and entered the country legally as
Kyriaki's husband.

That same year Kyriaki got pregnant and gave birth to Frank's daughter. In a
Greek setting, the first child is usually named after the grandparent from the fa-
ther's side. Nevertheless, they agreed to name her Danai, after Kyriaki's mother.
One of Frank's few entries in their marriage diary, after the birth of their child:

> I love my wife forever if she understands me and hear what I say. I will like to
> stay with my family until death comes. I will love my family and take care of
> them because is the only thing that I have. I will like my family to be together
> and have a better life and a good living. My family is all I have and I want to
> be proud of them. All I have is for my family and all they have is for me. I will
> like my family to be happy all the time and I pray that God will help us. All I
> wish my family is one love, one heart, and other things will be fine. I believe
> that one love can keep us together.[16]

The birth of their daughter was an important change in their relationship and
a new responsibility. With the onset of the Greek crisis, Frank and Kyriaki
could not earn enough to support their household and their daughter's upbringing. In February 2011, when Danai was just seven months old, Frank
and Kyriaki relocated to Amsterdam, where Chima and Katerina had already
migrated. Despite the harsh Dutch regulations for family migrants, Frank did

not face any problems in relocating to the Netherlands. He was a husband of an EU citizen who had exercised her right of free mobility and that right automatically extended to him.

FIRST YEAR IN AMSTERDAM, FIRST ATTEMPT TO DIVORCE

Kyriaki and Frank rented a room in Chima and Katerina's house. Although Frank's legal status was dependent on Kyriaki both in Greece and in the Netherlands, he had more autonomy in the Netherlands, where he could communicate in English and had the support of his social networks. With Chima's referral, Frank got a decently paid full-time job at the factory where Chima worked. Kyriaki's situation in the Netherlands, however, changed dramatically, and the reliance on her husband and his networks grew considerably. Frank's friends tried to help Kyriaki find a job, which was very difficult because she could speak only Greek. Finally, with the assistance of a Nigerian migrant's Greek wife, Kyriaki found a poorly paid job in a company owned by a Greek and worked as a cleaner in the houses of two Greek families.

In the first year of their stay in Amsterdam, Kyriaki observed many changes in Frank and became certain that he was not faithful. Frank opened a Facebook account in which he did not add any information about his wife and even declined Kyriaki's friend request. Kyriaki noticed that he talked too often on the phone with women whom he would simply present to her as his "sisters." Kyriaki was also disappointed in Frank because he did not spend as much time with her as he had done in Greece and preferred to hang out with Chima and other Nigerian friends. In addition, Frank was secretive about his earnings and, according to Kyriaki, contributed minimally to their daughter's upbringing and household costs. For all these reasons, Kyriaki decided to divorce Frank. She warned him about her thoughts. Frank responded that if they divorced, Kyriaki would be all alone and have to pay all the bills herself.

Frank had not taken Kyriaki's warning seriously until the day he received a letter from her lawyer. The letter contained information about Kyriaki's actions, her request to maintain full custody of Danai, and a proposal of €500 monthly alimony, calculated on the basis of Frank's income. Frank's reaction was to say that his income was not as high as the letter calculated. Kyriaki was furious:

> I said, "I'm sorry, you receive this letter, you see what I request, I ask you to see the kid every second weekend and your only comment is about money?" I have been with Frank for four years and I've realized that he is interested only

in two things: pussy and money. He doesn't want to run out of these two. If he
has these two, he's OK.

After a period of tension, during which sex was never absent, Frank and
Kyriaki discussed their marriage and what had gone wrong. Kyriaki proposed
withdrawing her divorce request on three conditions: Frank should contribute more money for Danai's upbringing and household costs; he should take
Kyriaki out more often; and he had to consistently pay more attention to
Kyriaki. Frank accepted. But in June 2012, Kyriaki told me she had lied to Frank
about withdrawing the divorce request; she had only put it on hold because
she wanted to see whether Frank would change. Kyriaki said he changed his
behavior but only for a few weeks.

In October 2012, Kyriaki shared with me another new negative change
in her relationship with Frank: although they had never stopped having sex,
Kyriaki's pleasure had been gradually disappearing:

> Well, it's different when you're used to nice situations in which your man lasts
> and does this and that. And it's different that you reach the point that he's so
> lazy and feels bored to move and expects you to fuck him until he finishes . . .
> Imagine that you have a woman who is used to this and that, and one two
> hours sex, etc. Forget the one, two hours. It's not necessary. We have been
> growing up and pleasure [idoni] can come in five minutes . . . What's the issue?
> It's a very bad thing when someone approaches you sexually only because he
> wants to empty his balls.

The sexual gift changed direction one more time.[17] In the beginning of their
relationship, Frank provided sexual pleasure and "put all his mastery to really
impress" Kyriaki to the extent of her forgiving everything he did "after a good
fuck." But now Frank would return home late at night and wake Kyriaki to
have sex. "Does he ask me how I can sleep after that?" Kyriaki asked frustrated.

Despite the disappearance of sexual pleasure for Kyriaki and Frank's re-
sumption of former behavior, Kyriaki decided to stay with him and asked her
lawyer to withdraw the divorce request. Her first decision to divorce Frank
was based on emotion. But when she started making concrete plans about
living without him, she realized it would be difficult to manage:

> It is not in my benefit to change country. In general, it is not in my benefit to
> stay alone. Things should be more mature. The kid is growing up and is stick-
> ing to her father little by little. And in general until I find a better job with
> higher salary, until I learn better the language, both English and Dutch, I need
> Frank next to me. Especially for the kid.

After reconsidering her divorce decision, Kyriaki considered her own respon-sibility in how her marriage had unfolded. She approached Frank and asked him what he wanted her to change for their marriage to be revived. Frank said that after her pregnancy she let herself go and asked her to take care of herself again. Kyriaki agreed. Frank also said that he wanted to decrease his contribution to household costs, which was €160 per month. Earlier, Kyriaki had proposed increasing it to €200; Frank's request to decrease it crossed the line. She became so angry that she decided he was not worth another chance. She made an appointment with her lawyer and they went together to see her.

On the way, in the metro, Frank and Kyriaki had a very heated discussion:

> I said to him, "You never wanted to admit that I married you mainly to help you because I know how it is to live without papers" . . . And he is such a selfish person who did not want to admit that. Because when I said that, he turned to me and said, "I don't want to hear that again. You married me only because you loved me." And I said, "No, Frank! If it was only because of love, I would not marry you but we would simply stay together. Love is not recognized with marriage but in the everyday life of a couple."

The lawyer asked Frank whether he wanted the divorce. Frank insisted that he did not want it. The lawyer explained that a divorce would not affect his legal status as he could already qualify for an indefinite residence permit. She advised him to consult another lawyer. According to Kyriaki, this changed Frank's strong reluctance to divorce. After visiting the lawyer, Frank went out alone and Kyriaki returned home. Frank came back late at night with a hickey on his neck.

In December 2012, Kyriaki told me she had finally made up her mind. She decided not to divorce him because it would be good for Danai to grow up with two parents. She also announced her plan to go on vacation in Greece. She said she needed to go to Greece, especially after her marriage crisis. I expected she wanted to see her friends and relax after the stressful period she had been through. To my great surprise, she wanted to see how the financial crisis was unfolding. It would help her appreciate better what she had achieved with her husband in the Netherlands, she said. When she went to Greece, I happened to be there too. We met in Thessaloniki and went out for coffee. Kyriaki did not miss a chance to show off that she was a migrant. "I want a Greek coffee. In the country where I live, I don't drink Greek coffee," she said to a waitress, inviting her to ask questions that she then answered with pride. I asked Kyriaki how she found Greece. She was disappointed. But, again, not for the reasons I expected: "Well, I was expecting it quite worse after all I hear on TV. People complain for poverty. But excuse me. I lived in poverty and know how it is and it is not like this!"

"THE BEST *KADOORTJE* OF MY LIFE! BABY *MOU*, I LOVE YOU"

In August 2015, Kyriaki organized a party to celebrate her thirty-fourth birthday. About fifteen friends and colleagues joined her in her small one-room apartment in the Bijlmer. When I arrived, almost all her guests were there: a Greek man with his Spanish girlfriend, a Polish woman with her Nigerian husband, a middle-aged Polish woman who had been a migrant in Greece and spoke Greek fluently and her daughter, two Surinamese neighbors, three of Frank's Nigerian male friends, and a few of Kyriaki's female Greek friends, most of whom were married to African men. Frank had just returned from work and immediately took charge of the party's music. He played mostly Afrobeats and asked us whether we had any preferences, especially for Greek or Polish music hits.

The tiny apartment was overcrowded with people. I went outside to the balcony and chatted with Olga, a Greek woman who had recently come to the Netherlands. My first meeting with her was a couple of months earlier in a café, where she was with Kyriaki. At the time, Olga shared her concerns with Kyriaki about the marriage proposal she received from her Nigerian boyfriend. She told Kyriaki it was unclear whether her boyfriend wanted to marry her for the papers or because he loved her: "I would really rather he say, 'I want you for my papers.' Then we would make an arrangement and I would do it. The situation would be clear and I wouldn't have all these doubts." Olga was confused because, on the one hand, she could see that her boyfriend would clearly benefit from their marriage by getting a residence permit, but on the other hand, he cared for and enjoyed having sex with her, just as she did with him. Kyriaki, then, warned Olga about the perils of telling him about her sexual satisfaction. Taking her relationship with Frank as an example, Kyriaki said that not only did she have sex with another man but she had told Frank about it. Olga was astonished: "Really, you said it to him? I can't believe you!" Kyriaki explained:

Yes, I did and I don't regret it at all. You know, these men think that they're the only ones who can water our garden. They think that because we have some extra kilos, no one else is interested in us. It's good for them to know that we have some value as women and they're not the only ones who offer it to us.

At the party, Olga told me she had decided to accept her boyfriend's proposal and marry him. But she was not very interested in talking about how and whether she overcame her frustrations. What she really wanted to talk about was "this slut over there." With these harsh words she referred to one of the Polish women who was at the party and danced with a Nigerian friend of Frank. "You see how she rubs herself on him?" she asked me. She explained to me that this Nigerian man was already married to a good friend of hers:

> My friend is also from Poland and is with him. They started it as a contract marriage but in the process their relationship developed into something else and they decided just to be together. And everything was going well until the moment this bitch appeared and started flirting with him. And you know what the irony is? That she was a good friend of my friend. With friends like that, who needs enemies! And now she is telling her, "Oh, I understood that you married him only for his papers" and so and so. Look at her! Look at her face and tell me: isn't she a whore?

Later, as I was talking with Olga and some of Kyriaki's Greek friends, a nineteen-year-old blonde woman approached and asked in Greek, "Are you Greeks?" She introduced herself as Iliana and said she was also Greek. She spoke Greek quite well, but her accent betrayed that she was not a native speaker. She said that she was born in the Netherlands and one of her parents was originally from Greece. The moment she joined our conversation, we had been discussing how many years each of us had been settled in the Netherlands. "I've been here about two years and I love it," said Vicky, another Greek woman married to a Nigerian. "I've been more than six years in Amsterdam and I liked it too," I commented. Iliana, surprised, said, "What are you talking about? I've been here nineteen years and I hate it!" Her eyes filled with tears. She said that she did not like her life in the Netherlands and felt socially excluded. She felt more comfortable when she socialized with Greeks, who, she thought, were more cheerful and friendly. She said that this was a strong motivation for her to improve her Greek, change her name from Ilse to Iliana, and participate regularly in ethnic Greek events and activities in the Netherlands. At that point, I learned that she was not a close friend of Kyriaki but they had gotten to know each other through a Facebook group for Greeks in the Netherlands. It was only the second time Kyriaki and Iliana had met in person.

Although Iliana's Greek identification enhanced her contacts with other Greeks with whom she felt at ease, it intensified her feelings and experiences of exclusion in the Netherlands. She told us about situations in which she had felt discriminated against: "One day at school, one of my classmates came to me with a newspaper which was writing something about the Greek crisis

and the debt and throw it on my desk and yelled at me, 'When are you going to pay it back?'" As she was recalling this incident, Iliana became very
emotional and started crying. Vicky shared with her that her employer in
the restaurant where she works also confronted her with the same question:
"My boss keeps asking me, 'When are you going to pay us back.' Some days
he jokes and says that he will not allow me to leave from the restaurant if I
do not give him a definite answer." Iliana continued to monopolize our attention with her sad stories, which became more and more private. She referred
to how strictly her parents still controlled her and were physically violent
with her. When she left us, she talked to other party guests and, I observed,
repeated what she told us and did not stop crying. Iliana became the party's
main character. Some people, such as Vicky and Kyriaki, sympathized with
her and advised her how to handle her issues. Others, such as Olga, found her
behavior inappropriate at the party of a person she hardly knew.

The party mood became more joyful when Kyriaki brought out her birthday cake. Iliana wiped her tears and joined us in singing birthday songs in
both English and Greek. Frank stood next to Kyriaki and held her with his
one arm and with the other held their daughter, Danai. Kyriaki blew out the
thirty-four candles, thanked us for the gifts, and asked us to pay attention to
what she wanted to say. She took Danai in her arms and addressed Frank: "I
want to thank my man. He's given of the best *kadoortje* of my life, my daughter. Baby *mou*, I love you!" Frank approached her and attempted to kiss her
on her right cheek, but Kyriaki turned her face and kissed him on the mouth.

The next day, Kyriaki called me to discuss several things that had happened at her party and complain about Frank: "He did not buy me any gift!
Not even a pint. Just to say that he brought me a present." I reminded her
about the "best *kadoortje* [gift]." She said she was referring to their daughter as Frank's most precious gift, but she had expected a birthday gift in the
conventional sense, too. The greatest part of our discussion was dedicated to
Iliana. We discussed her problems and whether or how we could help her.
Kyriaki told me that one of the Nigerian men at the party had called and
asked for Iliana's number.

"Oh, I didn't tell you," Kyriaki said. "Do you remember that friend of
Frank who was at the party with his wife, Agnieszka?"

"Yes, I do. Agnieszka is from Poland. Right?"

"Yes."

"She is skinny. The African men I know, who are married to Europeans,
usually prefer women with more curvy bodies."

"That's true. But she's not bad."

"No. Actually she is pretty."

"Yes indeed! Now she is pretty. Yesterday was the first time I saw her with her new teeth. All of her front teeth used to be rotten. Not very flattering. But anyways, this is the one I mean, Agnieszka's husband. He called me on phone after the party and started asking me questions 'about this Greek woman' and 'what is her number' . . . And I say, 'Why do you want her number? You are married!' And you know what he said? 'I don't ask it for me but in case a friend who does not have papers'! You see? You see what kind of men these Africans are? If they see a vulnerable woman, they want immediately to take advantage of her."

"So, what did you do?"

"Well, he irritated me and I talked badly to him. But then I thought that it might not be such a bad idea. It might be good for her to have someone who will pay some attention to her, who will take her to a house away from her parents, and in general, someone who will show some interest to her. So, in the end, I sent him her number."

Our conversation about Iliana ended there. Since then, neither of us has learned whether the Nigerian man contacted Iliana. Given everything she said at the party, I suspect she would be more interested in a Greek partner. Furthermore, and perhaps more important, it would have been disappointing for Agnieszka's Nigerian husband to realize that the Greek-identified Iliana was in fact a Dutch citizen who, as a young student relying on social assistance, could neither qualify for sponsorship of a foreign spouse nor benefit from the free movement within the EU as long as she was permanently settled in the Netherlands. Iliana's insecurities and weaknesses, as she exposed them at Kyriaki's party, might have made her a potential marriage partner for Agnieszka's husband's friend, but this was conditioned upon her Greek, and thus European, citizenship and not her Greek ethnicity.

Conclusion

In an era of restrictive immigration regimes, citizenship and legal status have become valuable scarce resources that migrants can access only with difficulty. In a setting of civic inequality, marriage remains one of the few channels for migrants to access those resources. Marriages between legally precarious African migrants and peripheral European migrant women in the Netherlands enable African spouses to legally reside in the Netherlands.

The shift in the marital trends of Nigerian and Ghanaian migrants from Dutch citizen spouses to EU citizen spouses takes place in the context of a twofold development. On the one hand, the imposition by the Netherlands of strict restrictions for family reunification has seriously affected legally precarious

African male migrants' marital preference for Dutch citizens (see chapter 4). On the other hand, a number of recent European Court of Justice decisions, especially in the Metock case, led to a more liberal interpretation of Community Law that enables unauthorized migrants to legalize their stay in a member state through marriage to an EU citizen. While marriage to a Dutch citizen is regulated by very strict Dutch legislation, marriage to a non-Dutch EU citizen (e.g., Greek in the Netherlands) is regulated by the Community Law that permits the immediate legalization of the migrant spouse. Several non-Dutch European women in the Netherlands exercise their right, as EU citizens, to free movement and residence, which is automatically extended to their African spouses, even those who, before their marriage, had resided unlawfully in Europe.

The responsiveness of West African migrants' marital practices to changes in the legal framework raised immigration authorities' concerns as to whether these marriages are shams. Dutch immigration authorities are generally suspicious of marriages that provide access to migrant legality, especially when the "sponsor" is a woman and the beneficiary is a migrant man. Perceiving women in these marriages as "vulnerable" and at risk of opportunistic men, immigration authorities assess whether the marriages are motivated by love and therefore are "genuine." Had I approached the marriages of West African migrant men using the state lens of sham versus genuine, I would have been concerned only with the question of love's authenticity, as Kyriaki originally was. Thus, I would have to limit myself to two competing, and misleading, interpretations. The first would be to analyze these marriages as material exchanges and frame the feelings of spouses as emotional labor (Hochschild 1983) or performances of love (Brennan 2004) or, second, as most usually happens, to emphasize love and neglecting the importance of material transfer. Furthermore, the concern about marriages' authenticity would have blurred a more fundamental issue: the consequences of romantic love on forms of exchange in marriage and why these have been different for women and men in these marriages. Instead of seeing interest and emotions as mutually exclusive elements of social relations, such as the dichotomy implied by the terms *marriage of convenience* and *love marriage*, I examined the various forms of exchange that take place within these marriages and involve different resources—both material and emotive.

As it became obvious from the analysis of these forms of exchange, West African men are interested in marriages with women from Europe's periphery not simply because they can get access to citizenship. In an effort to deal with the dependencies that marriage-based legalization generates, West African men married women who could also benefit from what they could offer them. The resources that West African men had at their disposal, mostly through their extensive transnational networks, were more appealing to migrant women from Europe's periphery than to Dutch or Western European women. With women from Europe's periphery, West African men could participate in various forms of exchanges both as recipients and as givers, and therefore could claim a less unequal position in the relationship. In their struggle to reverse their unequal position in marriage, given the dependency on their wives, some West African men found the ideal of romantic love unexpectedly in support of their efforts. While the norm of disinterested love was devised by immigration authorities to police cross-border marriages, supposedly in the name of women's protection, the appeal to love often had beneficial implications for West African migrant men, as it necessitated their wives' altruistic behavior. Recall Frank's emphasis that Kyriaki married him "only" because she loved him. And also Kyriaki's understanding that since their marriage was motivated by love, she should care for her husband without anticipating material returns. These insights remind us how the ideal of romantic love can be used to undermine the bargaining power of women in their relationships.

Unpredictable Dynamics of Kinship

In a Europe that is constantly changing, the Argonauts of West Africa try to find ways to fulfill their aspirations and build a future for themselves and their families. Kinship provides them the means to navigate the state's ever-more intensive interventions to curtail migration. In the preceding chapters, I examined how migrants generated kinship in response to new forms of exclusion and civic inequalities and how these novel kinship practices are linked to documents. Contrary to the modernization hypothesis that kinship will become less important in state-organized and capitalist societies, the ethnographic cases in this book demonstrate the persistent salience of kinship, at least for migrants—not despite but because of the growing presence of the state.

In *After Kinship*, an agenda-setting book for the so-called new kinship studies, Janet Carsten (2004, xi) explained that the message of her book "appears to be that 'after kinship' is—well, just more kinship (even if it might be of a slightly different kind)." The book, and Carsten's work in general, has been a source of inspiration for this study. Not only because it set the agenda for a new approach to kinship as a process, but also because Carsten's critique of dominant dichotomies in social theory (modern or traditional, Western or non-Western) with kinship as a marker of difference has been crucial to this study, especially her warning that the theorization of these dichotomies often relies on the methodological fallacy of comparing practices in so-called traditional or non-Western societies with norms in so-called Western or modern societies. It may seem obvious, but it is important to always be alert that practices may differ, sometimes quite considerably, from norms and discourses.

Citizenship is a case in point. Although citizenship as a norm is an institution of equality, in reality it is as much about exclusion as it is about inclusion. As any other form of membership, citizenship implies exclusion and therefore unequal relations between citizens and noncitizens. In a world where all citizens reside in the country of their citizenship, the exclusionary effect of citizenship is not—or more precisely should not be—an experience of everyday life. But this world can exist only hypothetically. Today more than ever, in a period that has been labeled "the age of migration" (Castles, De Haas, and Miller 2014) and "the age of involuntary immobility" (Carling 2002), the exclusionary aspect of state membership is experienced by citizens who live both within and outside their country of citizenship. This exclusionary side of citizenship has not received sufficient attention in its impact on social relations—not only between citizens but also between citizens and noncitizens. This study has shown that the new forms of inequality associated with state institutions offer kinship fertile ground to proliferate and regulate unequal relations as well as to facilitate the distribution of resources that state politics makes scarce. Conjuring with Carsten's words, I would say that the message of this study is that "after citizenship" is, well, just more kinship (even if it might be of a slightly different kind). But these dynamics of kinship can be understood only in relation to the new forms of inequality generated by the state.

Social Navigation and New Kinship Dynamics

As we have seen in the previous chapters, the kinship relations of West African migrants in Amsterdam are affected not only by state politics but also by wider changes that take place outside the realm of the nation-state, notably the 2008 financial crisis and the 2004 enlargement of the European Union. These political and economic developments had a deep impact on the lives of migrants, but this book has shown that the latter are anything but passive victims of these structural changes. Their tactics and strategies constantly change in their attempts to avoid new constraints, take advantage of emerging opportunities, and eventually attain a better position. The concept of social navigation proved useful in this context as well to describe their constantly changing practices in a constantly changing context (Vigh 2009).

The ethnographic cases analyzed here have shown that West African migrants rely especially on kinship to navigate new regulations, both national and EU, and the concomitant economic and political transformations. Kinship, therefore, becomes their ship to navigate overlapping forms of inequality. But kinship itself changes through this process, and the ship is rebuilt at sea. When the Dutch state took measures against informal employment, unauthorized migrants started using the identity documents of their "brothers"

and "sisters" that allowed them to work under their names. In that early period of identity loan—the 1990s—unauthorized West African migrants had
some degree of flexibility because their employers turned a blind eye to this
practice. Even though many of them hardly spoke Dutch, for instance, unauthorized West African migrants could use the documents of Dutch Afro-
Caribbeans without their employers protesting. However, the new law that
imposed severe fines on businesses employing unauthorized workers, the
growing presence of workers from Europe's east and south on the formal
labor market, and the decrease in job openings due to the economic crisis
changed the stance of employers toward unauthorized West African migrants.
This quickly resulted in the decline—almost disappearance—of identity loan.
The collaboration of West Africans with Afro-Caribbeans for identity loan
stopped, and nowadays, the few West Africans who work under the name of
someone else, usually without their employers' knowledge, use documents of
persons of the same ethnic background. Other unauthorized migrants earn
their living through informal economic activities that require the assistance
and support of their social networks (e.g., transnational trade). Furthermore,
more and more unauthorized migrants feel the pressure to get married, as this
appears to provide the best solution to their problem of legal and employment
uncertainty. Of course, marriage is not a new means to acquiring legality. But
in previous years, when migrants could earn their living by engaging in identity loan, marriage was not as important as it is today for the fulfillment of
their migratory aspirations. Quite ironically, the influx of European migrants
led, on the one hand, to a decrease in the number of unauthorized migrants
working in formal jobs, and of practices of identity loan; on the other hand, it
enabled unauthorized migrants to get legalized by marrying these newcomers.

　　Thus, kinship offered a way out of difficult situations and enabled West
African migrants to navigate through changing and hostile environments.
Nevertheless, as kinship is also changing through this process, its dynamics may have effects that migrants—and, I would argue, scholars—did not
anticipate. The intersubjectivity of kinship, its interpersonal character, has
consequences that are difficult to control for those who participate in the existence of one another. Consider, for example, the story of Sharon and Roberta (chapter 3). Although Sharon thought identity loan would be a temporary strategy for her to gain employment, she ended up assuming the identity
of her sister Roberta for almost two decades even after she stopped using
Roberta's identity documents. Another example is the marriage of Dennis
to Camelia (chapter 5), which in the beginning seemed to be "for papers"
(at least according to what Dennis's sister-in-law told me). However, soon
after Dennis and Camelia started living together, Camelia became pregnant

and decided to return to Romania, where she would have the support of her family. Dennis, whose legal status was tied to his marriage to Camelia and (later) to his relationship with his child, was left with no other option than to follow Camelia to Romania—despite his preference to reside in the Netherlands. These are just two of the many examples in which kinship developed a dynamic of its own and exceeded the control of those who, in the beginning, thought that they could control it.

Analyzing these practices through the lens of navigation allows us to capture the "motion within motion"—and I find great merit in this analytical concept. There are, however, possible limitations in our analysis if we employ the term uncritically. One is that *navigation*, a term associated with sailing, can too easily imply rationality in the decision-making and constant adjustment of strategies. This book has showed that, indeed, migrants often carefully assess the anticipated dangers and consequences of their actions. Nevertheless, the ethnographic cases also demonstrate the limits of interpreting their actions as rational choices. To trust someone and become kin with him or her is a decision that requires something more than a rational assessment of the consequence of intersubjective participation. If trust is the state of favorable expectation regarding other people's behavior and intentions (Möllering 2001, 404), can it be generated by a rational calculation of the risks involved? This is a fundamental question that diachronically tortures humans across all cultures.[1] In chapter 4, we saw how Judith took a hasty decision in replying positively to Jack's marriage proposal. As she said, what made her make that decision was that she did not "feel jumpy" about it. For Georg Simmel and other social scientists, trust requires a peculiar combination of knowledge and ignorance. But Simmel did not understand trust only as a mere outcome of this mixture. For him, a "further element of social-psychological quasi-religious faith" (Simmel [1900] 2004, 178) was crucial to explaining trust. This further element, as elaborated by Möllering (2001), is what makes people suspend their doubts, triggering "a leap of trust" that produces favorable expectations. Mama Clara's advice that it was important to find a Christian with whom to collaborate in identity loan (chapter 3); Kyriaki's forgiveness of Frank after "a good fuck" for "whatever bullshit he did" (chapter 5); Kelly's belief in Sam's rape story when she saw "the pain in his eyes" (chapter 4), and many other examples indicate that morality, emotions, and bodily sensations contribute to the "leap of trust" necessary to maintain a relationship. An analysis in terms of navigation must focus on the role of this quasi-religious element of trust in people's decisions.

Furthermore, the lens of navigation directs our attention to the interaction between people and shifting landscapes (or more precisely seascapes), emphasizing how the changing structural forces trigger actions. But can the concept capture the actor's ability to influence the structural conditions in which these actions take place? According to Massey et al. (1994, 1498), "Each act of migration generates a set of irreversible changes in individual motivations, social structures, and cultural values that alter the context within which future migration decisions are made." They maintained that these changes "accumulate across time to create conditions that make additional migration more likely." In a critical assessment of this approach, De Haas (2010) argued that these acts of migration affect not only the functioning of "endogenous" mechanisms of the migration process but also the "contextual" conditions such as income inequality and developmental disparities that initiated migration.[2] Moreover, De Haas pointed out that not all migration acts lead to more migration, and there are also migration-undermining effects. The migrant network approach, De Haas claimed, cannot explain negative effects on migration because it does not account for the downsides of social capital— migrants as bridgeheads and also gatekeepers (Böcker 1994). But beyond these points of contention, there is consensus among the migration scholars cited here that every migration act bears the possibility of changing—either positively or negatively—the conditions in which future acts of migration will take place. These effects on the wider context in which migration takes place cannot be captured by the lens of navigation.

"Givers Never Lack": Exchange and Inequality

The stories of migrants featured in this book, especially in chapters 2 and 3, demonstrate how West Africans manage to migrate and find work in the Netherlands by relying on the assistance of others—an interdependency they describe in kinship terms. Such reliance is even more necessary for those who do not fit into the categories that the Netherlands, as well as other states in the Global North, privilege for mobility and employment rights, such as "highly skilled migrants" (*kennismigranten*) and "wealthy foreign nationals" (*vermogende vreemdelingen*).

Other ethnographies have also shown the importance of exchange within kin networks to the survival of people who find themselves in marginal positions. For example, in the now-classic *All Our Kin*, Carol Stack (1974) documented the mutual aid between poor black Americans, which they called "swapping," as a survival strategy that enabled them to deal with the hardships of poverty. In her study of internal migrants in a Mexico City shantytown, Larissa Adler Lomnitz (1977) came up with similar findings. Her ethnography of urban poverty shed light on the vital role of kinship and the "networks of reciprocal exchange" in the daily survival of the shantytown dwellers.[3] Both studies, which have become influential in the social sciences, suggested that reciprocity was fundamental to the social organization of these disadvantaged communities.[4] In the ethnographic studies examined in this book, inequality necessitated forms of exchange between relatives as well. Nevertheless, these forms of collaboration between kin were not motivated by a shared inferior position in society but by the unequal access to resources that authorized and unauthorized migrants had as an outcome of their differing legal status. This unequal distribution of resources became fertile ground for the development of exchange relations between authorized and unauthorized migrants, citizens and noncitizens, which reinforced or produced kinship.

Various documents (e.g., passports, work permits) that prove civic membership became objects of exchange between citizens and legally precarious migrants. The exclusion of unauthorized West African migrants from civic membership in the Netherlands made citizenship a scarce and desirable status. At the same time, the inalienability of citizenship intensified the unequal quality of this exchange. The inalienability of things, according to Mauss, is a key characteristic of the gift economy that makes it different from the commodity economy, where people have alienable rights over their private property. In gift exchange, there is an "indissoluble bond of a thing with its original owner," and thus "it is wrong to speak here of alienation, for these things are loaned rather than sold and ceded" (Mauss [1924] 2002, 42). Similarly, citizenship cannot be sold, and the ownership rights of documents cannot be transferred. In fact, citizens who lent their identity documents to noncitizens never lost their civic status. This paradox of "keeping while giving" (Weiner 1992) reproduced the unequal relationship between citizens and noncitizens, and in fact strengthened the superior position of citizens who, without losing their civic status, could expect something in return—either material (e.g., money) or symbolic (e.g., recognition)—from noncitizens for their acts of giving (see also Eriksen 2007). These two features of citizenship—scarcity and inalienability—defined the conditions that made the exchange of identity documents and civic resources necessary and determined the social outcome of the exchange. "Givers never lack," a phrase from the Bible (Proverbs 28:27) that Pentecostal churches in the Netherlands and Ghana often distribute on stickers, describes very well the outcome of an exchange in which the gift is inalienable (fig. C.1).

The highly asymmetrical exchange relationships between document owners and document recipients were framed in kinship terms without kinship diminishing their inequality. Yet the relationships between lenders and borrowers of identity documents, as well as those who acted as intermediaries,

FIGURE C.1. "Givers Never Lack," bumper sticker seen in Accra, 2012. Photo by the author.

were still described as relationships of solidarity and mutual aid. The invocation of kinship was not meant to repress the asymmetrical character of these forms of exchange but rather, given the great risk to which the transactions exposed both parties, to reassure. When migrants appealed to siblinghood in the context of identity loan, they implicitly agreed that the exchange of identity documents would be regulated by a particular morality, different from the morality of a business relationship. What is important to stress here is that this particular morality of siblinghood stemmed not from a specific culture but from a convergence of different cultural meanings (see Baumann 1995). After all, as we have seen, migrants of different ethnic backgrounds participated in identity loan arrangements. No matter how migrants translated the terms into their native languages (Twi, Igbo, Yoruba, Sranan Tongo, Papiamentu, Dutch, and others), the English *brother* and *sister* came to denote— for all who used them in Amsterdam—social relationships of solidarity, care, support, and altruism. Of course, as the ethnographic cases showed, the practices of siblinghood were quite different from these ideals. As Narotzky and Moreno (2002, 301) stressed: "The emphasis on equality and balanced exchange as the starting point for a reciprocal relation has only served to hide the imbalance and ambiguity inherent in reciprocal relations and their capacity to generate, reproduce and transform systems of inequality in reference to a field of moral forces where conflict and ambivalence prevail."

Dynamics of Marriage

In the final two chapters of this book (chapters 4 and 5), we saw how legally precarious migrants accessed citizenship through marriage. The devaluation of Dutch citizenship, as a result of policies that restricted the family rights of many Dutch citizens, has gradually led to fewer marriages to, and fewer forms of exchange in general with, Dutch Afro-Caribbeans. At the same time, the new possibilities for legalization through marriage to an EU national made many legally precarious migrants, especially Nigerians, explore the possibilities of marrying citizens from the EU's periphery. Although both Dutch Afro-Caribbeans and peripheral Europeans have full Dutch and EU citizenship, respectively, their socioeconomic position is often lower than that of their fellow citizens. The ethnographic analysis of the practices of migrants showed that both of these characteristics—civic membership and socioeconomic position—were of utmost importance to these binational marriages and to the exchanges that took place within them.

State authorities and the media often suspect that these marriages, which provide African migrants access to long-term residence permits, are sham—that is, based not on love but on material interest. From the perspective of the state authorities, a marriage is considered "genuine" only when it is motivated and sustained by love in the absence of instrumental motives (Eggebø 2013; Bonjour and De Hart 2013; Satzewich 2014; D'Aoust 2013; Maskens 2015). Thus, immigration authorities seem to assess the authenticity of migrants' marriages on the basis of the modernist ideal of marriage as a "pure relationship" (Wray 2015; Eggebø 2013). According to Giddens (1992, 58), who coined the term, a *pure relationship* "refers to a situation where a social relation is entered into for its own sake, for what it can be derived by each person from a sustained association with another; and which is continued only in so far as it is thought by both parties to deliver enough satisfaction for each individual to stay within it." This normative ideal of marriage as a relationship in which acts of giving are not motivated by material returns can be seen as another example of Sahlins's equation of generalized reciprocity with minimal social distance. The danger, however, is that the pairing of generalized reciprocity with intimacy has gone beyond the academic debate and is now used by state bureaucrats as a model to assess the marriages of migrants.

The ethnographic cases analyzed in this book show that interest and emotions coexist in these marriages, and indeed are dynamically articulated, just as they are in other marital unions. Contrary to other scholars and civil society activists who defend the genuineness of these marriages by emphasizing the existence and prevalence of emotions over material benefits, this study has not neglected the importance of material transactions. Building on feminist interventions on the entanglement of love and money, this ethnographic study shows that material exchanges are embedded in a wider circulation of resources, including emotions and sexual pleasure—an embedding that is also found in non–migrant marriages whose authenticity is never officially questioned and scrutinized. The detailed ethnographic examination of the way interest, love, and sex are articulated in the marriages between legally precarious African migrants and Dutch or EU citizens can help us see the similarities with other marriages. But for this we certainly need studies that do not focus exclusively on the marriages of migrants—as is the usual tendency in migration studies (Dahinden 2016; Moret, Andrikopoulos and Dahinden 2021).

But let's return to Giddens and his consideration of pure relationship, which has so informed scholars' and state authorities' understandings about what a modern relationship is. According to Giddens, a pure relationship, and by extension a modern marriage, is a relationship that lacks ulterior or instrumental motives. It is a "relationship of emotional and sexual equality" (Giddens 1992, 2). However, what Giddens seems to forget is "the twofold truth of the gift," in Bourdieu's terms. On the one hand, the act of giving is experienced as disinterested and uncalculated generosity; on the other hand, it creates an obligation to return the gift. The time lapse between the initial gift giving and the countergift giving "makes it possible to experience the objective exchange as a discontinuous series of free and generous acts" (Bourdieu 2000, 192). The logic of exchange is disclosed when the gift giving is not returned or the recipient remains ungrateful. "You never wanted to admit that I married you mainly to help you," said Kyriaki to Frank, during a crisis in their marriage (chapter 5). "You married me only because you loved me," answered Frank—a response that made Kyriaki furious but would probably satisfy Giddens as well as immigration officers.

In a strikingly similar interaction, found in Euripides's work *Medea*, when Jason left Medea to marry another woman, Medea blamed Jason for being unappreciative of her help in acquiring the Golden Fleece. Jason angrily replied, "In return for my salvation, though, you got better than you gave" (534–35). And because she "started a contest of words" (546), he listed what Medea gained from her marriage to him, such as that Medea then lived in Greece and not in a "barbarian land" (Rayor 2013). Interestingly, an analogous argument was used by Sunny in reference to Natasha, who, according to him, should have appreciated that because of her Nigerian husband, she relocated from Greece to the Netherlands (chapter 5). But what made Jason's reaction so similar to Frank's was that Jason had refused to acknowledge the help of his wife Medea and instead said, "Since you raise a monument to gratitude, I consider Aphrodite alone the savior of my expedition—of all gods and humans." His gratitude for Aphrodite was because she sent Eros, the god of love, to help him. Jason continued: "You do have a subtle mind. Yet to detail the whole story of how Eros compelled you with his inescapable arrows to save my skin would cause resentment" (527–31). Jason and Frank did not deny that the assistance of their wives was crucial to surviving and achieving their goals. But they both did not want to see their wives' acts as gifts that generated the obligation of a countergift. Instead, they argued that these actions were only a manifestation of love and as such no expectation of acknowledgment or any other type of return could be expected.

The discrepancy between Giddens's and Bourdieu's views on the moral economy of exchange in intimate relations is crucial for arriving at a more sophisticated understanding of marriages between migrants and citizens. Such a broad view can help show how misleading it is to consider instrumentality a differentiating element in the marriages of African migrants to either Dutch citizens of Afro-Caribbean background or citizens from the EU periphery. What might be a significant difference is the difficulty for these couples themselves to think of the exchanges that take place in their marriages as unrelated and disinterested acts of giving. The moral panic around sham marriages, the dominant framing of these marriages by the state (e.g., the qualification of the citizen spouse as the "sponsor"), and the valorization of marriage as a channel to acquire scarce civic resources are all serious obstacles for African migrants and their spouses to fully experience the illusion of modern marriage as an emotional relationship in which the acts of generosity between spouses are unrelated.

This book may have shown that the old anthropological fascination with kinship is—maybe quite unexpectedly for many observers—highly relevant for understanding present-day problems of migration, with citizenship becoming an institution of exclusion rather than of equality. However, such relevance requires new orientations, emphasizing kinship as a dynamic process, allowing for novel adaptations in changing contexts (Andrikopoulos and Duyvendak 2020; Geschiere 2020; Carsten 2020). In this sense, such new contexts could outline new ways for reflecting on what kinship is. But instead of seeking a normative answer, this book preferred to examine what kinship enables and how it does so. Thus, I took a long journey, following the heroes and heroines of this book, the Argonauts of West Africa, and was attentive not only to their words but to their practices as well. The emphasis on the practices of kinship helped me uncover a less pleasant side of kinship that was hidden under the glossy cover of reciprocity and solidarity. In the shadow of exclusionary citizenship, this book sheds light on the dark side of kinship.

Acknowledgments

First of all, I want to express my deep gratitude to all those who participated in this study and shared their life stories with me. These are migrants from Ghana and Nigeria, who I call the Argonauts of West Africa. Like tragic heroes in Greek mythology, their lives are admirable and adventurous but also full of struggles, tensions, and existential dilemmas. Apart from West African migrants, my research participants are also migrants from other African countries, the Caribbean, Eastern and Southern Europe, with whom West Africans forge relations of kinship. I thank all of them for opening their homes and hearts to me.

I am incredibly grateful to four amazing scholars whose devoted mentorship has profoundly shaped my intellectual trajectory. I owe an enormous thank you to Peter Geschiere, even though words are too little to express my gratitude for his support, patience, and generosity. He has been my model of brilliance in scholarship and has shaped my intellectual thinking to an extent he may not realize. Peter taught me how to do ethnographic research, paying close attention to the uncertainties, seeming contradictions, and messiness of life, and then how to write ethnography that generously details the intricacies of social life and explores the articulation of people's everyday practices with structural conditions. Sébastien Chauvin's enthusiasm has been incredibly motivating and his rigorous comments on every single draft I sent him were invaluable. Our discussions about legal precarity and migrant legality have been formative for many of the ideas presented in this book. I appreciate him not only as a scholar but also because he is a wonderful person. I have been really lucky to cooperate with him. Jan Willem Duyvendak has been a voice of reason: his comments have always been to the point and particularly useful as to how I can make this study relevant to sociological debates. His contribution to this project was vital in helping me show how kinship, a classic anthropological topic, can be relevant to other fields in social sciences such as migration and citizenship studies. Like most European anthropologists of my generation, I have been trained in anthropology by the textbooks written by Thomas Hylland Eriksen. When I was excitedly reading his books, as a bachelor's student in Greece, I never could have imagined that one day I would cooperate with him and he would become my adviser. I learned so much from his books, then learned so much more from the man. A person of rare integrity and genuine kindness, Thomas has been for me a model of engaged anthropological work and an example of how anthropologists can have an impact on the social issues they study. All four of them offered insight and advice at different stages of this project. Thank you from the bottom of my heart for all you did for me.

In addition, advisers and mentors in earlier stages of my career have been very important in my intellectual development. Thank you so much to Georgios Agelopoulos, Effie Voutira, Fotini Tsibiridou, Flip Lindo, and Ilse van Liempt. Georgios Agelopoulos has been a longtime mentor and I cannot imagine how far I would have gone without him. Furthermore, I am really grateful to Akosua Adomako Ampofo, Janet Carsten, Hein De Haas, Barak Kalir, and Rachel Spronk, for their constructive criticism and engagement with my work.

The academic community at the University of Amsterdam was very welcoming and supportive. I wish to thank Rachel Spronk, with whom I collaborated on a new project in Kenya, Amade M'charek, Francio Guadeloupe, Mattijs van der Port, Jan Rath, Kristine Krause, Saskia Bonjour, Simona Vezzoli, Katerina Rozakou, Ahmet Akgündüz, Tesseltje de Lange, Jeroen Doomernik, Annelies Moors, Julie McBrien, Marleen De Witte, Christian Bröer, Niko Besnier, and Adnan Hossain. Unfortunately, Gerd Baumann, Sarah van Walsum, and Mario Rutten have passed away. I benefited a lot from my engagement with them. They will remain in my memory. Discussions with fellow colleagues and friends have also been stimulating: Robby Davidson, Manolis Pratsinakis, Dilys Amoabeng, Peter Miller, Naomi Van Stapele, Yannis Tzaninis, Sanderien Verstappen, Sanam Roohi, Anneke Beerkens, Paul Mepschen, Markus Balkenhol, Akwasi Osei, Tugba Öztemir, Rogier van Reekum, Carla Rodrigues, T. J. Schuitmaker, Eline van Haastrecht, Amisah Bakuri, Yannick Coenders, Marten Boekelo, Frank van As, Jeremy Bierbach, Aarthi Sridhar, Uroš Kovač, Valentina Di Stasio, Robert Pijpers, Maybritt Jill Alpes, and Mark Hann.

I am very grateful to Rogers Brubaker for inviting me to the Department of Sociology at UCLA right after I finished my ethnographic research in Amsterdam. During my visiting appointment at UCLA, I had the chance to meet and discuss my work with Roger Waldinger, Min Zhou, Andreas Wimmer, Gail Kligman, and Jaeeun Kim. Since then, Jaeeun has become a dear colleague and one of my first-line commentators.

I am also very grateful to Janine Dahinden, who invited me to Maison d'Analyse des Processus Sociaux at the University of Neuchâtel and arranged a magnificent working space, with a view of the lake and the Alps, where I wrote earlier versions of this book. My visit there was covered by a fellowship by the National Center of Competence in Research–On the Move. In Neuchâtel, I had thought-provoking discussions with Joëlle Moret, Yvonne Riaño, Shpresa Jashari, Tania Zittoun, Pathé Barry, and Katia Iglesias.

Furthermore, I am really grateful to George Paul Meïu for inviting me to the Department of Anthropology at Harvard, where I recently started a new postdoc fellowship. There, I worked on the final revisions of this book and had the opportunity to meet and engage with Myriam Lamrani, Oluwakemi Abiodun Adesina, Ashwin Subramanian, Emmanuel Akyeampong, Christine Chalifoux, Quincy Amoah, and Malavika Reddy.

At various times and locations, I had the opportunity to discuss my work with scholars from other universities who generously gave me feedback and made critical comments. I wish to thank Nicholas de Genova, Katherine Charsley, Charles Piot, Joris Schapendonk, Richard Jenkins, Susan Ossman, Irene Bloemrad, Sarah Horton, Erdmute Alber, Tatjana Thelen, Cati Coe, Pamela Feldman-Savelsberg, Rudolf Gaudio, Gloria Wekker, Blanca Garcés-Mascareñas, Michael Herzfeld, Melanie Griffiths, Anika Liversage, Jonathan Echeverri Zuluaga, Aiwha Ong, Basile Ndjio, Serena Dankwa, Rijk van Dijk, Edmond Préteceille, Kwame Edwin Otu, Mansah Prah, Dimitris Dalakoglou, Jack Ume Tocco, Tryfon Bampilis, Amber Gemmeke, and Helena Wray. Special thanks to Jojada Verrips, who gave me the idea for the title of this book. I want to express my thanks to Jeroen Slot, Harma Beenes, Zakaria Al Wahdani, and the late Hans de Waal from the Statistics Department of the municipality of Amsterdam (Onderzoek, Informatie en Statistiek). They provided access to unpublished data that were particularly useful for this study (see chapter 5).

I could not have imagined a better house for this book and a better editor to work with. I want to thank Mary Al-Sayed, my editor, for believing in this book from the beginning and for her incredibly helpful guidance throughout the process. Fabiola Enríquez and Tristan Bates offered excellent assistance. I want to thank Katherine Faydash for polishing my English in most creative ways. I also wish to thank the anonymous reviewers at the University of Chicago Press for the time and effort they put into engaging with the book and their excellent suggestions. I could not have hoped for more helpful feedback for the book!

The research project that the book is based on received funding and other forms of support from the Amsterdam Institute for Social Science Research and especially of the program group Political Sociology (formerly Dynamics of Citizenship and Culture). They have been generous with me in all possible ways. The Amsterdam Center for European Studies provided funding for the copyediting of the book. I worked on the revisions of the book while I started a Marie Skłodowska-Curie postdoc project, which received funding from the EU's Horizon 2020 research and innovation program under the grant agreement No. 894547. A revised portion of chapter 1 originally appeared in "After Citizenship: The Process of Kinship in a Setting of Civic Inequality" in *Reconnecting State and Kinship*, edited by Erdmute Alber and Tatjana Thelen. Copyright © 2018 University of Pennsylvania Press. I would also like to acknowledge that chapter 5 contains elements of a previous publication (Andrikopoulos 2021), and I thank Taylor & Francis for permission to republish revised parts of this publication.

I want also to say a big thank you to family and friends in the Netherlands, Greece, and Ghana, as well as in other parts of the world. The journey was long and their presence in my life made it more beautiful. Joël Illidge, now a fellow anthropologist, has been a solid pillar. There are so many reasons to thank him that it would be unfair to name only a few. I am sure he knows how much I appreciate him and care for him. Kim Kuo and Christel Peek have been very caring friends. Joanna Hardeman, my Dutch teacher, is now a dear friend and together with her partner Onno Schilstra has a special place in my heart. Anita Momodu has been a person to count on and I learned so much from her. Robby Davidson has been a friend and a great colleague. Valia Kalaitzi, Kostas Tikaidis, Alexandra Efraimidou, Vivian Kounio, Amalia Tzaneri, Apostolis Karabairis, and Katerina Tsekou have been great friends in Greece.

Where I am today, to a great extent, I owe to my late grandmother Anna. A hardworking farmer, she did everything she could to support my education. She spent almost her entire scant pension to back my bachelor's studies in Greece and was so happy to see me progressing. I was the first member of the family to obtain a higher education. But she supported everyone, especially her five grandsons. She was a person who lived for others. That's why her loss is so painful for us, felt so much. Especially for me. Much of what men achieve is often due to support by women, which remains invisible and unrecognized. The least I can do is to dedicate the fruit of my work, this book, to her.

Trust and Ethics

My long-term relationships with some research participants were vital to building up the necessary trust for carrying out this ethnographic research on quite sensitive topics. Still, conducting research on legally precarious migrants entails particular challenges. Why would migrants who are in a condition of legal uncertainty share with a researcher information about their lives, even more so, when this information concerns practices such as the exchange of identity documents and legalization strategies? The interviews with returnees in Ghana were indeed more relaxed than with unauthorized migrants in the Netherlands, and returnees were more open to sharing their life stories. However, I was interested not only in migrant's narratives but also in their practices.

At the early stage of my fieldwork, a Nigerian Pentecostal pastor asked me to help his brother get a job at the restaurant where I worked. I had known this pastor for quite some time and was planning to do my fieldwork at his church. The pastor told me that his brother did not have his own papers, but if I would help him to get the job, he would use the papers of someone else. On the one hand, I was interested to observe from such a close distance how identity loan operated in practice. I also felt that this was an opportunity to gain the trust of the pastor who, as a gatekeeper, could give me access to other members of his congregation engaged in similar practices. On the other hand, I was intimidated by the possible consequences of failure. Although I suspected that few of my restaurant colleagues worked with other people's documents, my impression was that the restaurant management, if aware of it, would not accept it. What would happen if they found out that the person they hired through my referral used someone else's identity document? Would they fire him, or would they also report him to immigration authorities, as some employers were doing at the time? After serious consideration, I discussed the risks with the pastor. We agreed that I would submit the job application, but I would inform my boss that the included identity document was not that of the person I referred. As I anticipated, the restaurant manager did not offer the job. I understood. Why would she take the risk and offer the job to person who used someone else's document when there are dozens of job applications every day from recently arrived migrants from Europe's periphery?

This event was a critical moment in my fieldwork and despite its outcome confirmed my loyalty to the pastor. It helped me gain his trust, which was invaluable in approaching other church members. Although he had called me his son since our first meeting, the way I handled the job application, putting at risk my relationship with the restaurant manager, added an emotional quality to the term "son." I felt that he started using it not only according to Christian etiquette but also as something more meaningful and sentimental. However, my relationship of mutual trust with him, as well as with all other research participants, was not a onetime, forever achievement (Kalir 2006). Trust was fragile, constantly assessed, and could be suspended at any moment. Every exchange with research participants had the potential to either strengthen or weaken the trust between us. After a while, the pastor came to me with a different request meant to help the unauthorized migrants of his church. Since employers were legally responsible for reporting unauthorized migrant labor (see chapter 3), he wanted to set up a small cleaning company and hire unauthorized migrants. This company, he said, would provide better working conditions to unauthorized workers, who would not have to use someone else's documents and would not need to fear that their employer might report them to immigration. He asked me, as a legal migrant (EU citizen), to register the company under my name. This meant that if the Labor Inspectorate (Inspectorate SZW) inspected us, I would have to pay a fine of €8,000 for each unauthorized worker. The risk of such an endeavor was great, and I did not seriously consider his proposal. But at the same time I had a hard time rejecting it. If I declined his proposal, the trust between us would suffer. To avoid this, I followed the advice of Nigerian friends and avoided giving a precise answer. Like my friends who changed their telephone numbers when requests from family members in Nigeria became persistent and unrealistic, I distanced myself from the pastor. This meant that I had to change my plans and choose another church as a field site. After a few months, when he was busy with other issues, I reconnected with him, without much having changed since.

The names of all individuals, as well as churches, in this book are pseud-onyms. To protect the anonymity of all these individuals, especially those whose lives are presented in great depth, I have altered details of minor im-portance. These alterations do not change the content of the stories, or at least not considerably, but they do effectively mislead anyone who might attempt to identify these individuals. To ensure that these alterations do not misdi-rect the analysis, I have discussed them with a close group of colleagues with firsthand knowledge of the field—more specifically, with Peter Geschiere and Sébastien Chauvin, who visited me in the Bijlmer and the restaurant where I worked and met some of the research participants, and Jan Willem Duyven-dak, who visited me in Ghana. Moreover, I provided drafts of chapters to some of my research participants, while with others I discussed their views about how they wanted their story to be included in the book.

Although I have been careful to protect individual identities, ethical ques-tions remain regarding the disclosure of collective practices. However, as I ex-plained earlier, the practices I describe constantly change and are well known to state authorities. Identity loan, for example, hardly takes place nowadays (chapter 3). In 2005, a new law shifted more responsibility for migration con-trol to employers and imposed a hefty administrative fine on those who em-ployed unauthorized migrants. Dutch authorities usually cite this regulation as the key reason for the disappearance of this particular type of "identity fraud." Nevertheless, my research shows that the most important reason for this development was the labor displacement of unauthorized migrants by the recently legalized migrants from the new EU member countries, espe-cially Poland.

The second part of the book (chapters 4 and 5) provides ethnographic mate-rial on the marriages of West African migrants to Afro-Caribbean Dutch citi-zens and European migrants. The academic debate on marriage and migra-tion has been influenced by how the state categorizes these marriages either as genuine and based on emotion, or as a sham and based on interest. Although the ethnographic material in these chapters confirms the presence of interest in these marriages, similar to other ethnographic studies, it shows the impos-sibility of separating interest from emotion. A closer look at sexual relations and how sexual pleasure is experienced in marriage helps us see how interest and emotion are strongly intertwined. "You cannot understand my marriage if we do not talk about sex," said a Greek woman married to an African man. This statement seemed quite reasonable to me. However, marriage and even sexuality research often gives short shrift to sex and sexual pleasure (Spronk 2014; see also Mai and King 2009). If, for reasons of academic prudence, I would ignore a crucial aspect of exchanges between spouses, how could I understand the ultimate outcome of all the exchanges that take place within marriage? Including sexual pleasure and bodily sensations in the context of marital relations in my ethnography is not meant to provoke but to help us explore how they are embedded in wider circles of exchange within marriage.

Notes

Chapter One

1. In Yoruba cosmology, *ori* has a special meaning. It is an ancestral guardian soul that resides in the head of people and determines their destiny. Every person is the owner of a unique *ori* that defines who the person is and the person's prospects in life. According to Yoruba beliefs, before persons come to life, they choose their *ori* from the storehouse of Àjàlà, a very skillful but nevertheless often careless and clumsy potter whose task is to shape human heads. It seems that in Yoruba cosmology, destiny is predetermined by the choice of *ori* persons make before they even are born. Nevertheless, while a person's destiny is seriously affected by choice of *ori*, there are ways a person's destiny can change, for either good (e.g., with sacrifices and struggles) or bad (through witchcraft and occult interventions) (see Babátúndé 2017; Balogun 2007; Ademuleya 2007). *Ori olori* appears to be a means for Nigerian migrants to change a destiny that they have not chosen themselves but that has been forced upon them by the increasingly hostile migration regimes in Europe and elsewhere in the Global North.

2. Peter Geschiere (1997, 2013) described witchcraft as "the dark side of kinship" to emphasize that witchcraft and kinship are not opposites but closely entwined. Although I borrow this term from Geschiere's work, I use it here more generally to refer to aspects of kinship that are unpleasantly experienced.

3. Scheel (2019) uses the notion of appropriation to denote migrants' capacity to subvert immigration controls. By engaging in a wide range of practices, such as unauthorized identity craft, migrants appropriate mobility.

4. Likewise, the difference between imposture and performance is not real and self-evident. Impostors are persons who are not authorized to perform certain identities (Goffman 1959, 38). Imposture, therefore, is contingent on the assessment of the authority that decides who is a "legitimate impostor" (Bourdieu 2000, 242) and on the sociohistorical context that this assessment takes place (Comaroff and Comaroff 2016).

5. Manchester School anthropologists have significantly contributed to the shift from tribe to ethnicity. In contrast to anthropologists from Cambridge and Oxford, such as Evans-Pritchard and Meyer Fortes, who studied small isolated African societies, Manchester anthropologists studied social transformations resulting from migration, urbanization, and colonialism. They argued that social relations were context bound (Gluckman 1940) and showed how the meaning of "tribe" changed (detribalization, retribalization) in new urban settings (Mitchell 1956;

Cohen 1969). Migration and ethnic studies scholars often forget that Fredrik Barth (1969) built on these insights for the theorization of boundaries in group formation process—arguably the most influential work in the constructivist and situationalist approach to ethnicity. For an intellectual history of the Manchester School, see Werbner (2020); and for an intellectual biography of Frederik Barth, see Eriksen (2015).

6. I use *peripheral* to refer to countries of Southern and Eastern Europe, such as Greece and Poland, not only because they are located on Europe's periphery but also because they are hierarchically included in the European Union and heavily dependent on countries of the EU core (see chapter 5).

7. Nowadays, the way that class is related to selectivity of migrants is different from in earlier periods, when state policies favored working-class migration. In the postwar era, Western democracies dealt with labor shortages by recruiting migrant workers from the lower socioeconomic strata of peripheral countries: Western European countries invited "guest workers" from southern Europe, Turkey, and North Africa (Akgündüz 2012); the United States imported "manual workers" (*braceros*) from Mexico (Cohen 2006); Australia launched the "assisted passage" program for low-skilled laborers from Europe (Colic-Peisker 2011).

8. It is important for me not only to rely on what West African migrants told me in interviews about their social relations but also to observe those relations in action and how the actors addressed one another. I do not suggest that we should take at face value the terms that West African migrants use in their daily interactions—such as *brother* and *sister*, which are used in the context of identity loan. However, we should "take seriously" (Archambault 2016) the terms that people use in their everyday interactions and try to understand why they choose them, and not others, and the outcome, or expected outcome, of such framings.

9. For my African interlocutors in the Netherlands, I was undoubtfully seen as "white." However, as a migrant from Europe's periphery, I was not placed in the same category as white Dutch people. In Ghana, my origin in Greece was of little relevance. For a reflection on my whiteness, see Andrikopoulos (n.d.).

10. In Cameroon (Alpes 2017; Atekmangoh 2017) and the Gambia (Gaibazzi 2015), migration is referred to as "bushfalling" or as going to "the bush"; in Nigeria (Adesina 2007), as "checking out"; in Francophone West Africa (Kleinman 2019), as "leaving on adventure" (*partir en/à l'aventure*) and migrants as "adventurers" (*aventuriers*).

11. Sometimes, after entering Europe, a person with a valid visa sends the passport back to Africa to be used by another, physically similar person (Carling 2006, 23–24; Okojie et al. 2003). Because immigration officers are quite careful when examining passports of Nigerian citizens—given that Nigeria has the reputation of being associated with drug smuggling, human trafficking, and fraud—some Nigerians use passports of other African nationals (e.g., Ghana, Senegal, Benin, Togo, or South Africa) (see also Prina 2003; Olaniyi 2009, 157), and others use European passports of naturalized Africans or Afro-Caribbeans. The use of new technologies in border controls (M'charek, Schramm, and Skinner 2014; Lyon 2009), including the control of biometric information in e-passports since the late 1990s, made entering Europe with someone else's passport more difficult but not impossible (see chapter 2).

12. These figures concern persons older than fifteen years. For the same year (2014), the percentage of account ownership at a financial institution was 99 percent in the Netherlands and 94 percent in the United States. See the World Bank's Global Findex Database, at https://www.worldbank.org/en/publication/globalfindex. See also Demirguc-Kunt and colleagues (2018).

13. Nigerians refer to counterfeit documents as *Oluwole* (e.g., an Oluwole passport). This term originates from the district of Oluwole in Lagos where producers of counterfeit documents are located (Ismail 2010; Adebanwni and Obadare 2022).

14. It was even possible at that time for migrants who were not legally residing in the Netherlands to receive welfare assistance, such as social housing and unemployment, health, and disability benefits (Van der Leun and Kloosterman 2006; Van der Leun 2003).

15. The unemployment rate fell from 9.5 percent in 1983 to 3.1 percent in 1996, and until the 2008 financial crisis, it did not rise above 6 percent (Eurostat data). From 1982 to 1996, the total number of jobs increased 25 percent, and 75 percent of new jobs were either flexible or part-time (Visser and Hemerijck 1997). In 2009, workers in the "flexible layer" (fixed-term contracts, agency workers, self-employed) of the Dutch economy reached 34 percent of the total workforce (Van Liempt 2013, 9).

16. Since the early 1980s, the Dutch state has implemented policies to promote labor flexibility. As a result, the Netherlands became Europe's champion in part-time employment—in 2002, 43.8 percent of total employment was part-time, while the European Union average was 18.2 percent (EUROFOUND 2007)—and obtained a rather flexible labor market, with temporary, on-call, and easily dissolvable job contracts (Van Oorschot 2004; Remery, van Doorne-Huiskes, and Schippers 2002, 480).

17. Transitional restrictions did not apply to citizens of Malta and Cyprus, which entered the European Union together with the other eight Eastern European countries.

18. In 2010, the European Court of Justice ruled that the 120 percent income requirement contradicted the 2003 European Directive on family reunification. As a result, the Netherlands had to lower the requirement to its previous level of 100 percent.

19. Indicatively, in January 2022, the monthly minimum wage for adults older than twenty-one was €1,725.

20. It goes without saying that that the percentage is larger in the total population, which includes unemployed persons and those who receive social benefits.

21. According to statistical data, "Surinamese" and "Antilleans" are in a better position than other "non-Western migrants," such as "Turkish" and "Moroccans," but a more disadvantaged position than "native Dutch" (Odé 2002, 49–66). In 2010, the labor force participation rate was 60 percent for Surinamese, 57 percent for Antilleans, and 69 percent for native Dutch. That year, 37 percent of Surinamese and 38 percent of Antilleans had elementary or lower occupations (compared to 28 percent of native Dutch) and 23 percent and 28 percent, respectively, had a flexible labor contract (compared to 16 percent of native Dutch) (De Boom et al. 2011).

22. By *European migrants* I refer to EU citizens who live in an EU member state different from the country of their citizenship.

23. The rights that migrants can claim through marriage with EU nationals was hotly debated in the United Kingdom before the Brexit referendum, as it was considered to undermine national sovereignty.

24. The logic of social evolution regarding the role of kinship in societal organization is also evident in the division of intellectual labor between anthropologists and sociologists. In the Global South, the "anthropology of kinship" focused mainly on societies with no or weak state organization, whereas in industrialized, capitalist societies of the Global North, the "sociology of the family" focused on nuclear families.

25. In an early critique of the anthropology of kinship, Ernest Gellner (1960) similarly wondered under which conditions anthropologists would categorize as "kinship" a social relation

they observe during fieldwork. Why did they not place this relation under other analytic categories such as politics or the economy? Gellner's answer to this question was that anthropologists
classified those relations as kinship that at least partially overlapped with their own conceptions
of kinship: "This is not primarily a discovery about societies," he asserted, "but rather about the
anthropologist's use of terms" (188).

26. This criticism of "relatedness" mostly targets the ways that other anthropologists employed
this term rather than how Janet Carsten herself used the concept. In her Langkawi ethnography,
Carsten's understanding of sharing as constitutive of relatedness is close to Gibson's (1986) critical
use of the term, as a negation of reciprocity, in his study of the Buid in the Philippines: "For the
Buid, sharing involves an obligation to give, but none to receive or to repay the giver. According to
this formulation, 'sharing' seems to fit the relation between houses of one compound in Langkawi
more closely than Sahlins's generalized reciprocity" (Carsten 1997, 166). Carsten (2004, 6) acknowledged "the intense, often too intense, emotional experiences that embody family relations." In a
later commentary on Sahlins's book on kinship, Carsten (2013, 246–47) criticized the notion of
mutuality of being because it "emanates a warm, fuzzy glow rather than a cold shiver. . . . Differentiation, hierarchy, exclusion, and abuse are, however, also part of what kinship does or enables."

27. The migrant network model considers reciprocal forms of exchange that take place
within social networks as reducing the risks and costs of migration and thus facilitating migration flows. For Massey and colleagues' 1987 study of Mexican migration, reciprocity is stronger
within the family and becomes weaker as social distance increases: "Kinship assistance is generally extended freely and openly up through parallel cousins. Among relatives more distant than
these, the strength of ties falls off rapidly, however, and their roles in the migratory process are
correspondingly smaller" (141). This approach to reciprocity, as dependent on social distance,
reflects Sahlins's (1972) theorization of the notion. In his more recent elaboration of the "mutuality of being," Sahlins (2013, 53) maintained the idea that generalized reciprocity exists in close
social relationships: "Broadly speaking, mutuality of being among kinfolk declines in proportion to spatially and/or genealogically reckoned distance."

28. Information from Onderzoek Informatie en Statistiek, Gemeente Amsterdam, Research,
Information and Statistics, City of Amsterdam (hereafter OIS), 2012, https://www.amsterdam
.nl/bestuur-organisatie/organisatie/dii/onderzoek-informatie/.

29. In total, I recorded sixty-three interviews with thirty-six individuals (from Ghana, Nigeria, Suriname, the Dutch Caribbean, the Netherlands, Greece, and other African countries).
For obvious reasons, however, most of my interviews, especially with unauthorized migrants,
were not recorded.

30. With most of my African research participants I communicated in English—the official language of both Ghana and Nigeria. Unauthorized migrants were usually not proficient
in Dutch. Unless they spoke the same "local language," English was the most common language
used between West African migrants in Amsterdam, even those from the same country. There
is a small number of French-speaking West African migrants in Amsterdam, but they have extremely limited contacts with Ghanaians and Nigerians. English was also the language West
Africans used in communication with Afro-Caribbeans and European migrants. Apart from
English, I conducted interviews in Greek with Greek migrants married to Africans, and very few
interviews in Dutch, with Surinamese migrants. Those who could not communicate in English
usually did not participate in the networks of legally precarious migrants.

31. I have recruited my research participants through four major avenues. First, I carried out
my ethnographic fieldwork and participant observation in a large fast-food restaurant where

I worked as a kitchen assistant. Second, I worked as a volunteer usher in a Pentecostal church in the Bijlmer, attended mostly by African and Afro-Caribbean migrants. Third, my living in the Bijlmer allowed me to develop a network through my participation in the daily life of the neighborhood. Additionally, I conducted complementary short-term fieldwork in Ghana, where I mostly interviewed Ghanaian migrants and their families.

32. OIS data from 2012.

33. Of the district's population, 63 percent is originally of "non-Western" background, including 29 percent from "Suriname" and 5 percent from the "Dutch Caribbean" (OIS data from 2017).

Chapter Two

1. *UK Border Force*, season 2, episode 8, 2008, https://www.youtube.com/watch?v=Amb KQmy4RZA.

2. Those who buy identity documents in the paper market are obviously aware that the documents were not produced by state authorities. Even when the documents are produced by state authorities (e.g., borrowed, stolen, or lost documents), buyers are well aware that buying or renting the documents does not turn them into their legitimate holders.

3. The services of migration brokers might be limited to assisting aspiring migrants in deciphering legal rules and procedures, organizing and submitting a visa application, and ensuring that it is complete. These services are in compliance with laws and regulations. Nevertheless, migration brokers often assist clients in ways that, should they come under the state's gaze, would be classified as illegal (Alpes 2017a; Kim 2018; Chu 2010).

4. With the goal of diversifying the US immigrant population, the visa lottery program offers green cards to a certain number of applicants in countries with low immigration to the United States.

5. Interestingly, other scholars described practices of unauthorized identity craft as "identity masking" (Horton 2016a; Mangena 2018; see also Fitzpatrick 2005).

6. Although dividuality became widely known through Strathern's work, it is not her own term. Earlier accounts of the divisible personhood can be found in the work of Roger Bastide (1973), who discussed the impact of Christianity on the shifting notions of the person in Melanesia and Africa. Marriot (1976), cited by Strathern, referred explicitly to "dividual" persons in India in contrast to "individuals" in Western societies, especially in the United States.

7. Kwame Edwin Otu (2022) builds on Gyekye's ideas of "amphibious" personhood to analyze how self-fashioned effeminate men in Accra navigate between local and global discourses of same-sex sexualities and more generally develop strategies and tactics to deal with uncertainties of everyday life. Along similar lines, Peter Geschiere and Rogers Orock (n.d.) draw inspiration from theorizations of the plasticity of the person (especially by Francis Nyamnjoh and Cécile Séverin Abega) to critically discuss the consideration of "the" homosexual as a particular kind of person in Cameroon and elsewhere.

8. See "The World Is Dancing a Masquerade—Chinua Achebe Interviewed by Ulli Beier," *Art Africa*, 2012, https://www.artafricamagazine.org/a-luta-continua-the-world-is-dancing-a-mas querade-chinua-achebe-interviewed-by-ulli-beier/.

9. For example, the mobility rights that a passport from the internationally unrecognized "Turkish Republic of Northern Cyprus" (TRNC) grants to its holders, citizens of the republic, are extremely limited. Despite the fact that these passports have been produced by civil servants

in the republic's Passports Unit, as long as the TNRC remains an internationally unrecognized state, passport holders can travel only to Turkey, the one state that has recognized the TRNC. Yael Navaro-Yashin (2007) referred to these passports and other TNRC documents as make-believe papers, differentiating them from counterfeits.

10. South Africa was infamous for the long electric border fence it constructed in the mid-1980s with the goal of discouraging unauthorized migration, especially from Mozambique. It was first set to "lethal mode," but in the 1990s was switched to "alarm mode" (Campbell 2010, 181).

11. It seems that this was also the strategy of the two young Iranian men who boarded the Malaysian Airlines flight MH370, which later went missing, from Kuala Lumpur to Beijing. In their attempt to travel to Europe and seek asylum there, these two men traveled with their Iranian passports to Malaysia and with an Italian and an Austrian stolen passports attempted to fly to Europe via Beijing. See Saeed Kamali Dehghan, "Iranians Travelling on Flight MH370 on Forged Passports 'Not Linked to Terror,'" *The Guardian*, March 11, 2014, https://www.theguardian.com/world/2014/mar/11/passengers-malaysian-plane-mh370-iranian-forged-passports.

12. As Mitchell and Coutin (2019) observed, a tension in the use of documents as a means of identification is that their reliability derives from their fixity, while their usefulness is produced by their fluidity.

13. Abarca and Coutin (2018, 10) mentioned the case of a Salvadoran unauthorized migrant who, while crossing Mexico on her way to the United States, put in her pocket a piece of paper with her name and the words "El Salvador." She did that because she wanted to be identified in case she died during the risky journey.

14. In September 2012, I participated in a conference ("Migration, Citizenship and Belonging: African, Caribbean and European Perspectives") organized by the University of Amsterdam and the University of Ghana in Accra. The organizers invited the Dutch ambassador to Ghana to deliver a welcome speech to the audience, which included academics, Ghanaian officers, and representatives of the Ghanaian immigration service. To the shock of organizers and all who attended, the ambassador announced that the Netherlands would consider cuts in development aid to Ghana if it did not cooperate more closely with Dutch authorities and agree to the repatriation of migrants who did not have residence permits in the Netherlands.

15. State bureaucrats have a very telling term for documents used for the production of other documents: *breeder documents*. A birth certificate is a breeder document for a passport because the passport uses information (e.g., name, year of birth) from the birth certificate. When it comes to biometric passports, biometric techniques (e.g., fingerprints) can verify the relation between the biometric document and the holder but not the relation of the holder and other documents, such as the birth certificate used to produce the passport. The unavoidable reliance of biometric documents on other types of documentation leaves open space for unauthorized identity craft practices (Cutolo and Banégas 2018; Banégas, Cutolo, and Kouyate 2021).

16. While Jason was a deportee, he had managed to return with money that allowed him to support his family and his people. He did not face stigmatization as other deportees who return emptyhanded because he managed to convert his wealth into local recognition for himself and his family (see Kleist 2020; Awedoba and Hahn 2014).

Chapter Three

1. The growth of cocoa production in the early twentieth century resulted in farmers migrating in search of adequate lands. According to Coe (2014, 50–51), migrant farmers in need of

capital to purchase land often pawned their relatives, especially their own children. But they also relied on their wives and children as sources of labor for their farms and thus wanted to have many wives to give birth to many children. For this chapter, it is relevant to note that the history of cocoa production in Ghana was from its onset tightly related to migration and kinship.

2. The system of *abusa* was neither unique to cocoa plantations nor the first time this labor relationship was observed in Ghana. For example, there are references to *abusa* in mining arrangements in the nineteenth-century Gold Coast: "Owners of land where gold and other minerals are found give permission to miners to work thereon. These men open mines and sink shafts, and the customary rent is known as *Ebusã*, which is a division into three parts of whatever the mines produce, whether gold, or quartz, or other minerals" (Sarbah 1904, 73). Furthermore, the system of *abusa* is also used, though to a lesser extent, in the production of citrus, palm oil, kola nut, and other food crops (Amanor and Diderutuah 2001).

3. In popular culture, there are also references to the practice of identity loan in African diasporic communities. For example, the Nigerian Igbo novelist Chimamanda Ngozi Adichie (2013) described in her book *Americanah* how unauthorized Nigerian migrants in the United Kingdom find employment under someone else's name (for other novels that refer to similar arrangements, see Nfon 2013; Umar 2017; Mbombo 2016). The song "Green Card" by the Ghanaian artist Wanlov the Kubolor narrates the life of a Ghanaian migrant in the United States and his struggles to find a job without a work permit: "Can't get a job without social security / A friend takes pity says 'Use ma I.D.' / 'Thanks, but um . . . I don't look like you / And I'm 6 foot / Your I.D. says 5′2″.'"

4. *Surprising Europe* is made and presented by African migrants. It is interesting that an episode on "cloning" focused exclusively on the risks posed to those engaged in identity loan by the controls of immigration authorities and employers. See "What to Do without Papers? Try to Become Someone Else," *Surprising Europe*, 2016, http://www.surprisingeurope.com/items/what-to-do-without-papers-cloning-try-to-become-someone-else. The coverage did not include any information about payments between migrants or the risks involved in loaning documents. However, in his autobiography, Ssuuna Golooba (2016), the initiator of the *Surprising Europe* project, focuses on its negative aspects and the problems he experienced in receiving the agreed amount from the document lender.

5. However, Horton (2016b, 208n2) noted that the tip by document lenders to document borrowers was a recent development. Until the late 1990s, those who received the documents had to pay document lenders $100 for each $1,000 earned. In 1996, it became possible for unauthorized migrants to obtain an Individual Taxpayer Identification Number, which enabled them to file taxes under their name. In anticipation of a future legalization program, which, paradoxically, often requires applicants to demonstrate evidence of good citizenship during their years of "illegality," such as paying taxes (Chauvin and Garcés-Mascareñas 2012; 2014; Horton 2020), unauthorized migrants preferred to work under their own name and use a fake social security number instead of borrowing one. To make identity loan more attractive to unauthorized migrants, and of course out of fear that they would lose unemployment payments, document lenders gave up their requests for money in exchange for their papers and instead started offering a tip to those who wanted to use their documents and work under their name.

6. Of course, as she also noted, this did not always prevent her interviewees from talking about their own practices.

7. A Ghanaian migrant who was formerly a cocoa farmer explained the connection between cocoa farming in Ghana and identity loan in the Netherlands: "Everything we do in this world is

based on experience. Probably those who started it [identity loan], they got this idea from farming. OK, when my father has a farm and someone comes from wherever, seasonal worker, coming to take the farm and work it, this is how they share it. They share it because he [the laborer] hasn't really put enough effort into it and want to get something. So we share it in three and then he takes one. But in this case here [in the Netherlands], it is a person who has to go up and down, buy bus ticket and all of that. So, the same thing works here but maybe the opposite direction [the laborer takes two-thirds of income] because I'm basically going to stay at home and receive it."

8. In the Netherlands, holiday allowance (*vakantiegeld*) is given by the employer to employees to cover vacation costs. It is a fixed percentage, about 8 percent, of the gross salary, which is kept every month and deposited annually in the employee's account at the end of May.

9. In an interview with an Afro-Surinamese man who worked as a recruiter in various employment agencies, he said that some Afro-Surinamese migrants, especially Maroons who used to live in the Surinamese inland rain forest, gave their documents to African migrants. He said these exchanges took place before 2004, and although employment agencies were aware of the practice, it was often not easy to tell the difference between an African and an Afro-Surinamese person: "They call them Bosland Creolen. They live in the woods and they are similar to African people. They speak the same. They don't speak Dutch. So you have a lot of them who came to Holland also. So, they have also the Dutch nationality and they could not speak Dutch. So, it was not easy to check. And between those two groups [Bosland Creolen and Africans] a lot of passports and work permits circulated. . . . They have their own language and it's very often exactly the same with what the Ghanaian or what the Nigerian people speak. Even for me it's difficult to see where they are from, if they are Surinamese or Africans." During my fieldwork, I came across a few Africans who had used the documents of Afro-Surinamese people. They told me that the Surinamese who gave them their documents could speak Dutch and that their own English was good enough to communicate with them.

10. Mama Clara was the only person I talked with who claimed that part of the money is meant for expenses for potential legal assistance in the case of being caught. Most people I talked with who had given their documents to unauthorized migrants considered it self-evident that they had to be paid without providing explanation as to how they would spend the payment.

11. "Many speculations and arguments abound as to most of the deaths; some alleged spiritual attacks, stress, eating habit, medication abuse, social conflicts and economic crisis, etc. . . . Attribution of the deaths to spiritual attacks has pitched the religious circles in collision with secular minds. It was said that a Ghanaian traditional priest that visited Netherlands some time ago predicted that about 35 persons of Ghanaian descent may die in the year 2012. This prediction has been making the rounds as to the prophesy coming to pass. To some, it is a curse, while others see it as a prophesy" ("Alarming Death Rate" 2012).

12. Pentecostal narratives very often appeal to witch-doctor testimonies to stress the protection of born-again Christians from occult powers. One of Daswani's (2015, 140) Pentecostal interlocutors, for example, said that after his stepmother attempted unsuccessfully to poison him, she returned to the witch doctor who gave her the poison. The witch doctor was surprised that the poison was not effective and used a magic mirror to look into the person's life. He then saw a ring of fire surrounding the person and asked the stepmother why she wanted to kill a child of God. Quite ironically, although witch doctors' confessions reassure born-again Christians that they are not at risk, they also reproduce and heighten the fear of witchcraft by those who are not "true" or "good" Christians.

13. Francis Nyamnjoh (2013, 653) describes African migrations "as an emotional, relational and social phenomenon captured in the complexities, contradictions and messiness of their

everyday realities." He notes that scholarly accounts cannot fully capture these complexities and thus advocates an engagement of ethnography with relevant works of fiction.

Chapter Four

1. Privileges that were, of course, relative to the disadvantaged position of legally unauthorized African migrants.

2. According to Howell (2006, 9), "kinning," the process in which an adopted baby develops permanent relations, expressed in kinship terms, with a new family often succeeds a process of "de-kinning" with the birth parents of the baby—especially if they abandoned their child. For other studies that consider the weakening or undoing of kinship, see Amrith and Coe (2022), Papadaki (2018); Bodenhorn (2000).

3. Many Ghanaian migrants who arrived in the Netherlands that period had stayed previously in Germany (Bakuri 2015).

4. According to Onderzoek Informatie en Statistiek (OIS) data, 24 percent of registered Ghanaians in 1992 and 30 percent in 2013 were dual nationals, but this does not necessarily mean that one of the two nationalities was Dutch. In 1992, 57 percent of Ghanaians had a single foreign nationality, compared to 30 percent in 2013. These numbers concern only registered residents of the municipality of Amsterdam.

5. OIS data from 2013.

6. This does not necessarily mean that this knowledge was important for their everyday life or their feelings of belonging (see Balkenhol 2021).

7. The Ghanaian historian Akosua Perbi (2004, 35) distinguished five different sources of slave supply to Dutch traders along the Ghanaian coast: warfare, market supply, raids and kidnapping, tribute, and pawning.

8. Trouw, June 12, 2002, quoted in (and translated by) Balkenhol (2021, 87).

9. The literature on marriage and migration has predominantly focused on cross-border marriages in economically developed counties, especially in North America, Europe, and some Asian countries. For a review of the literature on marriage and migration, see Brettell (2017).

10. At the time these posts were published online, they were open to public. This account no longer exists.

11. See "Grote actie tegen schijnhuwelijken," NOS, November 9, 2016, http://nos.nl/artikel /438594-grote-actie-tegen-schijnhuwelijken.html.

12. See "Phillips Onikoyi jailed for Nottingham sham marriages," BBC, February 1, 2012, https://www.bbc.com/news/uk-england-nottinghamshire-16789080.

13. See "Plastic Wedding Rings Used in Nottingham Sham Marriages," BBC, February 1, 2012, https://www.bbc.com/news/uk-england-nottinghamshire-14970873.

14. See "Broker Fake Marriages with Antillean Women in Court," Daily Herald: The Leading Newspaper for St. Maarten and the Northeast Caribbean, April 13, 2016, https://www.thedaily herald.sx/islands/56773-broker-fake-marriages-with-antillean-women-in-court.

Chapter Five

1. In the Netherlands, there are three types of unions that grant rights and obligations to two partners of the opposite or same sex: marriage (huwelijk), registered partnership (geregisteerd partnerschap), and cohabitation contract (samenlevingscontract).

2. "The Metock case" (*Metock v. Minister of Justice Equality and Law Reform*) was named after one of four African nationals (Cameroonian and Nigerian) who married EU citizens (from Britain, Poland, and Germany) in Ireland. The Irish government denied them residence permits, thereby denying them the right to free movement, on the grounds that they had resided unlawfully in Ireland and that some had married only after their European spouses exercised their right to free movement by coming to Ireland. Ireland justified its decision by claiming that the denial of permits would not have any impact on the economic activities of the EU citizen spouses and family members, who had already been in Ireland and exercised their freedom of movement. The European Court of Justice, however, ruled in favor of Metock and the other Nigerian and Cameroonian nationals, and Ireland was obliged to grant them residence permits. The decision had wide impact because other EU countries had interpreted and acted on Directive 2004/38 similarly to Ireland but became obliged to heed the court's interpretation (Arcarazo 2009; Bierbach 2017b; Tryfonidou 2009).

3. In 2009 in the Netherlands, there were 109,190 single women (i.e., unmarried, divorced, or widowed adults) from Germany, 34,717 from Belgium, and 24,169 from the United Kingdom; from Greece there were 4,169; from Poland, 24,382; and from other Eastern European countries, 6,865 (Centraal Bureau voor de Statistiek).

4. In 2022, Statistics Netherlands (Centraal Bureau voor de Statistiek) introduced a new system of categorization by country and continent of origin. See "CBS Introducing New Population Classification by Origin," March 18, 2022, https://www.cbs.nl/en-gb/news/2022/07/cbs-introducing-new-population-classification-by-origin.

5. For example, see Rijksoverheid, "Hogere Eisen Huwelijksmigratie En Inburgering," 2009, https://rijksoverheid.archiefweb.eu/#archive.

6. Love is not explicitly mentioned in legal definitions of sham marriage. Nevertheless, the romantic love ideal informs immigration officers' implementation of these laws and policies, judges' decisions in legal cases on sham marriages, and political discourse such as parliamentary debates on the topic (De Hart 2003; Bonjour and De Hart 2013; Pellander 2021; Scheel 2017).

7. Of sixty-nine court decisions for cases of sham marriages in the Netherlands from 2006 to 2017, in only ten cases the "sponsor" was a Dutch national. In all other cases the sponsors were EU citizens, predominantly women from Eastern Europe (particularly Poland) (De Hart 2017b, 401).

8. This dependency of a migrant spouse on the citizen spouse goes beyond the legal necessity for the residence permit. For example, the citizen partner has better knowledge of the country of settlement and better-established access to the labor market, speaks the country's language better, and has a larger network of friends and family who can potentially provide support.

9. In a different context, in coastal Kenya, where Samburu men engage in intimate relations with European female tourists, Meiu (2017) described the various forms of exchanges that result from these encounters as ethnoerotic economies. What makes this framing particularly interesting is that Meiu did not only focus on the commodification of African men's ethnosexuality and the transfers between Samburu men and European women. He also showed how the money produced in coastal Kenya through such encounters flowed back to the men's hometowns and was used by them to craft belonging and gain respect.

10. There is, however, a good side, according to Livingstone: "The good thing is that you get a free house and some clothes. They will never ask for your money like African women who are always begging money from their husbands" (Golooba 2016, 60)

11. As noted, the practices of migrants vary considerably. The search for a wife from Europe's periphery is most common among Nigerian men. Although the trend is similar among Ghanaian male migrants, they often marry non-Dutch EU citizens of Ghanaian descent. The history of Ghanaian migration to Europe is longer than that of Nigerian migration, which makes Ghanaian communities richer in civic resources. Figure 5.2 and table 5.2 depict these differences and show that Ghanaians marry more often with other Ghanaians than do Nigerians with other Nigerians. The figure and table are categorized by ethnicity, so a marriage between a Ghanaian migrant in the Netherlands and a British citizen of Ghanaian descent appears as a Ghanaian-Ghanaian marriage.

12. Certainly, not all migrants from Southern and Eastern Europe in the Netherlands are working class and poor. A great many of them are highly educated and work in prestigious and well-paid professions in Amsterdam. However, the contacts that legally precarious African migrants have with them are minimal because in their daily life, either in their working-class neighborhoods (e.g., the Bijlmer, parts of Amsterdam Noord) or at their workplace, the peripheral Europeans they come across mostly share a similar position to their own in Dutch society.

13. According to estimates for 2009, Nigerian migrants sent, on average, the greatest amount of money to their country of origin (around €3,000 per household). The list with the top 20 nationalities in the Netherlands by amount of money remitted to their home countries include: Romania (seventh), Bulgaria (tenth), Hungary (eleventh), Poland (twelfth), Portugal (thirteenth), Spain (fifteenth), Greece (sixteenth), Ghana (twentieth) (De Boom et al. 2011, 115).

14. From the French verb *consommer*, "to consume." Usually this job includes not sexual services but chatting with male customers to make them consume more and buy the women expensive drinks.

15. Of course not all women in Greece express their love in that way. The norms and practices of love differ across generations, social classes, place of residence, and so on.

16. All Frank's entries are in English and undated. All Kyriaki's entries are in Greek. Kyriaki could not read English and became aware of the content of these entries only when I translated them for her.

17. Sexual services and sexual pleasure are rarely reciprocal. In studies of sexual exchanges in African contexts, sex is usually framed as a gift from women to men (e.g., Hunter 2010; Tabet 1991; Adomako Ampofo 1997, 2007). For an exception, see Meiu (2017).

Conclusion

1. In Euripides's *Medea* (431 BC), the ancient Greek tragedy, the impossibility of a rational assessment of trust is expressed in Medea's rhetorical question to God: "Zeus, why did you give humans signs to clearly identify counterfeit gold, but no mark on a man's body to distinguish the bad among men?" (516–19) (Rayor 2013, 23). Medea said these words after her husband Jason, the leader of the Argonauts, left her to marry another woman. Medea had helped Jason steal the Golden Fleece from the kingdom of Colchis, where her father was king; abandoned her family to live with Jason; and even killed her little brother to make it possible for Jason and the Argonauts to sail away from Colchis. Feeling deeply betrayed by Jason, Medea eventually took revenge by killing their two children.

2. Interestingly, though, the outcome defies common sense. For example, elsewhere De Haas (2007; Flahaux and De Haas 2016) has shown that more development in migrant-sending regions did not lead to less migration but to more—at least in the short term.

3. In the theorization of the migrant network approach, in which reciprocity is associated with social distance (see chapter 1), Massey and colleagues (1987, 1994) did not refer directly to Sahlins's (1972) concentric-circle model. But they cited other anthropological studies, such as work by Adler Lomnitz (1977), which reproduced Sahlins's point that family is a site of generalized or positive reciprocity.

4. Other studies on urban marginality (e.g., Menjívar 2000; Fennell 2016) have also stressed the importance of mutual assistance as a survival strategy for disadvantaged populations. But they did emphasize the conflicts that the sharing of scarce resources may cause as well as the devastating burden of obligations for all those who engage in exchange relations. Elsewhere I have written about the necessity of collaboration between legally precarious Nigerian migrants in Thessaloniki who worked as street vendors and were in a more or less similar, unequal position. Nevertheless, I stressed that the strong solidarity relations, expressed as "brotherhood," between these migrants were also grounded in existential fear, shame, and a common economic interest (Andrikopoulos 2018, 226–30).

Bibliography

Abarca, Gray Albert, and Susan Bibler Coutin. 2018. "Sovereign Intimacies: The Lives of Documents within US State-Noncitizen Relationships." *American Ethnologist* 45 (1): 7–19.

About, Ilsen, James Brown, and Gayle Lonergan, eds. 2013. *Identification and Registration Practices in Transnational Perspective: People, Papers and Practices*. New York: Palgrave.

Adebanwni, Wale, and Ebenezer Obadare. 2022. "Paper Games: Consularity and Ersatz Lives in Urban Lagos." In *Everyday State and Democracy in Africa: Ethnographic Encounters*, edited by Wale Adebanwni, 70–96. Athens: Ohio University Press.

Ademuleya, Babasehinde A. 2007. "The Concept of Ori in the Traditional Yoruba Visual Representation of Human Figures." *Nordic Journal of African Studies* 16 (2): 212–20.

Adepoju, Aderanti, and Arie van der Wiel. 2010. *Seeking Greener Pastures Abroad: A Migration Profile of Nigeria*. Ibadan, Nigeria: Safari Books.

Adesina, Olutayo C., and Akanmu Adebayo. 2009. "Globalization and Transnational Migrations: An Overview." In *Globalization and Transnational Migrations: Africa and Africans in the Contemporary Global System*, edited by Akanmu Adebayo and Olutayo C. Adesina, 2–13. Newcastle upon Tyne, UK: Cambridge Scholars Publishing.

Adesina, Oluwakemi Abiodun. 2007. "'Checking Out': Migration, Popular Culture, and the Articulation and Formation of Class Identity." Paper presented at the African Migrations workshop "Understanding Migration Dynamics in the Continent," Accra, September 18–21.

Adichie, Chimamanda Ngozi. 2013. *Americanah*. New York: Alfred Knopf.

Adler Lomnitz, Larissa. 1977. *Networks and Marginality: Life in a Mexican Shantytown*. New York: Academic Press.

Adomako Ampofo, Akosua. 1997. "Costs and Rewards—Exchange in Relationships: Experiences of Some Ghanaian Women." In *Transforming Female Identities: Women's Organizational Forms in West Africa*, edited by Eva Evers Rosander, 177–94. Uppsala, Sweden: Nordiska Afrikainstitutet.

———. 2007. "'My Cocoa Is Between My Legs': Sex as Work among Ghanaian Women." In *Women's Labor in the Global Economy: Speaking in Multiple Voices*, edited by Sharon Harley, 182–205. New Brunswick, NJ: Rutgers University Press.

Akanle, Olayinka. 2009. "'Immigration Cultism' and Nigerian Migrants: Tidal Dynamism in the Age of Globalization." In *Globalization and Transnational Migrations: Africa and Africans in the Contemporary Global System*, edited by Akanmu Adebayo and Olutayo C. Adesina, 181–200. Newcastle upon Tyne, UK: Cambridge Scholars Publishing.

——. 2013. *Kinship Networks and International Migration in Nigeria*. Newcastle upon Tyne, UK: Cambridge Scholars Publishing.

Akanle, Olayinka, Olufunke A. Fayehun, Gbenga S. Adejare, and Otomi A. Orobome. 2021. "International Migration, Kinship Networks and Social Capital in Southwestern Nigeria." *Journal of Borderlands Studies* 36 (2): 319–32.

Akgündüz, Ahmet. 2012. "Guest Worker Migration in Post-War Europe (1946–1974): An Analytical Appraisal." In *An Introduction to International Migration Studies. European Perspectives*, edited by M. Martiniello and J. Rath, 181–209. Amsterdam: Amsterdam University Press.

Akyeampong, Emmanuel. 2000. "Africans in the Diaspora: The Diaspora and Africa." *African Affairs* 99 (395): 183–215.

"Alarming Death Rate in Ghana Community NL." 2012. *African Bulletin* 11 (121): 10.

Alfaro-Velcamp, Theresa, Robert H. McLaughlin, Gahlia Brogneri, Matthew Skade, and Mark Shaw. 2017. " 'Getting Angry with Honest People': The Illicit Market for Immigrant 'Papers' in Cape Town, South Africa." *Migration Studies* 5 (2): 216–36.

Alpes, Maybritt Jill. 2017a. *Brokering High-Risk Migration and Illegality in West Africa: Abroad at Any Cost*. New York: Routledge.

——. 2017b. "Papers That Work: Migration Brokers, State/Market Boundaries, and the Place of Law." *PoLAR: Political and Legal Anthropology Review* 40 (2): 262–77.

Amanor, Kojo, and Maxwell Kude Diderutuah. 2001. *Share Contracts in the Oil Palm and Citrus Belt of Ghana*. London: International Institute for Environment and Development.

Amrith, Megha, and Cati Coe. 2022. "Disposable Kin: Shifting Registers of Belonging in Global Care Economies." *American Anthropologist* 124 (2): 307–18.

Anderson, Bridget. 2020. "And about Time Too . . . Migration, Documentation, and Temporalities." In *Paper Trials: Migrants, Documents, and Legal Insecurity*, edited by Sarah Horton and Josiah Heyman, 53–73. Durham, NC: Duke University Press.

Andersson, Ruben. 2014. *Illegality, Inc. Clandestine Migration and the Business of Bordering Europe*. Oakland: University of California Press.

Andrikopoulos, Apostolos. 2013. "Migration, Class and Symbolic Status: Nigerians in the Netherlands and Greece." In *Long Journeys. African Migrants on the Road*, edited by Alessandro Triulzi and Lawrence McKenzie, 165–85. Leiden, Netherlands: Brill.

——. 2017. "Hospitality and Immigration in a Greek Urban Neighborhood: An Ethnography of Mimesis." *City & Society* 29 (2): 281–304.

——. 2018. "After Citizenship: The Process of Kinship in a Setting of Civic Inequality." In *Reconnecting State and Kinship*, edited by Erdmute Alber and Tatjana Thelen, 220–40. Philadelphia: University of Pennsylvania Press.

——. 2021. "Love, Money and Papers in the Affective Circuits of Cross-Border Marriages: Beyond the 'Sham'/'Genuine' Dichotomy." *Journal of Ethnic and Migration Studies* 47 (2): 343–60.

——. N.d. "Becoming White?" In *Migrant Academics' Narratives of Precarity and Resilience*, edited by Olga Burlyuk and Ladan Rahbari. Unpublished manuscript under review.

Andrikopoulos, Apostolos, and Jan Willem Duyvendak. 2020. "Migration, Mobility and the Dynamics of Kinship: New Barriers, New Assemblages." *Ethnography* 21 (3): 299–318.

Apter, Andrew. 2012. "Matrilineal Motives: Kinship, Witchcraft, and Repatriation among Congolese Refugees." *Journal of the Royal Anthropological Institute* 18 (1): 22–44.

Arcarazo, Diego Acosta. 2009. "Immigration in the European Union: Family Reunification After the Metock Case." *University College Dublin Law Review* 9: 64–89.

Archambault, Julie Soleil. 2016. "Taking Love Seriously in Human-Plant Relations in Mozambique: Toward an Anthropology of Affective Encounters." *Cultural Anthropology* 31 (2): 244–71.

Atekmangoh, Christina. 2017. *Les Mbengis-Migration, Gender, and Family: The Moral Economy of Transnational Cameroonian Migrants' Remittances.* Mankon/Bamenda, Cameroon: Langaa RPCIG.

Awedoba, Albert K. and Hans Peter Hahn. 2014. "Wealth, Consumption and Migration in a West African Society. New Lifestyles and New Social Obligations among the Kasena, Northern Ghana." *Anthropos* 109 (1): 45–55.

Babátúndé, Abosede Omowumi. 2017. "Orí and Ẹlẹ́dàá in Poverty Conceptualization in Traditional Yorùbá Religion: Challenging Developmental and Aid Organizations' Understandings of Poverty." *Journal of African Cultural Studies* 29 (3): 362–76.

Bakuri, Amisah Zenabu. 2015. "Ghanaian Migrants in the Netherlands: Germany as a Transit Zone." In *African Roads to Prosperity: People En Route to Socio-Cultural and Economic Transformations*, edited by Akinyinka Akinyoade and Jan-Bart Gewald, 232–63. Leiden, Netherlands: Brill.

———. 2018. "Ghanaian Migration to the Netherlands: Status Paradox?" *Cultural and Religious Studies* 6 (10): 561–77.

Balkenhol, Markus. 2021. *Tracing Slavery: The Politics of Atlantic Memory in the Netherlands.* New York: Berghahn Books.

Balogun, Oladele Abiodun. 2007. "The Concepts of Ori and Human Destiny in Traditional Yoruba Thought: A Soft-Deterministic Interpretation." *Nordic Journal of African Studies* 16 (1): 116–30.

Banégas, Richard, Armando Cutolo, and Souleymane Kouyate. 2021. "General Amnesty for all 'René Cailliés'! Falsifying Birth Certificates and Reforming Legal Identification in Côte d'Ivoire." In *Identification and Citizenship in Africa: Biometrics, the Documentary State and Bureaucratic Writings of the Self*, edited by Séverine Awenengo Dalberto and Richard Banégas, 122–26. London: Routledge.

Barth, Fredrik, ed. 1969. *Ethnic Groups and Boundaries: The Social Organization of Culture Difference.* Oslo: Universitetsforlaget.

Bastide, Roger. 1973. "Le principe d'individuation (contribution à une philosophie africaine)." In *La notion de personne en Afrique noire*, 33–43. Paris: Éditions du Centre National de la Recherche Scientifique.

Baumann, Gerd. 1995. "Managing a Polyethnic Milieu: Kinship and Interaction in a London Suburb." *Journal of the Royal Anthropological Institute* 1 (4): 725–41.

———. 1996. *Contesting Culture: Discourses of Identity in Multi-Ethnic London.* Cambridge: Cambridge University Press.

Beck, Ulrich, and Elisabeth Beck-Gernsheim. 2010. "Passage to Hope: Marriage, Migration, and the Need for a Cosmopolitan Turn in Family Research." *Journal of Family Theory & Review* 2 (4): 401–14.

Belloni, Milena. 2019. *The Big Gamble: The Migration of Eritreans to Europe.* Oakland: University of California Press.

Bierbach, Jeremy Benjamin. 2017a. "Family Life as a Civil Right for Some EU Citizens, but Not All: Reserve Discrimination in the EU and the US." *Asiel & Migrantenrecht* (6–7): 275–80.

———. 2017b. *Frontiers of Equality in the Development of EU and US Citizenship*. The Hague: T.M.C. Asser Press.

Block, Laura. 2021. "'(Im-)Proper' Members with '(Im-)Proper' Families? Framing Spousal Migration Policies in Germany." *Journal of Ethnic and Migration Studies* 47 (2): 379–96.

Böcker, Anita. 1994. "Chain Migration over Legally Closed Borders: Settled Immigrants as Bridgeheads and Gatekeepers." *Netherlands' Journal of Social Sciences* 30 (2): 87–106.

Bodenhorn, Barbara. 2000. "'He Used to Be My Relative': Exploring the Bases of Relatedness among Iñupiat of Northern Alaska." In *Cultures of Relatedness: New Approaches to the Study of Kinship*, edited by Janet Carsten, 128–48. Cambridge: Cambridge University Press.

Boehm, Deborah A. 2012. *Intimate Migrations: Gender, Family, and Illegality among Transnational Mexicans*. New York: NYU Press.

Bonjour, Saskia, and Betty De Hart. 2013. "A Proper Wife, a Proper Marriage: Constructions of 'Us' and 'Them' in Dutch Family Migration Policy." *European Journal of Women's Studies* 20 (1): 61–76.

Bonjour, Saskia, and Jan Willem Duyvendak. 2018. "The 'Migrant with Poor Prospects': Racialized Intersections of Class and Culture in Dutch Civic Integration Debates." *Ethnic and Racial Studies* 41 (5): 882–900.

Bosniak, Linda. 2008. *The Citizen and the Alien: Dilemmas of Contemporary Membership*. Princeton, NJ: Princeton University Press.

Bourdieu, Pierre. 2000. *Pascalian Meditations*. Stanford, CA: Stanford University Press.

Brennan, Denise. 2004. *What's Love Got to Do with It? Transnational Desires and Sex Tourism in the Dominican Republic*. Durham, NC: Duke University Press.

Brettell, Caroline. 2017. "Marriage and Migration." *Annual Review of Anthropology* 46: 81–97.

Brubaker, Rogers. 1992. *Citizenship and Nationhood in France and Germany*. Cambridge: Cambridge University Press.

———. 2004. *Ethnicity without Groups*. Cambridge, MA: Harvard University Press.

Bruner, Edward M. 1996. "Tourism in Ghana: The Representation of Slavery and the Return of the Black Diaspora." *American Anthropologist* 98 (2): 290–304.

Campbell, Eugene. 2010. "Irregular Migration within and to the Republic of South Africa and from the African Continent to the European Union: Tapping Latent Energy of the Youth." In *International Migration within, to and from Africa in a Globalised World*, edited by Aderanti Adepoju, 168–208. Accra: Sub-Saharan Publishers.

Caplan, Jane. 2001. "'This or That Particular Person': Protocols of Identification in Nineteenth-Century Europe." In *Documenting Individual Identity: The Development of State Practices in the Modern World*, edited by Jane Caplan and John Torpey, 49–66. Princeton, NJ: Princeton University Press.

Caplan, Jane, and John C. Torpey, eds. 2001. *Documenting Individual Identity: The Development of State Practices in the Modern World*. Princeton, NJ: Princeton University Press.

Carling, Jørgen. 2002. "Migration in the Age of Involuntary Immobility: Theoretical Reflections and Cape Verdean Experiences." *Journal of Ethnic and Migration Studies* 28 (1): 5–42.

———. 2006. *Migration, Human Smuggling and Trafficking from Nigeria to Europe*. Geneva: International Organization for Migration.

Carrithers, Michael, Steven Collins, and Steven Lukes, eds. 1985. *The Category of the Person: Anthropology, Philosophy, History*. Cambridge: Cambridge University Press.

Carsten, Janet. 1997. *The Heat of the Hearth: The Process of Kinship in a Malay Fishing Community*. Oxford: Oxford University Press.

———. 2000. *Cultures of Relatedness: New Approaches to the Study of Kinship*. Cambridge: Cambridge University Press.

———. 2004. *After Kinship*. Cambridge: Cambridge University Press.

———. 2013. "What Kinship Does—and How." *HAU: Journal of Ethnographic Theory* 3 (2): 245–51.

———. 2020. "Imagining and Living New Worlds: The Dynamics of Kinship in Contexts of Mobility and Migration." *Ethnography* 21 (3): 319–34.

Carver, Natasha. 2016. "'For Her Protection and Benefit': The Regulation of Marriage-Related Migration to the UK." *Ethnic and Racial Studies* 39 (15): 2758–76.

Castles, Stephen, Hein De Haas, and Mark J. Miller. 2014. *The Age of Migration: International Population Movements in the Modern World*. New York: Palgrave Macmillan.

Castles, Stephen, and Godula Kosack. 1972. "The Function of Labour Immigration in Western European Capitalism." *New Left Review* (73): 3–21.

Charsley, Katharine. 2005. "Unhappy Husbands: Masculinity and Migration in Transnational Pakistani Marriages." *Journal of the Royal Anthropological Institute* 11 (1): 85–105.

———. 2013. *Transnational Pakistani Connections: Marrying "Back Home."* London: Routledge.

Charsley, Katharine, and Anika Liversage. 2015. "Silenced Husbands: Muslim Marriage Migration and Masculinity." *Men and Masculinities* 18 (4): 489–508.

Chauvin, Sébastien. 2010. *Les agences de la précarité: Journaliers à Chicago*. Paris: Seuil.

———. 2017. "In the Shadow of Employment Precarity: Informal Protection and Risk Transfers in Low-End Temporary Staffing." In *Democracy and the Welfare State: The Two Wests in the Age of Austerity*, edited by Alice Kessler-Harris and Maurizio Vaudagna, 176–94. New York: Columbia University Press.

Chauvin, Sébastien, and Blanca Garcés-Mascareñas. 2012. "Beyond Informal Citizenship: The New Moral Economy of Migrant Illegality." *International Political Sociology* 6 (3): 241–59.

———. 2014. "Becoming Less Illegal: Deservingness Frames and Undocumented Migrant Incorporation." *Sociology Compass* 8 (4): 422–32.

Chauvin, Sébastien, Manuela Salcedo Robledo, Timo Koren, and Joël Illidge. 2021. "Class, Mobility and Inequality in the Lives of Same-Sex Couples with Mixed Legal Statuses." *Journal of Ethnic and Migration Studies* 47 (2): 430–46.

Choldin, Harvey M. 1973. "Kinship Networks in the Migration Process." *International Migration Review* 7 (2): 163–75.

Chu, Julie Y. 2010. *Cosmologies of Credit: Transnational Mobility and the Politics of Destination in China*. Durham, NC: Duke University Press.

Coe, Cati. 2014. *The Scattered Family: Parenting, African Migrants, and Global Inequality*. Chicago: University of Chicago Press.

Cohen, Abner. 1969. *Custom and Politics in Urban Africa: A Study of Hausa Migrants in Yoruba Towns*. London: Routledge and Kegan Paul.

Cohen, Adrienne. 2018. "Occult Return, Divine Grace, and Saabui: Practising Transnational Kinship in Postsocialist Guinea." *Journal of the Royal Anthropological Institute* 24 (2): 275–92.

Cohen, Deborah. 2006. "From Peasant to Worker: Migration, Masculinity, and the Making of Mexican Workers in the US." *International Labor and Working-Class History* 69 (1): 81–103.

Cole, Jennifer. 2009. "Love, Money, and Economies of Intimacy in Tamatave, Madagascar." In *Love in Africa*, edited by Jennifer Cole and Lynn M. Thomas, 109–34. Chicago: University of Chicago Press.

———. 2014a. "Producing Value among Malagasy Marriage Migrants in France: Managing Horizons of Expectation." *Current Anthropology* 55 (S9): S85-S94.

———. 2014b. "Working Mis/Understandings: The Tangled Relationship between Kinship, Franco-Malagasy Binational Marriages, and the French State." *Cultural Anthropology* 29 (3): 527–51.

———. 2016. "Giving Life: Regulating Affective Circuits among Malagasy Marriage Migrants in France." In *Affective Circuits: African Migrations to Europe and the Pursuit of Social Regeneration*, edited by Jennifer Cole and Christian Groes, 197–222. Chicago: University of Chicago Press.

Cole, Jennifer, and Christian Groes. 2016a. "Affective Circuits and Social Regeneration in African Migration." In *Affective Circuits: African Migrations to Europe and the Pursuit of Social Regeneration*, edited by Jennifer Cole and Christian Groes, 1–26. Chicago: University of Chicago Press.

———. 2016b. *Affective Circuits: African Migration to Europe and the Pursuit of Social Regeneration*. Chicago: University of Chicago Press.

Colic-Peisker, Val. 2011. "A New Era in Australian Multiculturalism? from Working-Class 'Ethnics' to a 'Multicultural Middle-Class.'" *International Migration Review* 45 (3): 562–87.

Collier, Jane. 1988. *Marriage and Inequality in Classless Societies*. Palo Alto, CA: Stanford University Press.

———. 1997. *From Duty to Desire: Remaking Families in a Spanish Village*. Princeton, NJ: Princeton University Press.

Comaroff, Jean, and John L. Comaroff. 2016. *The Truth about Crime*. Chicago: University of Chicago Press.

Constable, Nicole. 2003. *Romance on a Global Stage: Pen Pals, Virtual Ethnography, and "Mail Order" Marriages*. Berkeley: University of California Press.

Constable, Nicole, ed. 2010. *Cross-Border Marriages: Gender and Mobility in Transnational Asia*. Philadelphia: University of Pennsylvania Press.

Cooper, Elizabeth, and David Pratten, eds. 2015. *Ethnographies of Uncertainty in Africa*. New York: Palgrave Macmillan.

Cornwall, Andrea. 2002. "Spending Power: Love, Money, and the Reconfiguration of Gender Relations in Ado-Odo, Southwestern Nigeria." *American Ethnologist* 29 (4): 963–80.

Cutolo, Armando, and Richard Banégas. 2018. "Les margouillats et les papiers kamikazes." *Genèses* (3): 81–102.

Dahinden, Janine. 2016. "A Plea for the 'De-Migranticization' of Research on Migration and Integration." *Ethnic and Racial Studies* 39 (13): 2207–25.

Dalberto, Séverine Awenengo, and Richard Banégas. 2021. "The Social and Political Life of Identity Papers in Contemporary Africa." In *Identification and Citizenship in Africa: Biometrics, the Documentary State and Bureaucratic Writings of the Self*, edited by Séverine Awenengo Dalberto and Richard Banégas, 1–26. London: Routledge.

Dalberto, Séverine Awenengo, Richard Banégas, and Armando Cutolo. 2021. "African Citizenships—A Biometric Turn?" In *Identification and Citizenship in Africa: Biometrics, the Documentary State and Bureaucratic Writings of the Self*, edited by Séverine Awenengo Dalberto and Richard Banégas, 29–48. London: Routledge.

D'Aoust, Anne-Marie. 2013. "In the Name of Love: Marriage Migration, Governmentality, and Technologies of Love." *International Political Sociology* 7 (3): 258–74.

———. 2022. "Thinking in Constellations: Marriage and Partner Migration in Relation to Security, Citizenship, and Rights." In *Transnational Marriage and Partner Migration: Constella-*

tion of Security, Citizenship, and Rights, edited by Anne-Marie D'Aoust, 1–27. New Brunswick, NJ: Rutgers University Press.

Darkwah, Akosua K. 2019. "Fluid Mobilities? Experiencing and Responding to Othering in a Borderless West Africa." *Contemporary Journal of African Studies* 6 (2): 54–72.

Darkwah, Akosua K., and Akosua Adomako Ampofo. 2008. "Race, Gender and Global Love: Non-Ghanaian Wives, Insiders or Outsiders in Ghana?" *International Journal of Sociology of the Family* 34 (2): 187–208.

Daswani, Girish. 2015. *Looking Back, Moving Forward: Transformation and Ethical Practice in the Ghanaian Church of Pentecost.* Toronto: University of Toronto Press.

De Boom, Jan, A. Weltevrede, Y. Seidler, P. Van Wensveen, Erik Snel, and Godfried Engbersen. 2011. *Migration and Migration Policies in the Netherlands 2011. Dutch SOPEMI Report.* Rotterdam: Risbo and Erasmus University.

De Genova, Nicholas. 2002. "Migrant 'Illegality' and Deportability in Everyday Life." *Annual Review of Anthropology* 31: 419–47.

De Haas, Hein. 2007. "Turning the Tide? Why Development Will Not Stop Migration." *Development and Change* 38 (5): 819–41.

———. 2008. *Irregular Migration from West Africa to the Maghreb and the European Union: An Overview of Recent Trends.* Vol. 32. Geneva: International Organization for Migration.

———. 2010. "The Internal Dynamics of Migration Processes: A Theoretical Inquiry." *Journal of Ethnic and Migration Studies* 36 (10): 1587–1617.

De Haas, Hein, Katharina Natter, and Simona Vezzoli. 2018. "Growing Restrictiveness or Changing Selection? The Nature and Evolution of Migration Policies." *International Migration Review* 52 (2): 324–67.

De Hart, Betty. 2003. "Onbezonnen Vrouwen: Gemengde Relaties in Het Nationaliteitsrecht En Het Vreemdelingenrecht." PhD diss., Nijmegen University.

———. 2017a. "The Europeanization of Love. the Marriage of Convenience in European Migration Law." *European Journal of Migration and Law* 19 (3): 281–306.

———. 2017b. "Wanneer is Er Sprake Van Een 'Oprecht' Huwelijk? Europeesrechtelijke Grenzen Aan De Controle Op Schijnhuwelijken." *Asiel & Migrantenrecht* 2017 (9): 398–404.

———. 2022. "The Odd Couple: Gender, Securitization, Europeanization, and Marriages of Convenience in Dutch Family Migration Policies (1930–2020)." In *Transnational Marriage and Partner Migration: Constellations of Security, Citizenship, and Rights*, edited by Anne-Marie D'Aoust, 31–48. New Brunswick, NJ: Rutgers University Press.

Delaney, Carol. 2001. "Cutting the Ties that Bind: The Sacrifice of Abraham and Patriarchal Kinship." In *Relative Values: Reconfiguring Kinship Studies*, edited by Sarah Franklin and Susan McKinnon, 445–67. Durham, NC: Duke University Press.

De Lange, Tesseltje. 2011. "The Privatization of Control Over Labour Migration in the Netherlands: In Whose Interest?" *European Journal of Migration and Law* 13 (2): 185–200.

Del Real, Deisy. 2019. "Toxic Ties: The Reproduction of Legal Violence within Mixed-Status Intimate Partners, Relatives, and Friends." *International Migration Review* 53 (2): 548–70.

Demirguc-Kunt, Asli, Leora Klapper, Dorothe Singer, Saniya Ansar, and Jake Hess. 2018. *Global Findex Database 2017: Measuring Financial Inclusion and the Fintech Revolution.* Washington, DC: World Bank.

De Witte, Marleen. 2019. "Black Citizenship, Afropolitan Critiques: Vernacular Heritage-making and the Negotiation of Race in the Netherlands." *Social Anthropology* 27 (4): 609–25.

Dobash, R. Emerson, and Russell Dobash. 1979. *Violence against Wives: A Case against the Patriarchy*. London: Open Books.

Doomernik, Jeroen. 2008. "Report from the Netherlands." In *Modes of Migration Regulation and Control in Europe*, edited by Jeroen Doomernik and Michael Jandl, 129–45. Amsterdam: Amsterdam University Press.

Drotbohm, Heike. 2020. "Care and Reunification in a Cape Verdean Family: Changing Articulations of Family and Legal Ties." *Ethnography* 21 (1): 48–70.

Dumont, Louis. 1979. *From Mandeville to Marx: The Genesis and Triumph of Economic Ideology*. Chicago: University of Chicago Press. Originally published as *Homo aequalis: Genèse et épanouissement de l'idéologie économique*.

———. 1980. *Homo Hierarchicus: The Caste System and its Implications*. Chicago: University of Chicago Press.

Duyvendak, Jan Willem, Peter Geschiere, and Evelien Tonkens, eds. 2016. *The Culturalization of Citizenship: Belonging and Polarization in a Globalizing World*. London: Palgrave Macmillan.

Dzobo, N. K. 1992. "African Symbols and Proverbs as Source of Knowledge and Truth." In *Person and Community. Ghanaian Philosophical Studies, I*, edited by Kwasi Wiredu and Kwame Gyekye, 85–98. Washington, DC: The Council for Research in Values and Philosophy.

Echeverría, Gabriel. 2020. *Towards a Systemic Theory of Irregular Migration: Explaining Ecuadorian Irregular Migration in Amsterdam and Madrid*. Cham, Switzerland: Springer Nature.

Effevottu, Efetobor Stephanie. 2021. "Unravelling the Nigerian Irregular Migration Quandary to Southern Europe in the Twenty-First Century." In *Intra-Africa Migrations: Reimaging Borders and Migration Management*, edited by Innocent Moyo, Jussi P. Laine, and Christopher Changwe Nshimbi, 31–49. London: Routledge.

Eggebø, Helga. 2013. "A Real Marriage? Applying for Marriage Migration to Norway." *Journal of Ethnic and Migration Studies* 39 (5): 773–89.

Eriksen, Thomas Hylland. 1994. *Ethnicity and Nationalism: Anthropological Perspectives*. London: Pluto Press.

———. 2007. "Trust and Reciprocity in Transnational Flows." In *Holding Worlds Together: Ethnographies of Knowing and Belonging*, edited by Marianne Elisabeth Lien and Marit Melhuus, 1–16. New York and Oxford: Berghahn Books.

———. 2015. *Fredrik Barth: An Intellectual Biography*. London: Pluto Press.

EUROFOUND. 2007. *Part-Time Work in Europe*. Dublin: Eurofound.

Faist, Thomas. 2000. *The Volume and Dynamics of International Migration and Transnational Social Spaces*. Oxford: Oxford University Press.

Fassin, Didier, and Estelle d'Halluin. 2005. "The Truth from the Body: Medical Certificates as Ultimate Evidence for Asylum Seekers." *American Anthropologist* 107 (4): 597–608.

Feldman-Savelsberg, Pamela. 2016. *Mothers on the Move: Reproducing Belonging between Africa and Europe*. Chicago: University of Chicago Press.

Fennell, Catherine. 2016. "The Family Toxic: Triaging Obligation in Post-Welfare Chicago." *South Atlantic Quarterly* 115 (1): 9–32.

Fernandez, Nadine T. 2013. "Moral Boundaries and National Borders: Cuban Marriage Migration to Denmark." *Identities* 20 (3): 270–87.

Fichte, J. G. (1796) 1889. *The Science of Rights* [Grundlage des Naturrechts nach Principien der Wissenschaftslehre]. Translated by A. E. Kroeger.

Fitzpatrick, Sheila. 2005. *Tear Off the Masks! Identity and Imposture in Twentieth-Century Russia*. Princeton, NJ: Princeton University Press.

Flahaux, Marie-Laurence, and Hein De Haas. 2016. "African Migration: Trends, Patterns, Drivers." *Comparative Migration Studies* 4 (1): 1–25.

Fleischer, Annett. 2011. "Marriage Across Space and Time among Male Migrants from Cameroon to Germany." In *Gender, Generations and the Family in International Migration*, edited by Albert Kraler, Eleonore Kofman, Martin Kohli and Camille Schmoll, 243–64. Amsterdam: Amsterdam University Press.

Fortes, Meyer. 1987. *Religion, Morality and the Person: Essays on Tallensi Religion.* Cambridge: Cambridge University Press.

Foucault, Michel. 1990. *Power/Knowledge. Selected Interviews and Other Writings, 1972–1977.* Edited by Colin Gordon. New York: Pantheon Books.

Freeman, Caren. 2011. *Making and Faking Kinship: Marriage and Labor Migration between China and South Korea.* Ithaca, NY: Cornell University Press.

Gaibazzi, Paolo. 2014. "Visa Problem: Certification, Kinship, and the Production of 'Ineligibility' in the Gambia." *Journal of the Royal Anthropological Institute* 20 (1): 38–55.

———. 2015. *Bush Bound: Young Men and Rural Permanence in Migrant West Africa.* New York: Berghahn Books.

Gallo, Ester. 2006. "Italy Is Not a Good Place for Men: Narratives of Places, Marriage and Masculinity among Malayali Migrants." *Global Networks* 6 (4): 357–72.

Garcés-Mascareñas, Blanca, and Jeroen Doomernik. 2007. *Exploratory Study on Trafficking and Labour Exploitation of West African Immigrants in the Netherlands.* Vol. 55. Geneva: International Labour Organization.

Gelles, Richard J. 1972. *The Violent Home: A Study of Physical Aggression between Husbands and Wives.* Beverly Hills, CA: Sage.

———. 2017. *Intimate Violence and Abuse in Families.* 4th ed. Oxford: Oxford University Press.

Gellner, Ernest. 1960. "The Concept of Kinship: With Special Reference to Mr. Needham's' Descent Systems and Ideal Language." *Philosophy of Science* 27 (2): 187–204.

Geschiere, Peter. 1997. *The Modernity of Witchcraft: Politics and the Occult in Postcolonial Africa.* Charlottesville: University of Virginia Press.

———. 2013. *Witchcraft, Intimacy, and Trust: Africa in Comparison.* Chicago: University of Chicago Press.

———. 2014. "The Funeral in the Village: Urbanites' Shifting Imaginations of Belonging, Mobility, and Community." In *The Arts of Citizenship in African Cities: Infrastructures and Spaces of Belonging*, edited by Mamadou Diouf and Rosalind Fredericks, 49–66. New York: Palgrave Macmillan.

———. 2020. "'The African Family is Large, very Large': Mobility and the Flexibility of Kinship—Examples from Cameroon." *Ethnography* 21 (3): 335–54.

Geschiere, Peter, and Rogers Orock. N.d. *Conspiracy Narratives from Postcolonial Africa: Freemasonry, Homosexuality, and Illicit Enrichment.* Unpublished manuscript under review.

Gibson, Thomas. 1986. *Sacrifice and Sharing in the Philippine Highlands: Religion and Society among the Buid of Mindoro.* London: Athlone Press.

Giddens, Anthony. 1992. *The Transformation of Intimacy: Sexuality, Love and Eroticism in Modern Societies.* Cambridge: Polity.

Gluckman, Max. 1940. "Analysis of a Social Situation in Modern Zululand." *Bantu Studies* 14 (1): 1–30.

Goffman, Erving. 1959. *The Presentation of Self in Everyday Life.* New York: Penguin Books.

Golooba, Ssuuna. 2016. *Illegal Immigrant in the Land of Milk and Honey.* Rothersthorpe, UK: Paragon Publishing.

Goody, Jack. 1990. *The Oriental, the Ancient and the Primitive: Systems of Marriage and the Family in the Pre-Industrial Societies of Eurasia*. Cambridge: Cambridge University Press.

Griffiths, Melanie. 2013. "'Establishing Your True Identity': Immigration Detention and Contemporary Identification Debates." In *Identification and Registration Practices in Transnational Perspective*, edited by James Brown, Ilsen About, and Gayle Lonergan, 281–301. New York: Springer.

Groebner, Valentin. 2007. *Who Are You? Identification, Deception, and Surveillance in Early Modern Europe*. New York: Zone Books.

Groes, Christian. 2016. "Men Come and Go, Mothers Stay: Personhood and Resisting Marriage among Mozambican Women Migrating to Europe." In *Affective Circuits: African Migrations to Europe and the Pursuit of Social Regeneration*, edited by Jennifer Cole and Christian Groes, 169–96. Chicago: University of Chicago Press.

Grütters, Carolus, and Karin Zwaan. 2010. *Migration-Related Identity Fraud*. Nijmegen, Netherlands: Radboud University.

Guadeloupe, Francio. 2022. *Black Man in the Netherlands: An Afro-Antillean Anthropology*. Jackson: University Press of Mississippi.

Gyekye, Kwame. 1988. *The Unexamined Life: Philosophy and the African Experience*. Accra: Ghana Universities Press.

Herzfeld, Michael. 2016. *Cultural Intimacy: Social Poetics and the Real Life of States, Societies, and Institutions*. London: Routledge.

Hill, Polly. 1956. *The Gold Coast Cocoa Farmer: A Preliminary Survey*. Oxford: Oxford University Press.

———. 1963. *The Migrant Cocoa-Farmers of Southern Ghana: A Study in Rural Capitalism*. Cambridge: Cambridge University Press.

Hirsch, Jennifer S., and Holly Wardlow, eds. 2006. *Modern Loves: The Anthropology of Romantic Love and Companionate Marriage*. Ann Arbor: University of Michigan Press.

Hochschild, Arlie. 1983. *The Managed Heart: Commercialization of Human Feeling*. Berkeley: University of California Press.

Hollis, Martin. 1985. "Of Masks and Men." In *The Category of the Person: Anthropology, Philosophy, History*, edited by Michael Carrithers, Steven Collins, and Steven Lukes, 217–33. Cambridge: Cambridge University Press.

Holsey, Bayo. 2008. *Routes of Remembrance: Refashioning the Slave Trade in Ghana*. Chicago: University of Chicago Press.

Hoogenraad, Henrike A. 2021. *African-Australian Marriage Migration: An Ethnography of (Un)Happiness*. Leiden, Netherlands: Brill.

Horton, Sarah. 2015. "Identity Loan: The Moral Economy of Migrant Document Exchange in California's Central Valley." *American Ethnologist* 42 (1): 55–67.

———. 2016a. "Ghost Workers: The Implications of Governing Immigration through Crime for Migrant Workplaces." *Anthropology of Work Review* 37 (1): 11–23.

———. 2016b. *They Leave Their Kidneys in the Fields: Illness, Injury, and Illegality among US Farmworkers*. Oakland: University of California Press.

———. 2020. "Paper Trails: Migrants, Bureaucratic Inscription, and Legal Recognition." In *Paper Trails: Migrants, Documents, and Legal Insecurity*, edited by Sarah Horton and Josiah Heyman, 1–26. Durham, NC: Duke University Press.

Howell, Signe. 2006. *The Kinning of Foreigners: Transnational Adoption in a Global Perspective*. New York: Berghahn Books.

Hull, Matthew S. 2012. "Documents and Bureaucracy." *Annual Review of Anthropology* 41: 251–67.

Hunter, Mark. 2010. *Love in the Time of AIDS: Inequality, Gender and Rights in South Africa.* Bloomington: Indiana University Press.

Ikuteyijo, Lanre Olusegun. 2020. "Irregular Migration as Survival Strategy: Narratives from Youth in Urban Nigeria." In *West African Youth Challenges and Opportunity Pathways*, edited by Mora L. McLean, 53–77. Cham, Switzerland: Palgrave Macmillan.

Illouz, Eva. 2007. *Cold Intimacies: The Making of Emotional Capitalism.* Cambridge: Polity.

Immigratie en Naturalisatiedienst. "Marriage of Convenience." https://ind.nl/en/about-ind/back ground-themes/pages/marriage-of-convenience.aspx.

Ismail, Olawale. 2010. "Deconstructing 'Oluwole': Political Economy at the Margins of the State." In *Encountering the Nigerian State*, edited by Wale Adebanwni and Ebenezer Obadare, 29–53. New York: Palgrave Macmillan.

Jung, C. G. 1972. *Two Essays in Analytical Psychology.* Princeton, NJ: Princeton University Press.

Kalir, Barak. 2006. "The Field of Work and the Work of the Field: Conceptualising an Anthropological Research Engagement." *Social Anthropology* 14 (2): 235–46.

———. 2017. "State Desertion and 'out-of-Procedure' Asylum Seekers in the Netherlands." *Focaal: Journal of Global and Historical Anthropology* 2017 (77): 63–75.

Kim, Jaeeun. 2011. "Establishing Identity: Documents, Performance, and Biometric Information in Immigration Proceedings." *Law & Social Inquiry* 36 (3): 760–86.

———. 2018. "Migration-Facilitating Capital: A Bourdieusian Theory of International Migration." *Sociological Theory* 36 (3): 262–88.

Kleinman, Julie. 2016. "From Little Brother to Big Somebody: Coming of Age at the Gare Du Nord." In *Affective Circuits: African Migrations to Europe and the Pursuit of Social Regeneration*, edited by Jennifer Cole and Christian Groes, 245–68. Chicago: University of Chicago Press.

———. 2019. *Adventure Capital: Migration and the Making of an African Hub in Paris.* Oakland: University of California Press.

Kleist, Nauja. 2020. "Trajectories of Involuntary Return Migration to Ghana: Forced Relocation Processes and Post-Return Life." *Geoforum* 116: 272–81.

Kofman, Eleonore. 2018. "Family Migration as a Class Matter." *International Migration* 56 (4): 33–46.

Konadu-Agyemang, Kwadwo. 1999. "Characteristics and Migration Experience of Africans in Canada with Specific Reference to Ghanaians in Greater Toronto." *Canadian Geographer* 43 (4): 400.

Kopytoff, Igor, and Suzanne Miers. 1977. "African 'Slavery' as an Institution of Marginality." In *Slavery in Africa: Historical and Anthropological Perspectives*, edited by Suzanne Miers and Igor Kopytoff, 3–81. Madison: University of Wisconsin Press.

Kringelbach, Hélène Neveu. 2016. "'Marrying Out' for Love: Women's Narratives of Polygyny and Alternative Marriage Choices in Contemporary Senegal." *African Studies Review* 59 (1): 155–74.

Kritzman-Amir, Tally. 2021. "Swab before You Enter: DNA Collection and Immigration Control." *Harvard Civil Rights–Civil Liberties Law Review* 56 (1): 77–114.

Kulu-Glasgow, Isik, Monika Smit, and Roel Jennissen. 2017. "For Love or for Papers? Sham Marriages among Turkish (Potential) Migrants and Gender Implications." In *Revisiting Gender and Migration*, edited by Murat Yüceşahin and Pinar Yazgan, 61–78. London: Transnational Press.

Kuper, Adam. 1988. *The Invention of Primitive Society: Transformations of an Illusion*. London: Routledge.

La Fontaine, J. S. 1985. "Person and Individual: Some Anthropological Reflections." In *The Category of the Person: Anthropology, Philosophy, History*, edited by Michael Carrithers, Steven Collins, and Steven Lukes, 123–40. Cambridge: Cambridge University Press.

Lakoff, George, and Mark Johnson. 2003. *Metaphors We Live By*. Chicago: University of Chicago Press.

Lambek, Michael. 2011. "Kinship as Gift and Theft: Acts of Succession in Mayotte and Israel." *American Ethnologist* 38 (1): 2–16.

Le Courant, Stefan. 2019. "Imposture at the Border: Law and the Construction of Identities among Undocumented Migrants." *Social Anthropology* 27 (3): 472–85.

Leerkes, Arjen, and Isik Kulu-Glasgow. 2011. "Playing Hard(er) to Get: The State, International Couples, and the Income Requirement." *European Journal of Migration and Law* 13 (1): 95–121.

Lewis, Michael. 1993. *The Culture of Inequality*. Amherst: University of Massachusetts Press.

Lipsky, Michael. 1980. *Street-Level Bureaucracy: Dilemmas of the Individual in Public Service*. New York: Russell Sage Foundation.

LiPuma, Edward. 2001. *Encompassing Others: The Magic of Modernity in Melanesia*. Ann Arbor: University of Michigan Press.

Litwak, Eugene. 1960. "Geographic Mobility and Extended Family Cohesion." *American Sociological Review* 25 (3): 385–94.

Liversage, Anika. 2012. "Gender, Conflict and Subordination within the Household: Turkish Migrant Marriage and Divorce in Denmark." *Journal of Ethnic and Migration Studies* 38 (7): 1119–36.

———. 2013. "Gendered Struggles Over Residency Rights when Turkish Immigrant Marriages Break Up." *Oñati Socio-Legal Series* 3 (6): 1070–90.

Lucht, Hans. 2011. *Darkness before Daybreak: African Migrants Living on the Margins in Southern Italy Today*. Berkeley: University of California Press.

Lyon, David. 2009. *Identifying Citizens: ID Cards as Surveillance*. Cambridge: Polity.

MacDonald, John S., and Leatrice D. MacDonald. 1964. "Chain Migration Ethnic Neighborhood Formation and Social Networks." *The Milbank Memorial Fund Quarterly* 42 (1): 82–97.

Mahler, Sarah J. 1995. *American Dreaming: Immigrant Life on the Margins*. Princeton, NJ: Princeton University Press.

Mai, Nicola, and Russell King. 2009. "Love, Sexuality and Migration: Mapping the Issue(s)." *Mobilities* 4 (3): 295–307.

Malinowski, Bronislaw. (1922) 1984. *Argonauts of the Western Pacific: An Account of Native Enterprise and Adventure in the Archipelagoes of Melanesian New Guinea*. Prospect Heights, IL: Waveland Press.

Mangena, Tendai. 2018. "(Re)Negotiating Illegal Migrant Identities in Selected Zimbabwean Fiction." *South African Journal of African Languages* 38 (3): 277–84.

Mariner, Kathryn A. 2019. " 'Who You Are in These Pieces of Paper': Imagining Future Kinship through Auto/Biographical Adoption Documents in the United States." *Cultural Anthropology* 34 (4): 529–54.

Marriott, McKim. 1976. "Hindu Transactions: Diversity without Dualism." In *Transaction and Meaning: Directions in the Anthropology of Exchange and Symbolic Behavior*, edited by Bruce Kapferer, 109–42. Philadelphia: ISHI Publications.

Maskens, Maïté. 2015. "Bordering Intimacy: The Fight against Marriages of Convenience in Brussels." *Cambridge Journal of Anthropology* 33 (2): 42–58.

Massey, Douglas S., Rafael Alarcón, Jorge Durand, and Humberto González. 1987. *Return to Aztlan: The Social Process of International Migration from Western Mexico.* Berkeley: University of California Press.

Massey, Douglas S., Jorge Durand, and Nolan J. Malone. 2002. *Beyond Smoke and Mirrors: Mexican Immigration in an Era of Economic Integration.* New York: Russell Sage Foundation.

Massey, Douglas S., Luin Goldring, and Jorge Durand. 1994. "Continuities in Transnational Migration: An Analysis of Nineteen Mexican Communities." *American Journal of Sociology* 99 (6): 1492–1533.

Mauss, Marcel. (1924) 2002. *The Gift: The Form and Reason for Exchange in Archaic Societies.* London: Routledge.

———. 1985. "A Category of the Human Mind: The Notion of the Person, the Notion of Self." In *The Category of the Person: Anthropology, Philosophy, History*, edited by Michael Carrithers, Steven Collins, and Steven Lukes, 1–25. Cambridge: Cambridge University Press.

Mays, Devi. 2020. *Forging Ties, Forging Passports: Migration and the Modern Sephardi Diaspora.* Stanford, CA: Stanford University Press.

Mazzucato, Valentina. 2008. "The Double Engagement: Transnationalism and Integration—Ghanaian Migrants' Lives between Ghana and the Netherlands." *Journal of Ethnic and Migration Studies* 34 (2): 199–216.

Mbembe, Achille. 2001. *On the Postcolony.* Berkeley: University of California Press.

Mbombo, Timothy Keyeke. 2016. *The Last Bush Faller: Saga in the Diaspora.* N.p.: CreateSpace.

M'charek, Amade, Katharina Schramm, and David Skinner. 2014. "Topologies of Race: Doing Territory, Population and Identity in Europe." *Science, Technology & Human Values* 39 (4): 468–87.

McKinnon, Susan. 2013. "Kinship within and Beyond the 'Movement of Progressive Societies.'" In *Vital Relations: Modernity and the Persistent Life of Kinship*, edited by Susan McKinnon and Fenella Cannell, 39–62. Sante Fe, NM: SAR Press.

———. 2016. "Doing and Being: Process, Essence, and Hierarchy in Making Kin." In *The Routledge Companion to Contemporary Anthropology*, edited by Simon Coleman, Susana B. Hyatt, and Ann Kingsolver, 161–82. London: Routledge.

McKinnon, Susan, and Fenella Cannell, eds. 2013. *Vital Relations: Modernity and the Persistent Life of Kinship.* Santa Fe, NM: SAR Press.

Medick, Hans, and David Warren Sabean, eds. 1984. *Interest and Emotion: Essays on the Study of Family and Kinship.* Cambridge: Cambridge University Press.

Meeteren, Masja. 2014. *Irregular Migrants in Belgium and the Netherlands: Aspirations and Incorporation.* Amsterdam: Amsterdam University Press.

Meiu, George Paul. 2017. *Ethno-erotic Economies: Sexuality, Money, and Belonging in Kenya.* Chicago: University of Chicago Press.

Menjívar, Cecilia. 1995. "Kinship Networks among Immigrants: Lessons from a Qualitative Comparative Approach." *International Journal of Comparative Sociology* 36 (3): 219–32.

———. 2000. *Fragmented Ties: Salvadoran Immigrant Networks in America.* Berkeley: University of California Press.

Menjívar, Cecilia, and Olivia Salcido. 2002. "Immigrant Women and Domestic Violence: Common Experiences in Different Countries." *Gender & Society* 16 (6): 898–920.

4

Mitchell, James Clyde. 1956. *The Kalela Dance: Aspects of Social Relationships among Urban Africans in Northern Rhodesia*. Manchester, UK: Manchester University Press for the Rhodes-Livingstone Institute.

Mitchell, Julie, and Susan Bibler Coutin. 2019. "Living Documents in Transnational Spaces of Migration between El Salvador and the United States." *Law & Social Inquiry* 44 (4): 865–92.

Moliner, Christine. 2011. "'Did You Get Papers?' Sikh Migrants in France." In *Sikhs in Europe: Migration, Identities and Representations*, edited by Kunt Jacobsen and Kristina Myrvold, 163–77. Surrey, UK: Ashgate.

Möllering, Guido. 2001. "The Nature of Trust: From Georg Simmel to a Theory of Expectation, Interpretation and Suspension." *Sociology* 35 (2): 403–20.

Moret, Joëlle, Apostolos Andrikopoulos, and Janine Dahinden. 2021. "Contesting Categories: Cross-Border Marriages from the Perspectives of the State, Spouses and Researchers." *Journal of Ethnic and Migration Studies* 47 (2): 325–42.

Muller Myrdahl, Eileen. 2010. "Legislating Love: Norwegian Family Reunification Law as a Racial Project." *Social & Cultural Geography* 11 (2): 103–16.

Narotzky, Susana, and Paz Moreno. 2002. "Reciprocity's Dark Side: Negative Reciprocity, Morality and Social Reproduction." *Anthropological Theory* 2 (3): 281–305.

National Document Fraud Unit. 2016. *Guidance on Examining Identity Documents*. London: Home Office UK.

Navaro-Yashin, Yael. 2007. "Make-Believe Papers, Legal Forms and the Counterfeit: Affective Interactions between Documents and People in Britain and Cyprus." *Anthropological Theory* 7 (1): 79–98.

Nave, Carmen. 2016. "One Family: Defining Kinship in the Neighbourhoods of Kumasi, Ghana." *Journal of the Royal Anthropological Institute* 22 (4): 826–42.

Nfon, Charles. 2013. *Greener from a Distance: Stories from the Diaspora*. Mankon/Bamenda, Cameroon: Langaa RPCIG.

Nieswand, Boris. 2014. "The Burgers' Paradox: Migration and the Transnationalization of Social Inequality in Southern Ghana." *Ethnography* 15 (4): 403–25.

Nimako, Kwame, and Stephen Small. 2010. "Collective Memory of Slavery in Great Britain and the Netherlands." Paper presented at the annual meeting of the American Sociological Association Annual Meeting, Atlanta.

Nshimbi, Christopher Changwe. 2020. "Life in the Fringes: Informality, African Migrants' Perception of the Border and Attitudes Towards Migrating to Europe." In *Migration Conundrums, Regional Integration and Development*, edited by Innocent Moyo, Christopher Changwe Nshimbi, and Jussi P. Laine, 165–91. Singapore: Palgrave Macmillan.

Nyamnjoh, Francis B. 2013. "Fiction and Reality of Mobility in Africa." *Citizenship Studies* 17 (6–7): 653–80.

———. 2017. "Incompleteness: Frontier Africa and the Currency of Conviviality." *Journal of Asian and African Studies* 52 (3): 253–70.

———. 2021. "Being and Becoming African as a Permanent Work in Progress: Inspiration from Chinua Achebe's Proverbs." *Acta Academica* 53 (1): 129–37.

Odé, Arend. 2002. *Ethnic-Cultural and Socio-Economic Integration in the Netherlands: A Comparative Study of Mediterranean and Caribbean Minority Groups*. Assen, Netherlands: Koninklijke Van Gorcum.

Okali, Christine. 1983. *Cocoa and Kinship in Ghana: The Matrilineal Akan of Ghana*. London: Routledge.

Okojie, Christiana E. E., Obehi Okojie, Kokunre Eghafona, Gloria Vincent-Osaghae, and Victoria Kalu. 2003. *Trafficking of Nigerian Girls to Italy: Report of Field Survey in Edo State, Nigeria*. Turin, Italy: UN Interregional Crime and Justice Research Institute.

Okunade, Samuel Kehinde. 2021. "Irregular Emigration of Nigeria Youths: An Exploration of Core Drivers from the Perspective and Experiences of Returnee Migrants." In *Intra-Africa Migrations: Reimaging Borders and Migration Management*, edited by Innocent Moyo, Jussi P. Laine, and Christopher Changwe Nshimbi, 50–69. London: Routledge.

Olaniyi, Rasheed. 2009. "'We Asked for Workers but Human Beings Came': A Critical Assessment of Policies on Immigration and Human Trafficking in the European Union." In *Globalization and Transnational Migrations: Africa and Africans in the Contemporary Global System*, edited by Akanmu Adebayo and Olutayo C. Adesina, 140–61. Newcastle upon Tyne, UK: Cambridge Scholars Publishing.

Olwig, Karen Fog. 2012. "The 'Successful' Return: Caribbean Narratives of Migration, Family, and Gender." *Journal of the Royal Anthropological Institute* 18 (4): 828–45.

Oostindie, Gert. 2005. "The Slippery Paths of Commemoration and Heritage Tourism: The Netherlands, Ghana, and the Rediscovery of Atlantic Slavery." *New West Indian Guide/ Nieuwe West-Indische Gids* 79 (1–2): 55–77.

Ordóñez, Juan Thomas. 2016. "Documents and Shifting Labor Environments among Undocumented Migrant Workers in Northern California." *Anthropology of Work Review* 37 (1): 24–33.

———. 2020. "Strategies of Documentation among Kichwa Transnational Migrants." In *Paper Trails: Migrants, Documents, and Legal Insecurity*, edited by Sarah Horton and Josiah Heyman, 208–28. Durham, NC: Duke University Press.

Osei, Akwasi. 2014. "'Ya Ba no Dεε Na Ya Ba': Residence Strategies of Ghanaian Illegal Migrants in Amsterdam." MA thesis, University of Amsterdam.

Ossman, Susan. 2013. *Moving Matters: Paths of Serial Migration*. Stanford, CA: Stanford University Press.

Otu, Kwame Edwin. 2022. *Amphibious Subjects: Sasso and the Contested Politics of Queer Self-Making in Neoliberal Ghana*. Oakland: University of California Press.

Padilla, Mark B., Jennifer S. Hirsch, Munoz-Laboy, Miguel, Sember, Robert E., and Richard G. Parker, eds. 2007. *Love and Globalization: Transformations of Intimacy in the Contemporary World*. Nashville, TN: Vanderbilt University Press.

Papadaki, Eirini. 2018. "Undoing Kinship: Producing Citizenship in a Public Maternity Hospital in Athens, Greece." In *Reconnecting State and Kinship*, edited by Tatjana Thelen and Erdmute Alber, 178–99. Philadelphia: University of Pennsylvania Press.

Partridge, Damani James. 2008. "'We Were Dancing in the Club, Not on the Berlin Wall': Black Bodies, Street Bureaucrats, and Exclusionary Incorporation into the New Europe." *Cultural Anthropology* 23 (4): 660–87.

Paul, Anju Mary. 2011. "Stepwise International Migration: A Multistage Migration Pattern for the Aspiring Migrant." *American Journal of Sociology* 116 (6): 1842–86.

Pauli, Julia. 2013. "'Sharing Made Us Sisters': Sisterhood, Migration, and Household Dynamics in Mexico and Namibia." In *The Anthropology of Sibling Relations: Shared Parentage, Experience, and Exchange*, edited by Erdmute Alber, Cati Coe, and Tatjana Thelen, 29–50. New York: Palgrave Macmillan.

Paxson, Heather. 2007. "A Fluid Mechanics of Erotas and Aghape: Family Planning and Maternal Consumption in Contemporary Greece." In *Love and Globalization: Transformations of Intimacy in the Contemporary World*, edited by Mark B. Padilla, Jennifer S. Hirsch, Miguel

Munoz-Laboy, Robert E. Sember, and Richard G. Parker, 120–38. Nashville, TN: Vanderbilt University Press.

Pellander, Saara. 2021. "Buy Me Love: Emotions and Income in Regulating Cross-Border Marriages." *Journal of Ethnic and Migration Studies* 47 (2): 464–79.

Perbi, Akosua Adoma. 2004. *A History of Indigenous Slavery in Ghana: From the 15th to the 19th Century*. Accra: Sub-Saharan Publishers.

Piot, Charles. 1996. "Of Slaves and the Gift: Kabre Sale of Kin during the Era of the Slave Trade." *Journal of African History* 37 (1): 31–49.

———. 2019. *The Fixer: Visa Lottery Chronicles*. Durham, NC: Duke University Press.

Prina, Franco. 2003. *Trafficking of Nigerian Girls to Italy. Trade and Exploitation of Minors and Young Nigerian Women for Prostitution in Italy*. Turin, Italy: UN Interregional Crime and Justice Research Institute.

Rayor, Diane J. 2013. *Euripides' Medea. A New Translation*. Cambridge: Cambridge University Press.

Rebhun, L. A. 1999. *The Heart Is Unknown Country: Love in the Changing Economy of Northeast Brazil*. Stanford, CA: Stanford University Press.

Reeves, Madeleine. 2013. "Clean Fake: Authenticating Documents and Persons in Migrant Moscow." *American Ethnologist* 40 (3): 508–24.

Remery, Chantal, Anneke van Doorne-Huiskes, and Joop Schippers. 2002. "Labour Market Flexibility in the Netherlands Looking for Winners and Losers." *Work, Employment & Society* 16 (3): 477–95.

Riaño, Yvonne. 2011. " 'He's the Swiss Citizen, I'm the Foreign Spouse': Binational Marriages and the Impact of Family-Related Migration Policies on Gender Relations." In *Gender, Generations and the Family in International Migration*, edited by Albert Kraler, Eleonore Kofman and Martin Kohli, 265–83. Amsterdam: Amsterdam University Press.

———. 2015. "Latin American Women Who Migrate for Love: Imagining European Men as Ideal Partners." In *Rethinking Romantic Love. Discussions, Mobilities and Practices*, edited by Begonya Enguix and Jordi Roca, 45–60. Newcastle upon Tyne, UK: Cambridge Scholars Publishing.

Riles, Annelise, eds. 2006. *Documents: Artifacts of Modern Knowledge*. Ann Arbor: University of Michigan Press.

Robertson, A. F. 1982. "Abusa: The Structural History of an Economic Contract." *Journal of Development Studies* 18 (4): 447–78.

Sabar, Galia. 2010. "Witchcraft and Concepts of Evil amongst African Migrant Workers in Israel." *Canadian Journal of African Studies/La Revue Canadienne des Études Africaines* 44 (1): 110–41.

Sahlins, Marshall. 1972. *Stone Age Economics*. New York: Aldine de Gruyter.

———. 2013. *What Kinship Is—and Is Not*. Chicago: University of Chicago Press.

Salcedo Robledo, Manuela. 2011. "Bleu, blanc, gris . . . La couleur des mariages: Altérisation et tactiques de résistance des couples binationaux en France." *L'Espace Politique* 13.

Salcido, Olivia, and Madelaine Adelman. 2004. " 'He Has Me Tied with the Blessed and Damned Papers': Undocumented-Immigrant Battered Women in Phoenix, Arizona." *Human Organization* 63 (2): 162–72.

Sapir, J. David. 1977. "The Anatomy of Metaphor." In *The Social Use of Metaphor*, edited by J. David Sapir and J. Christopher Crocker, 3–32. Philadelphia: University of Pennsylvania Press.

Sarbah, John Mensah. 1904. *Fanti Customary Laws: A Brief Introduction to the Principles of the Native Laws and Customs of the Fanti and Akan Districts of the Gold Coast*. London: W. Clowes and Sons.

Satzewich, Vic. 2014. "Canadian Visa Officers and the Social Construction of 'Real' Spousal Relationships." *Canadian Review of Sociology/Revue Canadienne de Sociologie* 51 (1): 1–21.

Şaul, Mahir. 2017. "The Migrant in a Plotted Adventure: Self-Realisation and Moral Obligation
in African Stories from Istanbul." *Journal of Modern African Studies* 55 (1): 129–53.

Schapendonk, Joris. 2020. *Finding Ways through Eurospace: West African Movers Re-Viewing
Europe from the Inside*. New York: Berghahn Books.

Scheel, Stephan. 2017. "Appropriating Mobility and Bordering Europe through Romantic Love:
Unearthing the Intricate Intertwinement of Border Regimes and Migratory Practices." *Migration Studies* 5 (3): 389–408.

———. 2019. *Autonomy of Migration? Appropriating Mobility within Biometric Border Regimes*.
London: Routledge.

Schneider, David Murray. (1968) 1980. *American Kinship: A Cultural Account*. Chicago: University of Chicago Press.

———. 1972. "What Is Kinship All About?" In *Kinship Studies in the Morgan Centennial Year*,
edited by P. Reining, 32–63. Washington, DC: Anthropological Society of Washington.

———. 1984. *A Critique of the Study of Kinship*. Ann Arbor: University of Michigan Press.

Schramm, Katharina. 2009. "Negotiating Race: Blackness and Whiteness in the Context of
Homecoming to Ghana." *African Diaspora* 2 (1): 3–24.

———. 2016. *African Homecoming: Pan-African Ideology and Contested Heritage*. London: Routledge.

Simmel, Georg. (1900) 2004. *The Philosophy of Money*. 3rd ed. London: Routledge.

Siskind, Janet. 1978. "Kinship and Mode of Production." *American Anthropologist* 80 (4): 860–72.

Smart, Carol. 2007. *Personal Life: New Directions in Sociological Thinking*. Cambridge: Polity.

Smith, Daniel Jordan. 2009. "Managing Men, Marriage, and Modern Love: Women's Perspectives on Intimacy and Male Infidelity in Southeastern Nigeria." In *Love in Africa*, edited by
Jennifer Cole and Lynn M. Thomas, 157–80. Chicago: University of Chicago Press.

———. 2017. *To Be a Man Is Not a One-Day Job: Masculinity, Money, and Intimacy in Nigeria*.
Chicago: University of Chicago Press.

Sociale Inlichtingen en Opsporingsdienst. 2005. *Beleidsdocument "Labyrint": Onderzoek Naar
West-Afrikaanse Criminele Netwerken in De Sociale Zekerheid*. The Hague: Ministerie van
Sociale Zaken.

Spronk, Rachel. 2014. "Sexuality and Subjectivity: Erotic Practices and the Question of Bodily
Sensations." *Social Anthropology* 22 (1): 3–21.

Stack, Carol B. 1974. *All Our Kin: Strategies for Survival in a Black Community*. New York: Harper &
Row.

Stipriaan, Andrew Alexander van. 2000. *Creolisering: Vragen Van Een Basketbalplein, Antwoor-
den Van Een Watergodin*. Rotterdam: Erasmus Universiteit Rotterdam.

Strathern, Marilyn. 1988. *The Gender of the Gift: Problems with Women and Problems with Society in Melanesia*. Berkeley: University of California Press.

———. 1992. *After Nature: English Kinship in the Late Twentieth Century*. Cambridge: Cambridge
University Press.

Suksomboon, Panitee. 2011. "Cross-Border Marriages as a Migrant Strategy: Thai Women in the
Netherlands." In *Gender, Generations and the Family in International Migration*, edited by
Albert Kraler, Eleonore Kofman, Martin Kohli, and Camille Schmoll, 221–41. Amsterdam:
Amsterdam University Press.

Tabet, Paola. 1991. "'I'm the Meat, I'm the Knife': Sexual Service, Migration, and Repression in
some African Societies." *Feminist Issues* 11 (1): 3–21.

Thelen, Tatjana, and Erdmute Alber. 2018a. *Reconnecting State and Kinship*. Philadelphia: University of Pennsylvania Press.

———. 2018b. "Reconnecting State and Kinship: Temporalities, Scales, Classifications." In *Reconnecting State and Kinship*, edited by Tatjana Thelen and Erdmute Alber, 1–35. Philadelphia: University of Pennsylvania Press.

Thelen, Tatjana, Cati Coe, and Erdmute Alber. 2013. "The Anthropology of Sibling Relations: Explorations in Shared Parentage, Experience, and Exchange." In *The Anthropology of Sibling Relations: Shared Parentage, Experience, and Exchange*, edited by Erdmute Alber, Cati Coe, and Tatjana Thelen, 1–26. New York: Palgrave Macmillan.

Thomas, Lynn M., and Jennifer Cole. 2009. "Thinking through Love in Africa." In *Love in Africa*, edited by Jennifer Cole and Lynn M. Thomas, 1–30. Chicago: University of Chicago Press.

Tilly, Charles, and C. Harold Brown. 1967. "On Uprooting, Kinship, and the Auspices of Migration." *International Journal of Comparative Sociology* 8: 139–64.

Torpey, John. 2000. *The Invention of the Passport: Surveillance, Citizenship and the State*. Cambridge: Cambridge University Press.

Tryfonidou, Alina. 2008. "Reverse Discrimination in Purely Internal Situations: An Incongruity in a Citizens' Europe." *Legal Issues of Economic Integration* 35 (1): 43–67.

———. 2009. "Family Reunification Rights of (Migrant) Union Citizens: Towards a More Liberal Approach." *European Law Journal* 15 (5): 634–53.

Turner, Bryan S. 1986. "Personhood and Citizenship." *Theory, Culture & Society* 3 (1): 1–16.

Umar, Mohammed. 2017. *The Illegal Immigrant*. London: Salaam Publishing.

Van der Geest, Sjaak. 2000. "Funerals for the Living: Conversations with Elderly People in Kwahu, Ghana." *African Studies Review* 43 (3): 103–29.

———. 2013. "Kinship as Friendship: Brothers and Sisters in Kwahu, Ghana." In *The Anthropology of Sibling Relations: Shared Parentage, Experience and Exchange*, edited by Erdmute Alber, Cati Coe, and Tatjana Thelen, 51–70. New York: Palgrave Macmillan.

Van der Leun, Joanne. 2003. *Looking for Loopholes: Processes of Incorporation of Illegal Immigrants in the Netherlands*. Amsterdam: Amsterdam University Press.

Van der Leun, Joanne, and Robert Kloosterman. 2006. "Going Underground: Immigration Policy Changes and Shifts in Modes of Provision of Undocumented Immigrants in the Netherlands." *Tijdschrift Voor Economische En Sociale Geografie* 97 (1): 59–68.

Van Dijk, Rijk. 2004. "Negotiating Marriage: Questions of Morality and Legitimacy in the Ghanaian Pentecostal Diaspora." *Journal of Religion in Africa* 34 (4): 438–67.

Van Hear, Nicholas. 1998. *New Diasporas: The Mass Exodus, Dispersal and Regrouping of Migrant Communities*. Seattle: University of Washington Press.

Van Liempt, Gijsbert. 2013. *Private Employment Agencies in the Netherlands, Spain and Sweden*. Geneva: International Labour Office.

Van Liempt, Ilse. 2007. *Navigating Borders: Inside Perspectives on the Process of Human Smuggling into the Netherlands*. Amsterdam: Amsterdam University Press.

Van Oorschot, Wim. 2004. "Flexible Work and Flexicurity Policies in the Netherlands: Trends and Experiences." *Transfer: European Review of Labour and Research* 10 (2): 208–25.

Vasta, Ellie. 2011. "Immigrants and the Paper Market: Borrowing, Renting and Buying Identities." *Ethnic and Racial Studies* 34 (2): 187–206.

Vasta, Ellie, and Leander Kandilige. 2010. "'London the Leveller': Ghanaian Work Strategies and Community Solidarity." *Journal of Ethnic and Migration Studies* 36 (4): 581–98.

Vigh, Henrik. 2009. "Motion Squared: A Second Look at the Concept of Social Navigation." *Anthropological Theory* 9 (4): 419–38.

———. 2016. "Life's Trampoline: On Nullification and Cocaine Migration in Bissau." In *Affective Circuits: African Migrations to Europe and the Pursuit of Social Regeneration*, edited by Jennifer Cole and Christian Groes, 223–44. Chicago: University of Chicago Press.

Visser, Jelle, and Anton Hemerijck. 1997. *A Dutch Miracle: Job Growth, Welfare Reform and Corporatism in the Netherlands*. Amsterdam: Amsterdam University Press.

Wallerstein, Immanuel. 2003. "Citizens All? Citizens Some! The Making of the Citizen." *Comparative Studies in Society and History* 45 (4): 650–79.

Weiner, Annette B. 1992. *Inalienable Possessions: The Paradox of Keeping While Giving*. Berkeley: University of California Press.

Wekker, Gloria. 2016. *White Innocence: Paradoxes of Colonialism and Racism*. Durham, NC: Duke University Press.

Werbner, Richard. 2020. *Anthropology after Gluckman: The Manchester School, Colonial and Postcolonial Transformations*. Manchester, UK: Manchester University Press.

White, Jenny. 2004. *Money Makes Us Relatives: Women's Labor in Urban Turkey*. Hove, UK: Psychology Press.

Williams, Lucy. 2010. *Global Marriage: Cross-Border Marriage Migration in Global Context*. London: Palgrave Macmillan.

———. 2012. "Transnational Marriage Migration and Marriage Migration: An Overview." In *Transnational Marriage: New Perspectives from Europe and Beyond*, edited by Katharine Charsley, 23–37. New York: Routledge.

Wimmer, Andreas. 2004. "Does Ethnicity Matter? Everyday Group Formation in Three Swiss Immigrant Neighbourhoods." *Ethnic and Racial Studies* 27 (1): 1–36.

———. 2009. "Herder's Heritage and the Boundary-Making Approach: Studying Ethnicity in Immigrant Societies." *Sociological Theory* 27 (3): 244–70.

Wimmer, Andreas, and Nina Glick Schiller. 2002. "Methodological Nationalism and Beyond: Nation-State Building, Migration and the Social Sciences." *Global Networks* 2 (4): 301–34.

Winfrey, Oprah. 2012. "Oprah's Letter to Her Younger Self." *O, the Oprah Magazine*. https://www.oprah.com/spirit/oprahs-letter-to-her-younger-self-oprah-wisdom.

Wray, Helena. 2015. "The 'Pure' Relationship, Sham Marriages and Immigration Control." In *Marriage Rites and Rights*, edited by Joanna Miles, Rebecca Probert, and Perveez Mody, 141–65. Oxford, UK: Hart Publishing.

Yanagisako, Sylvia, and Carol Delaney, eds. 1995. *Naturalizing Power: Essays in Feminist Cultural Analysis*. New York: Routledge.

Yngvesson, Barbara, and Susan Bibler Coutin. 2006. "Backed by Papers: Undoing Persons, Histories, and Return." *American Ethnologist* 33 (2): 177–90.

Zelizer, Viviana A. 2005. *The Purchase of Intimacy*. Princeton, NJ: Princeton University Press.

Zuluaga, Jonathan Echeverri. 2015. "Errance and Elsewheres among Africans Waiting to Restart Their Journeys in Dakar, Senegal." *Cultural Anthropology* 30 (4): 589–610.

Index